STONEYBATTER

Dublin's Inner Urban Village

By the same author

Georgian Dublin: Ireland's Imperilled Architectural Heritage
Dublin's Vanishing Craftsmen

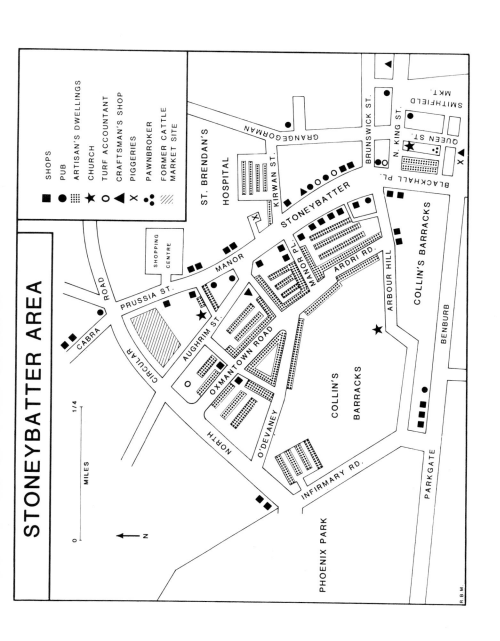

STONEYBATTER AREA

N →

MILES
0   1/4

Legend:
- ■ SHOPS
- ● PUB
- ▦ ARTISAN'S DWELLINGS
- ★ CHURCH
- ○ TURF ACCOUNTANT
- ◀ CRAFTSMAN'S SHOP
- ✕ PIGGERIES
- ∴ PAWNBROKER
- ▨ FORMER CATTLE MARKET SITE

St. Brendan's Hospital
Grangegorman
Kirwan St.
Brunswick St.
Stoneybatter
N. King St.
Queen St.
Smithfield Mkt.
Blackhall Pl.
Manor
Manor Pl.
Ardri Rd.
Arbour Hill
Collin's Barracks
Benburb
Prussia St.
Shopping Centre
Cabra Road
Circular Road
Aughrim St.
Oxmantown Road
O'Devaney
North
Infirmary Rd.
Collin's Barracks
Parkgate
Phoenix Park

R.B.M.

1 View of Stoneybatter Street looking northward

2 View of east side of Stoneybatter Street looking southward

STONEYBATTER

Dublin's Inner Urban Village

KEVIN C. KEARNS

GLENDALE

First published in Ireland by
THE GLENDALE PRESS
1 Summerhill Parade
Sandycove
Co. Dublin

© Kevin C. Kearns 1989

British Library Cataloguing in Publication Data
Kearns, Kevin Corrigan
    Stoneybatter: Dublin's inner urban village.
    1. Dublin. Stoneybatter. Social life, history —
    Biographies — Collections
    I. Title
    941.8'35

    ISBN 0-907606-73-3

Typeset by Wendy A. Commins, The Curragh
Make-up by Paul Bray Studio
Printed by The Camelot Press Plc., Southampton.

For my mother, Virginia Corrigan Kearns,
in eternal gratitude for imbuing me with
a fierce pride in my Irish heritage

'Upon my honour, nothing here is a sham'.

('Stoneybatter — An Unfinished Prologue',
The Irish Builder, 1871)

'Places around Arbour Hill, Stoneybatter, Oxmantown Lane ... it was the other side of the Dublin coin because the people in the area are as Dublin as those of the Liberties'.

(Paddy Crosbie, *Your Dinner's Poured Out!*, 1981)

Contents

List of Illustrations

Acknowledgements

A book of such personal social and oral history could never have been written without the kindness, cooperation, and trust of the people of the Stoneybatter community. Unfailingly, they welcomed me into their homes, shops, pub cliques, and family circles and with uncommon candour shared life's most intimate experiences. I feel great sadness that a number of persons whose poignant oral histories are featured passed away before this book was published. But it is hoped that surviving family and friends will find lasting meaning and comfort in their words which imbue this work with its originality and relevance. During the long course of my research mutual friendships were formed which will endure over a lifetime and allow me in heart and mind to forever remain a part of Stoneybatter.

A particular debt of gratitude is owed to the following individuals for their valuable contributions to this book: Eamonn O'Brien, head of the Stoneybatter Development Committee, who, from the outset, provided me with vital information, prudent guidance, and indispensable contacts; Paula Howard, head librarian at the Gilbert Collection of the Pearse Street Library, for untiring assistance with archival research; Deirdre Kelly, head of the Dublin Living City Group, for sharing insights and perceptions of the inner-city life; Lisa Collins for field research assistance; and academic colleagues Steven Scott and Charles Collins for critical and constructive reading of manuscript sections. Special heartfelt thanks are extended to Leslie Lauren Smith, kindred spirit and companion explorer, who shared with me the discovery of Stoneybatter and the quest to find its heart.

Formal acknowledgement is gratefully given to the National Geographic Society and the University of Northern Colorado Research and Publications Committee for their financial funding of my research, both over the past several years and for on-going research in the Stoneybatter community. Without their faith and investment in my project this book could not have been produced.

3 A neighbourhood institution. The little 'Corner Shop' in Smithfield at the corner of Red Cow Lane

Introduction

'This is a very historic part of the city. It has a village atmosphere, very unique, like a country town. Other Dublin people didn't know where this was. It's been a nice secret. There was no development. Time here stood still'.

(Leslie Foy, Third Generation Stoneybatter Dweller)

'There's a lot of oral history left in the old residents. You'd really want to pry it out of some of the old lads in the pub over several drinks'.

(Thomas Linehan, Fourth Generation Stoneybatter Dweller)

Stoneybatter is a splendid anachronism, a tranquil village community surviving in the heart of frenetic, modern Dublin. The serendipity of stumbling upon the scene is like entering some historical time warp. One is immediately struck by the antiquity of the place. Cobblestones, artisan's dwellings, small family-owned shops, eighteenth-century pubs, white-washed stone cottages, piggeries up narrow lanes, and horse fairs all tell of a bygone age. The genteel pace of local life and intimate socialisation are conspicuously characteristic of small Irish towns. To the unsuspecting wanderer it is the most delightful discovery on Dublin's cityscape. Indeed, Cathal O'Byrne, writing in 1946 of a personal 'voyage of discovery to Stoneybatter', gave this vivid account:[1]

A busy, sonsy, wholesome, bustling place this Stoneybatter, a place that seemed to enjoy the blessings of life and health and faith in God. The famous old thoroughfare lined on either side with shops and the aromatic scents from the apothecaries' establishments and the odours of ripened fruit and great piles of green stuffs were heavy in the warm air. On the sagged roofs of the little shops the moss grew in little green cushions and however spick and span their frontages, their interiors seemed ages old and lost nothing in being picturesque for that reason.

Similarly, Paddy Crosbie, recounting the Stoneybatter of his youth in *Your Dinner's Poured Out!*, portrays it as a sort of forgotten world suspended in a past era.[2] As locals like to explain, it has simply been a well kept 'secret'. Other Dubliners exhibit remarkably little knowledge of the district. When doing preparatory work for this book at the Dublin Corporation, the ranking officer to whom I had been directed unabashedly confessed that he had 'never heard of Stoneybatter ... are you certain it's in Dublin?' I later found that it is precisely because of such benign neglect by urban planners and developers that Stoneybatter has been providentially preserved.

Every Dubliner knows of the famed Liberties, heralded in books for its history, traditions, and characters. But precious little has been written about Stoneybatter. This is curious and unfortunate because, in actuality, this area is equally rich in antiquity, heritage, and local lore. The oldest settled community on the northside of Dublin, Stoneybatter comprises the ancient Viking settlement of Oxmantown and its environs. Stoneybatter street itself, once part of the royal highway from Tara to Wicklow and trekked over by St. Patrick, is the oldest surviving thoroughfare in the city, dating back 1700 years.

Linked directly by road to the midlands, this northwest frontier of Dublin was a major market and trading hub for over a thousand years. It was the last part of the city in which Irish was spoken. Because of its sprawling cattle markets, the area became known as 'cowtown'. Here was the real 'wild west' of Dublin, a maelstrom of shuffling cattle, sheep, pigs, horses, drovers, farmers, dealers, traders, Tinkers, craftsmen and shopkeepers. Close association with the Royal Barracks, British occupation, and Black and Tan quarters brought people into personal confrontation with tumultuous historical events. Few parts of the capital have known such a convoluted and lively history. Even today, street names such as Viking Road, Norsemen Place, and Oxmantown Lane harken back unmistakably to distant origins, and local lore is thick with tales of saints, scoundrels, and classical characters. History and heritage here are a fair match for the Liberties.

Owing to its sequestered location, unique social-economic evolution, and freedom from predatory developers, Stoneybatter has survived rather miraculously into the 1980's physically and socially intact. Despite its inner-urban setting, it retains the basic character of a village as defined by urban geographers and sociologists. The traditional working-class population shares common geographical, historical, and social roots. Family, friends, and religion form the basis of daily life and old customs and traditions remain highly cherished. The enclosed maze-like structure of the artisan's dwel-

4 Observing a goat for sale at the Smithfield horse fair

lings is conducive to intimate social interaction and mutual dependency. Consequently, the old-fashioned, small town practice of 'neighbouring' still flourishes along every street.

In contrast to the rest of Dublin, people's lives here revolve around a small nub of support systems largely within a 200-yard radius — church, shops, pubs, betting offices, bank, post office, doctors, and community centre. It forms a very self-contained little universe. To be sure, most residents venture beyond for special shopping and visiting but the great part of their lives is spent in a relatively small sphere. There persists a distinct feeling of physical and psychological separateness from the rest of Dublin. People still habitually speak of 'going into town', though it only means a short jaunt by bus or foot to Henry or O'Connell Street. The cultural distance, however, is considerably greater.

The significance of Stoneybatter's survival is manifest in light of the widespread destruction experienced in central Dublin over the past twenty-five years. Historical architecture and venerable neighbourhoods have been obliterated with impunity by insensitive government authorities, urban planners, and greedy developers to make way for new roads, housing estates, and office buildings. Entire neighbourhoods, full of life and tradition, have been whittled away bit by bit or simply bulldozed into oblivion with bewildering speed, the local residents uprooted and transplanted in a sterile, suburban housing complex. Old Dublin communities, created over a great span of time, around Sean McDermott Street, Gardiner Street, Sheriff Street, and Summerhill have been stricken from the cityscape, all in the name of progressive urban redevelopment. Even the fabled Liberties, largely lost or tattered, now exists mostly in 'folk memory' and imagination.[3] Demolished, depopulated, drained of its very life-blood, much of the once-vibrant inner-city has been reduced to what Deirdre Kelly, head of the Dublin Living City Group, sadly terms 'dreary, dead Dublin'.

Stoneybatter stands alone as the conspicuous exception to the litany of destruction scarring Dublin's heartland. Not only has the physical environment been spared in terms of buildings, shops, houses, and streetscapes but the social milieu has been preserved as well. Thus, Stoneybatter constitutes a truly *living* inner-urban community retaining customs, traditions and city lifeways passed down over many generations. Furthermore, the area boasts the largest and most concentrated elderly population in Dublin. These 'old-timers' comprise an invaluable repository of local oral history and urbanlore.

Countless volumes have been written about Ireland's rural life, settlements, and folklore. To many writers and scholars, the terms 'tradition' and 'heritage' seem to have exclusive application to the rural realm. They hasten to study rural communities in decline before they vanish.[4] Since such settlements typically die a prolonged death through gradual emigration or economic stagnation, there is normally sufficient time in which to record their history and folkways. Conversely, there is a glaring absence of literature documenting the decline and demise of Dublin's inner-city settlements. This is regrettable because urban communities are as endowed with tradition, customs, heritage, and lore as their country counterparts. This omission is doubtless due, in part, to the inherent bias of many Irish against cities – Dublin in particular for its British connections. Also, the mistaken notion that urban neighbourhoods don't possess their own unique history worth recording may dissuade some from the task. But another explanation is certainly that city communities are often depopulated and demolished so swiftly that there is simply not time to record oral narratives and collect historical data.

What normally occurs when beloved parts of old Dublin perilously decline or disappear is that someone writes about them in a nostalgically retrospective and recreative manner. Some works are more seriously recollective than others. Such books as Mairin Johnston's *Around the Banks of Pimlico*, Bill Kelly's *Me Darlin' Dublin's Dead and Gone*, and Eamonn MacThomais' *Gur Cake and Coal Blocks* and *Me Jewel and Darlin' Dublin* are delightful and valuable personal reminiscences of the 'old days' around the city. Reflecting on the old neighbours, shops, activities, characters, and events, they paint a colourful picture of past time and place. But because these are *retrospective* accounts based on *singular personal memories* they are necessarily limited in scope and perspective. As eloquent as such authors may be, they can, at best, only recall and describe the past through their own vision and in their own words. They cannot speak for the people whom they remember nor tell us what was in the minds and hearts of bygone shopkeepers, neighbours, craftsmen of their childhood days. Nonetheless, considering that the communities they so lovingly recall no longer exist, their descriptive volumes stand as an important record.

In contrast to vanished Dublin neighbourhoods which must be recreated through memory, Stoneybatter offers a unique case – and a rare opportunity. Here is an inner-urban village community still alive, thriving, teeming with robust locals quite capable of telling their own tales. But many are of advanced age and their days are numbered. Residents are also confronted with threats to their home environment by impending urban redevelopment schemes. Stoneybatter stands starkly vulnerable and the future is uncertain. Preservationists regard it as the grand 'last stand' on the Dublin preservation scene. A decade from now it may no longer be a healthy and intact community. Mindful of such reality, the purpose of this book is to chronicle in a most human way the local history, heritage, lifeways, traditions, customs, characters and lore. To capture the very spirit and *ethos* of this living community before it changes drastically or perishes.

Chronicling the life and character of the community is best accomplished through the oral historical method. To create the richest human mosaic, widely disparate types must be included, from pig raiser to publican to parish priest — the humble to the exalted. Therefore, I assiduously sought out and tape recorded local folk of all sundried sorts — grocer, butcher, baker, fishmonger, cattle drover, horse dealer, pig raiser, tailor, pawnbroker, undertaker, stone carver, shoemaker, publican, pub 'regular', newspaper vendor, bookie, bettor, midwife, postman, cinema usher, priest, pensioner, housewife — and many more. They are the common folk who comprise the community.

Because no author could contrive the purity and poignancy of their speech and expressions, they are left to speak for themselves in their own inimitable fashion. Theirs is no nostalgic, romanticized account of life, but the hard truths. With great candour they share life's most personal experiences — childhood, poverty, schooldays, family struggles and strife, illness, work, drinking, courting, sexuality, religion, weddings, rearing children, losing infants, aging, death, wakes, and the 'beyond'. Their words are variously joyful and sad — often profound.

What emerges is an intensely human collage of life in Stoneybatter over the past century in the exact words and intonations of the participants themselves. The resulting range of experience and emotion allows one to feel the very pulse of the community. Simply stated, it is the most personal, undiluted type of social history and urbanlore. No such intimate historical account of an old Dublin community has ever been written. It is hoped that the originality of expression and testimony in this book will stand as an enduring document to the life and spirit of Stoneybatter, for here, in the truest sense, is the 'last of old Dublin'.

Geographical Identity

Historically, the term 'Stoneybatter' has had multiple meanings. Originally, it was known as *Bothar-na-gCloch*, or 'Road of the Stones'. In the second century it formed part of the royal road from Tara to Wicklow which crossed the Liffey River at the Ford of the Hurdles. Later, the name was changed to simpler Stoney-*Bothar* ('Stoney Road') and in more modern times corrupted to Stoneybatter. By the Middle Ages the name Stoneybatter transcended its road meaning and came gradually to refer to the area covering the old Viking settlement of Oxmantown and its adjoining green. Oxmantown, once a village completely separate from Dublin, encompassed the present-day area around Church Street, Smithfield, Bow Street, Queen Street, Blackhall Place, the western half of North King Street, Parkgate Street, Arbour Hill and Montpelier Hill.

In contemporary vernacular, Stoneybatter is still subject to varying interpretations. To historical purists, the term strictly applies to the street itself which extends only about one hundred yards and connects with Manor Street (See Map). To most local residents, Stoneybatter covers the old Oxmantown district generally corresponding with the Parish of the Holy Family on Aughrim Street. But the 1985 *Stoneybatter Development Plan* extends the area south to Benburb Street and west to the edge of Phoenix Park.

For the purpose of this book, Stoneybatter is defined generally as that area bounded by Grangegorman and Smithfield on the east, Benburb Street on the south, Infirmary Road on the west, and North Circular Road at the top. But the *core* of the greater Stoneybatter region, that part which actually constitutes the *urban village community*, centres on the complex of artisan's dwellings known to all as 'the buildings'. These stretch from Thor Place on the west to Kirwan Street on the east and Arbour Hill on the south up to the North Circular Road. This nucleus covers a radius of about one-third of a mile. Through its centre runs the Stoneybatter-Manor Street thoroughfare which is the principal axis.

5 *Small stone cottages at Arbour Hill. In harmonious scale with man*

Chapter 1

History and Heritage

'The story of the Parish is one of sinners as well as saints'.

(Record of the Parish of the Holy Family, Aughrim Street, Dublin, 1940)

'Oxmantown inhabitants presented a character which partook of that simplicity and homeliness that indicated constant intercourse with their rustic neighbours of Meath, whilst they were at the same time prevented from a disregard for the requisite qualities of civilized life by their close proximity to the capital.'

(Rev. Nathaniel Burton, *Oxmantown and Its Environs*, 1845)

ST. PATRICK AND THE 'STONEY ROAD'

Stoneybatter's history may be traced back 1700 years to the ancient thoroughfare of *Bothar-na-gCloch*. It formed part of *Sligh Cuallann*, one of the five great roads of Ireland, running from Tara in County Meath to Glendalough in County Wicklow. Paved with large stones similar to the Roman roads, this royal Irish highway crossed the Liffey River at the Ford of the Hurdles (a little upstream from present-day Church Street Bridge) by means of the Wattle Bridge. St. Patrick trod these stones in the middle part of the fifth century on his journeys to Tara. The strong imagery of St. Patrick's treks through Stoneybatter, so pridefully imprinted in local history and lore, is envisioned in the *Record of the Parish of the Holy Family*:[1]

One can picture his journey over the Wattle Bridge, through Stoneybatter, and then up Cabragh Lane, for such was the course of the old road. In his hand he bears his miraculous staff — the *Bachal Iosa*. How the tip of that staff resounded on the stones of *Bothar-na-gCloch* as Patrick went

23

on his way through North Dublin that day in the year 448; how gently
did he lay it on the sick, presented to him along the way, restoring
them, by its touch, to health and life.

Following in St. Patrick's steps were saintly students and founders of
learning centres, such as Kevin at Glendalough, Finnian of Clonard,
and Brendan at Birr, all of whom traversed the old stoney road and
left their mark on its early history.

THE VIKINGS AND OXMANTOWN

Towards the end of the eighth century the Norseman's invasion of
Ireland began. They established Dublin as their stronghold and
trading centre and it became a Scandanavian kingdom whose kings
had such hibernicised names as Sitric MacAuliffe and Hasculph
MacTorkill. Although the Viking's hold was broken by Brian Boru
in 1014 at the Battle of Clontarf, it wasn't until the Norman and
Saxon conquest of 1170 that they were actually displaced. When
the new invaders flocked to Dublin following the conquest, the
Vikings were either expelled or chose to migrate north of the Liffey.
Here they founded a settlement called Ostmentown, derived from
Ostmen or Eastman, a name given to the Scandanavians who lived
east of Ireland and England. Ostmentown and its great adjoining
green was later corrupted into 'Oxmantown'. This Norse settlement
generally covered the area north of the Liffey between what is today Phoenix Park on the west and Church Street on the east. The
ground on which the Bluecoat School now stands marked the
approximate centre and there were great surrounding oak forests.
    Oxmantown evolved as a village quite separate from Dublin,
carrying on substantial husbandry in livestock and agriculture and
trading extensively by using the river to reach other ports. Throughout the eleventh century portions of the vast woods were cleared.
Magnificent oaks were shipped over to England to make the roof
beams for Westminster Abbey. These made a 'glorious roof invin-
cible by time or worm' and about which it has since been claimed
'no English spider webbeth or breedeth to this day'.[2] The adjacent
green was used for various festivals and events, a bowling green,
and a Maypole celebration. Fairs and their attendant sideshows were
also held here. By the end of the century the independent village
of Oxmantown, which probably had its own walls and gates, was
linked to Dublin by what was known as Dubhgall's Bridge.
    It was around this period that one of Stoneybatter's most legend-

ary figures made his appearance. Gilbert, in his *History of the City of Dublin*, confirms that Little John, Robin Hood's robust lieutenant, fled to Oxmantown when Robin and his merry men were dispelled from Scotland.[3] Local lore has it that Robin, too, spent time in the vicinity but there is no proof to validate this. It is known, however, that Little John, coaxed by local admirers into showing his prowess in archery, proceeded, to their amazement and delight, to shoot an arrow from the Liffey bridge to Arbour Hill, a distance of some seven hundred yards. To this day, virtually every child in Stoneybatter can recount the mighty feat of Little John.

THE SCOUNDREL SCALDBROTHER

Oxmantown continued through the whole of the Middle Ages to form an entirely separate part of Dublin, its green constituting what Falkiner calls the 'great lung of the old city'.[4] Eventually, parts of the green were divided up to make space for the Bluecoat School and the Ormond Market. For over a millennium this northwest frontier of the city, linked by roads directly to nearby farms and the midlands, served as a major market and trading site. As an area of trading prosperity and much activity, it proved to be fertile territory for the exploits of one of Stoneybatter's most notorious scoundrels, known as Scaldbrother (a Danish name). This sixteenth century rogue and robber roamed the environs accosting people, snatching their possessions, and fleeing with his booty to a vast maze of subterranean passages extending from Smithfield to Arbour Hill. Not only was he a cunning thief but 'the varlet was so swift on foot as he has oftsoon outrun the swiftest and lustiest young men of Osmantown' in the chase.[5] It was his arrogant habit after a robbery to deride his victims. Knowing that no one was swift enough to catch him in pursuit, he would dash well ahead, pause beside a tavern called the 'gallows' and, within view of his frustrated pursuers, proceed to mock them by placing a rope around his neck and pretending to hang himself. When they approached, he sped safely away to his underground hideout known as Scaldbrother's Hole. Though everyone knew of the dark labyrinthian caverns, no one dared to venture into them.

Eventually, Scaldbrother was outwitted and caught. Several hardy young men were chosen to wait in ambush along his habitual course. Surprised and captured cold when crossing Hennockemagennocke Hill, he was the next day hanged publicly to the delight of a great throng there to witness the event. His legend outlived his deeds.

Centuries later when digging foundations for houses around Smith-field the ground sometimes caved in revealing the mysterious pas-sages. It is also reputed that local brewers used the cool under-ground chambers for their vats. And boys of the Bluecoat School have always believed that the caves lie directly beneath their school rooms. Images of hidden booty underground still intrigue local children and adults alike and some hold the fanciful notion that one day an archaeological excavation will expose Scaldbrother's hidden treasury.

MARTYRS ON ARBOUR HILL

As the Parish Record confirms, Stoneybatter's history is one of saints and heroes as well as sinners. Two seventeenth-century saintly figures occupy a prominent place in local history. By this period 'no longer did Osmantown see St. Patrick or scholars on their way to centres of learning; all that glory had gone, but for that which had passed something else had come – an Age of Martyrs'.[6] In 1612 the ground at Arbour Hill was sanctified by the blood of two such martyrs, Cornelius O'Devaney, a Franciscan and Bishop of Down and Connor, and a young priest, Father Patrick Loughran, on whose hands the oil of consecration was scarcely dry.

Bishop O'Devaney was arrested in the North of Ireland and brought to Dublin Castle for imprisonment. The following month Father Loughran was placed beside him. They were accused of treason to the Crown and of assisting the Catholics at war by saying Masses and administering the Sacraments to them. Government authorities used every persuasive means to induce them to publicly reject their faith, but in vain. Hence, they were sentenced to be hanged, drawn and quartered at the gibbet on Arbour Hill. As they were dragged along to the gallows-site a great crowd compassionately accompanied them. A last offer was made to declare themselves Protestant and have their life and possessions spared. Upon rejection, the rope was promptly fastened about their necks and they were cast off the scaffold:[7]

> The whole multitude gave one great shout of anguish, and then ensued an unbroken silence. They cut down the body very soon, cut off the head, opened the body, burned the entrails and then divided the body into four quarters.

Local history has it that the women of Stoneybatter courageously

6 *Sign pointing to historic Arbour Hill*

7 *Cobblestones and tram tracks are visible relics of a past age*

broke through the ranks of English soldiers and soaked their hand-
kerchiefs in the blood of the two martyrs (ostensibly, a relic of one
of these is preserved in Rome). After execution the remains were
ordered to be interred at the site. However, 'to the eternal honour
and glory of the young men of the district', that night about twelve
Catholic youths risked death themselves by secretly retrieving the
quartered, bloody bodies, ferrying them across the Liffey and bury-
ing them in coffins in a 'decent place with other martyrs'.[8] The
housing estate built in the northwest section of Stoneybatter is
named O'Devaney Gardens after the martyred Bishop.

LIFE IN THE SEVENTEENTH AND EIGHTEENTH CENTURIES

The latter part of the seventeenth and early eighteenth centuries
marked a period of growth and development in the area. In the 1660's
a large market place was established on Queen Street and at Smithfield a great cattle market was opened. In 1704 the Royal Barracks
were built in the western section of the village and with this development came a change in the character of surrounding streets. Benburb
Street, filled with traders, shops, infirmaries, workhouses, hotels,
and singing halls, became one of the busiest streets on the northside
during most of the eighteenth century. It was a raucous district
with a reputation for licentious behaviour, quite at odds with the
rest of 'respectable' Stoneybatter.

In *Life in Old Dublin* Collins describes Stoneybatter around the
middle of the eighteenth century as still 'a somewhat primitive
place'.[9] It was rustic and countrified compared with progressive
Dublin entering its glorious Georgian Age of grand architecture and
gay social life. In contrast to sophisticated city culture, Stoneybatter's social and economic character reflected close ties to rural
life, marketing and trade. In addition to the busy cattle and hay
markets around Smithfield there was the corn and frieze market on
the village green at the apex formed by the meeting of Aughrim,
Prussia and Manor streets. Nearby farm folk converged on Stoneybatter for their trade and shopping. The Irish language was widely
spoken because local traders and shopkeepers were obliged to understand and speak the language in order to carry out transactions with
farmers and their families from the nearby Meath Gaeltacht.

By the 1760's the so-called 'primitive' nature of Stoneybatter
began to hold great appeal to Dubliners coping with an increasingly
hectic pace of life in the crowded city. As Burton explains in his
book *Oxmantown and Its Environs*, the 'simplicity and homeliness'
were inticing:[10]

Many, tired of the bustle of the city, retired to Oxmantown where they erected houses suited to the quiet taste, amidst decaying woodlands and increasing orchards. Cabragh Lane (now Prussia Street) became a desirable and fashionable retreat. This may be accounted for from the amenite of the air which visits it from the park ... its balmy influence to salute the persons depressed by the density of the city, its avocations and cares, induced to stray towards this village in quest of recreation and the health that results from the use of genuine milk and dairy air.

With Dublin expanding, portions of Oxmantown green were let by lots to replenish city coffers. Stoneybatter became a locale much favoured by those seeking a countrified residence. But the solitude of the semi-rural setting, so relished by native and newcomer alike, was soon despoiled by the opening of the North Circular Road in 1768. The multitudes of equestrians, pedestrians, and vehicles of all sorts not only disrupted the traditional repose but interfered with the natural flow of farmers with their animals and goods filtering in from small country roads that intersected with it. While many openly disdained the intrusion, others revelled in witnessing the exciting flurry of activity — 'simpler folk loved to see the quality flashing by, such as the beautiful Duchess of Rutland, who delighted in the new thoroughfare as a speedway on which she could handle her pony phaeton with grace and skill'.[11]

Village tranquility was further marred by a riotous event in Oxmantown Green on 1 May, 1773. At this time, surrounding villages had their own customs and annual festivities, such as Donnybrook with its famous fair. Stoneybatter had a grand Mayday celebration on its green. On this occasion, however, unruly British soldiers attempted to pull down the Maypole as it was being erected. The local populace attacked them with fury, driving them back into their barracks and breaking windows. Soon thereafter, the soldiers returned and retaliated by firing muskets, thus disbanding the crowd. In the days following, newspapers condemned the violence and, as a consequence, the popular Mayday ceremony was eventually abolished.

'BILLY-IN-THE-BOWL' AND THE 'HANGING JUDGE'

This was also the period in which one of Stoneybatter's most infamous 'sinners' enacted his deeds. By birth he was a *lesus naturae* ('freak of nature'), possessing no legs. As he grew into childhood he transported himself about in a bowl-shaped vehicle on wheels, using his powerful arms to propel it along the ground with wooden pegs. Thus, he became known as 'Billy-in-the-Bowl'. Despite his pitiable disability, he was a handsome and charming lad:[12]

> Nature had compensated for his curtailment by giving him fine, dark eyes, an aquiline nose, and a well formed mouth, with dark curling locks and a body and arms of Herculean power. He certainly won the hearts of the plebeian fair north of the Liffey.

He survived by begging, relying upon charm and sympathy to elicit a few coins. He was capable of evoking great pity and initially people were generously compassionate. Billy plied all the streets of Stoneybatter, attended every fair, and was known to everyone. But behind the comely face there existed a 'ruffian at heart' who freely indulged his pet vices of gambling and drinking to great excess.[13] To support these dual addictions, he resorted to robbing and eventually murdering some of his hapless victims. His scheme was to situate himself at lonely places along dark roads awaiting vulnerable women victims. Upon their approach, he would, in plaintive tone, beg for a few coins. Once within reach, he would lock upon them with his powerful hands, strangle them, rob them, then drag their body into the ditch. Simple servant girls proved his favourite targets. These crimes became known locally as the 'Grangegorman Lane Murders'. At first, nobody suspected the pathetic, deformed beggar. The end of his preying came one night when he attempted foolishly to rob two stoutly-constructed cooks trudging home from their place of employment. They proved too much for him, one ripping his face open with her sharp nails while the other ran for assistance. Billy was caught, tried and sentenced for robbery but it could never be proved that he had committed the murders. Upon conviction he was imprisoned and to the end of his days remained an attraction for curiosity mongers of north Dublin.

Another historical culprit lived in nearby Cabra at the northern extremity of Stoneybatter. He was John Toler, better known as Lord Norbury, the 'Hanging Judge'. He earned the title when he presided over the trials of many of the 1798 leaders and that of Robert Emmet. Detested by local people for his cruel acts, he was mythologised upon death. As the tale goes, the 'bloodthirsty judge was, on his death, changed into a phantom black dog, condemned for eternity to prowl around the area dragging a large chain behind him'.[14] His house was reputed to be haunted and people customarily avoided it at night by crossing to the far side of the road. Although the house was demolished in 1940 ghostly stories still persist.

NINETEENTH CENTURY SCENE

At the dawning of the 1800's Stoneybatter was a lively, flourishing place. Smithfield was renowned throughout Ireland as a great market for cattle and hay and most of the city's dairies were concentrated in the area. Strewn along the Prussia-Manor-Stoneybatter thoroughfare were coach stops, inns, pubs, boarding houses and numerous provision shops. The corn and frieze market thrived and many local women found employment cleaning and riddling seeds for the hay-seed dealers. Country folk flooded in with carts heaped with hay, vegetables and turf. Street life was congested and haphazard. Rowdy drovers, known as 'penny boys' and carrying bludgeons for their task, herded hordes of unruly cattle, sheep and pigs through the streets as pedestrians dodged the beasts. At this time cattle were often slaughtered on the spot where they were sold. To accommodate the country people, animal dealers and buyers, the area was filled with cheap boarding houses of every description. A good many people got a free night's sleep in the warm, soft hay in the lofts at Smithfield. At the popular eating houses, such as Stickfoot's opposite St. Michan's, one could feast on a generous plate of cabbage, pig's head and potatoes for four pence. To cater to the early-rising market crowd, all the local pubs had a licence to open at seven in the morning and too many took advantage of it.

A number of important developments occurred during this century. Following the Act of Union (1801), the military presence in the city was reduced for a time and some of the area's houses gradually fell into tenement use, setting the stage for poverty and congestion. However, the building of new houses continued on some main streets and along North Circular Road. In the 1860's a new cattle market was opened at the top of Prussia Street and soon thereafter the city abattoir was constructed adjacent to it. This triggered a decline in business around Smithfield. Completion of the stately Parish Church of the Holy Family on Aughrim Street in 1880 instilled within the community a great pride and a feeling of solidarity. But the most ambitious and far-reaching project of this period was a massive construction of the artisan's dwellings. This impressive undertaking put an end to many of the open fields and orchards and gave Stoneybatter the physical and architectural form it retains to the present day.

CREATION OF THE ARTISAN'S DWELLINGS

Dublin in the latter part of the nineteenth century was a city in great housing distress. It had become the principal urban catchbasin for rural masses fleeing the horrors of the Great Famine. During the period 1841-1900 the population of Ireland declined but Dublin increased from 236,000 to 290,000. Once-lordly Georgian houses were converted into tenements crammed with as many as sixty to ninety people. Dublin became noted for its poverty, unemployment, squalor and slums. The northside was the most depressed and some streets around Stoneybatter, such as Brunswick Street, North King Street and Queen Street, suffered virulent poverty and tenementation.

An article written a century ago in *The Irish Builder* noted with alarm the urgent need to alleviate the housing crisis. It was argued that the honest, respectable, industrious artisans and labourers of the city were entitled to decent housing but suggested that some impoverished souls 'leading immoral lives' might best be isolated in a 'species of ghetto'.[15] There were, at this time in Dublin's history, clear distinctions made between the 'deserving' and the 'undeserving'. Artisans were regarded as a higher order than their less-skilled brethren. Consequently, in the 1870's the Dublin Artisan's Dwellings Company (DADC) was established to help solve the housing problem for the city's respectable working classes.

This private company, working in cooperation with the Dublin Corporation, was managed by leading Protestant and Quaker businessmen who stated clearly that theirs was not a philanthropic undertaking but a commercial one. Furthermore, their avowed objective was not merely to provide physical shelter for labouring families but also to 'socially and morally elevate' them by encouraging a more civilised, sanitary lifestyle.[16] Consistent with this lofty goal, they implemented a policy of carefully screening prospective tenants. It was deemed essential that 'applicants were thoroughly respectable'.[17] Over the next three decades the DADC operated as the only substantial private builder on the Dublin scene constructing new housing for the working classes. By 1900, the company had built some 3,000 separate dwellings accommodating nearly 15,000 people. Most of the new houses were actually outside the areas of hardcore poverty and catered to tradesmen and skilled workers. Nonetheless, the activity did benefit the poor because as the artisans moved into their new dwellings it freed housing space for the lower-income classes.

The Stoneybatter district, because of its open spaces of land on the former Oxmantown green site, was designated as one of the DADC's major building zones. Old orchard land here was sold to the company for construction. It was noted that during the clear-

*8 Typically well-kept and personalised front of artisan's dwelling
on Viking Road*

ing process 'golden groves have been sawn down to the earth level ... some measured two feet in diameter, denoting, for fruit trees, a growth of many centuries'.[18] Local residents hold that they were planted by the Danes themselves.

One particular strategy of the DADC needs to be emphasised because it is responsible for the physical and social character of Stoneybatter as it exists to this day. This was the company's visionary idea of not merely constructing housing tracts but actually endeavouring to create social communities where people of like kind would live closely and in harmony. They set out to achieve this in two ways. First, by creating a physically integrated housing structure; second, by populating their dwellings with selected groups of related families.

The objective of producing communities was accomplished in significant part by the physical lay-out itself. Both architecture and streetscapes were designed with this human concept strongly in mind. Characteristically, each block contained two parallel rows of houses whose small rear yards with privies and coalhouses were separated by a narrow lane or 'cleansing passage'. Another vital integrating feature was that of housing site density, some sections having as many as fifty dwellings to the acre. This high concentration of small, compact houses, directly facing each other and arranged in a linear and maze-like pattern proved highly conducive to close social interaction and a sense of community. Also, since no designated areas with recreation facilities were provided, frontal footpaths, streets and corners served as space for socialising, recreation, and sports – thus naturally drawing people together. The only initial criticism was that the streetscapes, lined with stereotyped, unimaginative row houses were visually austere and boring (this was later changed dramatically). But if the dwellings were dreary in appearance they were solid in construction and provided the basic amenity for decent living.

Formation of a community was equally engendered by the policy of giving preferential treatment to new tenants with relatives already established in the area. Since there were long waiting lists for the new houses, company authorities conveniently selected newcomers on this basis. Consequently, a whole clan of parents, children, grandparents, uncles, aunts, and cousins could be clustered in the same vicinity literally within shouting distance. And children always had the right of inheriting the family home. As Eamonn O'Brien, third generation artisan's dweller, puts it, 'it was the *history* of the artisan's dwellings that to qualify for a house you had to be born in them. Outsiders couldn't come in ... it went from children to children.

Grandparents and parents and children all tended to live in the one area. We were very close'.

Children were, of course, free to depart and take up residence elsewhere, especially upon marriage. But in practice the majority have always remained as close to their parents as possible — in the same house, next door, down the street. Thomas Linehan, born and reared on Murtagh Road, can trace his family back to the dwellings when they were built a century ago. 'Families perpetuated themselves', he explains, 'it was a *tradition* that people *born* in the "buildings" *stayed* in the "buildings". Genuine, honest Dublin working-class people ... the salt of the earth. A lot of the elderly people today, their people came from the same street'. This type of social cohesion and continuity forged the village community into the mould it still possesses.

A PROSPEROUS PERIOD: 1900-1916

The period 1900-1916 was a 'prosperous time for Stoneybatter', years during which many individuals in this book were born.[19] Prosperity in this particular part of the city was due in large measure to the expanded contingent of British soldiers stationed there. Local trade and business boomed. The British army required massive general supplies as well as great amounts of foodstuffs and fodder for their horses. Demand was so great that there were five weighbridges at Smithfield, two in the Haymarket and even one in Blackhall Street. Apart from official army purchases, soldiers did most of their personal shopping and drinking at nearby establishments. Though they are remembered for having bought up the best steaks, fruit and whiskey, their business was much appreciated by local merchants. Grocers, butchers, hairdressers, publicans and shopkeepers of all sorts profited handsomely from their presence and their money filtered throughout the Stoneybatter economy.

In retrospect, most people here remember the British soldiers as a 'decent enough sort' simply carrying out an unpleasant assignment. Invariably, careful distinction is made between the 'tolerated' British troops and the 'despised' Black and Tans. Merchants almost unfailingly treated British soldiers respectfully. Mary Kinane's father owned the most popular Gent's Hairdresser's shop on Stoneybatter Street. Since her family lived above the shop she regularly mixed with customers. 'We had an awful lot of British army all around here. "Tommies" we called them. They were customers in the shop but no distinction was made. Never minded British soldiers in the shop, my father got on all right with them. But the Black and Tans, they were a different type altogether.'

In addition to the army's contribution, the rest of the local economy was healthy as well. The cattle market atop Prussia Street had become the largest in the British Isles, selling weekly nearly 5,000 cattle, 7,000 sheep and 1,000 pigs. British, German, Dutch and other European buyers came every Wednesday and Thursday to conduct big business. They, too, pumped much money into the economy through their patronisation of boarding houses, shops and pubs. The favourite haven of big cattle buyers was the City Arms Hotel on Prussia Street. As a young man, Billy Ennis worked at the hotel as, variously, a messenger boy, bootblack, bellboy, waiter and barman. 'It was really a cattleman's hotel. The British and Dutch, oh, they had money. They'd throw money around just the same as water ... live it up drinking and eating. It was no bother handing you a five shillings tip and that was a week's wages nearly at that time.' Beyond the income generated by the cattle market, many people found good employment in Jameson's Distillery, Guinness's Brewery and Jacob's Biscuit Factory.

SMITHFIELD CLAMOUR AND CHARACTERS

Smithfield, though having lost its cattle business to the new market, still enjoyed huge sales of hay, grain, fruits, vegetables, horses and turf. Farmers, drovers, traders and Tinkers all mixed on the cobblestones in a swirl of activity that entranced Moira Lysaght as an impressionable young girl. Now a sprightly eighty-five years of age, she still delights in reminiscing about childhood experiences before local groups or through radio broadcasts. As an active member of the Old Dublin Society, she put some of her memories in print in the *Dublin Historical Record*:[20]

> The area around Smithfield of my youthful memory, it resembled a country town, except for the cobblestones which contributed a far greater noise. Early in the morning the iron-covered wheels and the steel-shod horse's hooves of the milk carts clattered along accompanied by their jangling milk cans, all providing an orchestral overture to the commercial day. There was an even much earlier shattering of the brief silence of night on Thursdays when the lowing of cattle and the padding of their hooves were rounded off by loud 'Ho, Hoo, Ho's' from their drovers en route to the cattle market on the North Circular Road.
>
> Haymarket days held in Smithfield created a hum of industry, the horse-

9 The 'menfolk scene' at horse fair in Smithfield

10 Horse and cart in cobblestoned Red Cow Lane outside of potato merchant's

drawn carts top heavy with hay adding their fragrance to the picturesque scene. Grainwash from the nearby Jameson's Distillery was shovelled from big vat-like lorries into farmer's carts for animal feeding. Farmers strode along with their whips tied in bandolier fashion over their shoulders and unpretentious restaurants and sleeping accommodations were to be found to facilitate visiting farmers and dealers. And there were coach builders, harness makers, and farriers, many with living quarters above their premises. Tinkers dealt in horses, asses and mules. On those market days the usual occupational sounds were occasionally drowned by the braying of a Tinker's ass, but much more blood-curdling was the cry of some of its owners with all the troup joining in and blood being spilt and hair flying in the faction fighting fashion of olden days.

Such was life in Stoneybatter around 1915. As many old-timers recall, the scene was further enlivened by the antics and eccentricities of local characters. One of the most memorable and amusing was 'Jack the Tumbler', a familiar figure in Stoneybatter's streets. A small man of dishevelled appearance with shaggy black beard, he tramped around barefooted and hatless but 'attired in a "claw-hammer" coat with trousers of somewhat clerical aspect'.[21] He would wait for a hackney car or cab to come along and then, positioning himself alongside or behind it, would double up and comically tumble after it for five or six yards, hopefully to the amusement of passengers and observers. When he would hear the ring of a few coppers striking pavement he would scurry to scoop up the coins. He would also perform along footpaths and in front of shops, fascinating children and bringing smiles to adults. When his pocket was filled with sufficient coinage he would stomp into a pub, place his order, and dump the heap of coppers onto the counter from which the publican could extract the correct sum.

There was also 'Blind Joe' Sadler, the local newspaper delivery man. Despite his blindness, he was able to distinguish papers by feel and unerringly delivered them to the proper hands. He delighted in advertising his trade by shouting out the news of the day after being so informed by a friend. However, some waggish friends occasionally took mischievous fun in fuelling him with bogus news stories which he excitedly disseminated throughout the neighbourhood — until he sheepishly learned the truth. These are but two of the many entertaining local characters fondly recalled by those who saw them as just a natural part of daily life early in the century.

1916–1922: TURBULENT TIMES

The fateful years from 1916 to 1922 saw Stoneybatter swept up in political turmoil. With the British barracks and Black and Tan quarters in their very midst, people were personally confronted with all the dangers and dramas of the times. Military manoeuvrings, surveillance, curfews, home raids, searching, ransacking, looting and shooting were part of local life. Molly Baker, eighteen years of age when the Rising occurred, witnessed all the activity surrounding her home on Blackhall Place:

> In 1916 you didn't go near a window. You dare not open a door. You'd pull the blinds and get inside. When there was curfew everyone was in fear. There was a terrific lot of shooting. You could be knocked up at night and your house ransacked and you questioned. We'd hear rumours of people being shot at night and things taken from their homes and people being taken out, even women. There was a terrible lot of atrocities during that period.

Since many local men were actively involved in the Movement the area was rife with clandestine IRA activity and intrigue. Chris Carr, aged ninety, knew it first-hand since her father participated in the Movement, served as a gun-runner at Howth, and hid weapons in the home. Politicised by the experience, she became a member of one of the first *Cumann na mBan* formed during the Hostilities. Her feelings still run strong, especially hatred of the dreaded Black and Tans:

> The Black and Tans, they weren't in the army. They were a bunch of their own kind. They murdered an awful lot. They were desperate. They used to come out at night when the curfew would start, used to raid public houses and come out with bottles of whiskey and they'd drink it and then they'd raid a house. And when they raided your home, they *raided* it! They'd come and rap on your door at 4:00 in the morning with their gun. They'd pull everything out of the wall and throw it around the place and put bayonets through the cushions. They went around breaking into shops and robbing and terrorising everybody. They were drunk and could do what they liked because there was no control.

Children growing up amid such strife were traumatised to varying degrees. Many individuals today, looking back at these experiences, marvel that they came through it so well and liken it to the situation in Northern Ireland at present. In old age, some are forgiving and philosophical; others still carry deep hostility and scars. Harry John-

son, eighty-four, had many an unpleasant encounter with the Black
and Tans as a youth and does not easily forget:

> Oh, Jesus, I ran into them. The Black and Tans were the worst curse on
> the earth. If you were on the street after ten you'd see the point of a
> rifle. They might say 'Bring him up!' and you'd get a boxing. We could
> do nothing because they had the guns. Couldn't even use our hands
> because they'd pull the trigger and you were gone. Some were brutal.
> They'd go into Mulligan's Pub down there, maybe twenty or thirty of
> them. 'Bloody Irish pigs' they used to call us. The Black and Tans were
> scurrilous. Men of my age now, we still have that little stigma against the
> British Crown. I still have it. It'll only leave you when you die. It'll die
> with you.

In 1922 the people of Stoneybatter turned out *en masse* to cheer
and jeer the British soldiers as they marched down the streets to
the quays for the last time. 'When Independence came there was
great excitement', recalls Chris Carr, 'the soldiers all marched out
of the barracks down to their boats. They were laughing and singing 'A Long Way to Tipperary'. The crowd down on the quays gave
them plenty of clapping and plenty of boo's, I can assure you. And
I gave them a few boo's as well.'

THE HUNGRY TWENTIES AND THIRTIES

With political peace came a time of economic hardship and struggle.
The 1920's and 1930's have been described as the 'worst period
Stoneybatter had ever known', characterised by high unemployment, low wages, emigration, poverty and hunger.[22] Barefooted
children and adults in tattered clothing were common sights. Apart
from the general economic malaise of the times, the local economy
suffered its own problems. By the Twenties, Stoneybatter's rural-
based economy had begun to falter. Trading in livestock declined,
horse dealing was dealt a blow by the arrival of motor vehicles,
adjacent farmland and farm families were waning, traditional crafts
dying out, and small factories closed or laid off workers. Jobs were
few and times lean. Financial struggle was exacerbated in the Stoneybatter community where large families of typically five to nine
children were still dictated by Church teaching and social tradition.
Vincent Muldoon, seventy-three, was born and reared above the
little family fishmonger shop on North King Street which served
the poorest of the poor:

Around the 1920's there was no work, only poverty. Mass unemployment and mass hunger where we lived, and all tenement houses. Fish, shell coco, margarine and rabbits, that was the staple diet. And you'd have 'blind stew' without meat in it. People were *really hungry*. A woman, ah, she'd take your life to feed her family. It was a necessity at that point. There was nine of us in my family. If you hadn't got eight or nine it would be a stigma. It was a sin not to have large families.

The condition of hardship served to heighten the sense of community and increased cooperation and sharing among neighbours. John Byrne, a young man during the Thirties, reflects on how 'people just *existed*. They helped each other. If you had a little something extra you'd give it to your neighbour next door. But drinking was terrible heavy ... it was to forget their misery.' During troubled times women normally carried the heaviest burden of caring for the family, a fact readily conceded by men. 'Women held the families together' is a common refrain. Within community culture wives and mothers sometimes became heroines — even saintly figures. Survivors of that period today take great pride in their personal struggle and that of the community, remembering it as a period of selflessness, deep faith, sharing and character-building. Inevitably, they tend to compare the modern age of materialism and comfort to this past time and experience — and wonder about the values of present generations.

POST-WAR CONDITIONS

During the Forties things improved, though it was still a time of scarcity and unemployment. Government social and economic benefits had increased and at least there was more food on the table and children had shoes. In the post-war period when most of Dublin was entering the modern age, Stoneybatter, as one observer wrote, still retained its 'old world appearance'.[23] It was the very last section of the inner-city between the canals to be built up and even into the Fifties there remained patches of open fields. But in 1954 O'Devaney Gardens, an extensive flats complex, was built in the northwest sector. Although this development altered the traditional economic and social composition of the greater area by bringing in lower-income families with no local roots, it did not change the physical or social character of the artisan's dwellings community. If anything, it tended to reinforce the feelings that they were a separate and inviolable community with their separate territory, history and traditions.

The last quarter century has seen some significant changes in Stoneybatter. In the 1960's the old DADC policy of excluding outsiders from tenancy gave way to a more open, democratic system when the company began selling its housing stock to a private commercial firm and, in turn, houses were offered for sale to individuals. This allowed anyone to purchase a vacant dwelling and brought in some newcomers. But the long tradition of retaining the home within the family is still predominant and along most streets the 'blow-ins' have been welcomed as an injection of fresh social life.

In the 1970's a triple blow was struck. First, Jameson's Distillery terminated operations and left the city, then the great cattle market, in decline for years, finally closed down, and shortly thereafter, the abattoir followed suit. Considerable local employment was lost. Closure of the cattle market had the most adverse effect, not only because of the economic impact but also due to its psychological status within the community. Since anyone could remember, the cattle market had been the central focus of identity. Virtually everyone had some personal identification with it. All were 'cowtowners' by simple virtue of shared proximity and history. Predictably, the elderly were most unsettled by this loss, many finding it hard to accept that the old cattle market had really perished and been built over with a new housing estate.

The most recent threat to traditional Stoneybatter came in the early 1980's when a new supermarket and shopping centre were built at the top of Prussia Street. Local small shopkeepers viewed the development with great apprehension. Though the sleek, modern stores have siphoned off some trade, the local clientele have remained loyal and the majority of family-owned shops have survived.

Stoneybatter has experienced a long, illustrious, sometimes checkered, and often traumatic history. Among Dublin's old communities it must surely be regarded as the undisputed 'survivor'. In the late 1980's the physical environment, artisan's dwellings, and most shops remain basically intact and the village community alive and thriving. The coming decade may not be so kind.

11 Children swinging on lamp-post as their grandparents used to do

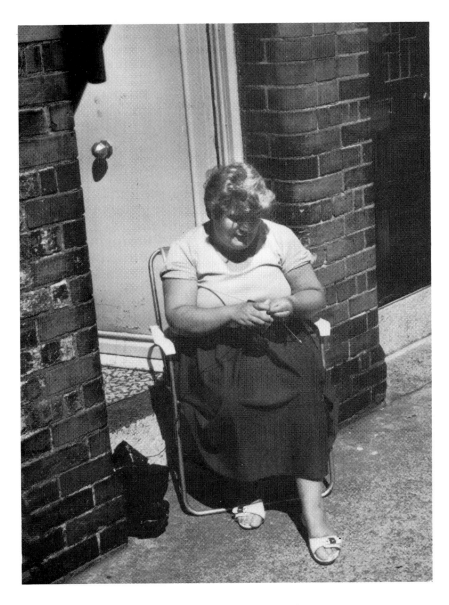

12 Knitting on a warm summer afternoon

Chapter 2

Survival as an Urban Village Community

'Stoneybatter was a pleasant place, like a little country district. There were little white-washed cottages on both sides of Chicken Lane and yards up there that had cows, sheep, goats, pigs and poultry running around. It was like a little village in Galway, something like the Claddagh.'

(Sarah Murray, aged 87 — oldest resident in Chicken Lane)

CONCEPT OF THE URBAN VILLAGE

The terms 'urban' and 'village' may appear incongruous. Yet there are such geographical and sociological entities as 'urban villages'. A few generations ago they were still quite common in many large European and American cities. They were usually associated with particular ethnic, racial, or cultural groups. These social enclaves, often known simply as 'old world neighbourhoods', had their distinctive character and customs which provided invigorating cultural diversity within the larger urban system. Most have been eradicated by war or urban development.

Judged by the criteria defined by Gans in his classic work *The Urban Villagers*, Stoneybatter is more than a community or network of linked neighbourhoods — it is an authentic inner-urban village.[1] Communities require only a shared area, common ties, and social interaction; hence, we even have newly-formed suburban communities.[2] But, as Gans explains, a true urban village community possesses its own unique history, geographical territory, deep ancestral roots, cherished customs and traditions, urbanlore and social character. Clearly, such characteristics — all of which are evident in Stoneybatter — can only be formed over generations. Another typical mark of villages, be they rural or urban, is a central roadway along which most pubs, shops and services are concentrated. This, too, is found in Stoneybatter.

The distinctive atmosphere of a village community is perceived

45

by outsiders as well as residents. McLoughlin notes in his current
Guide to Historic Dublin that in Stoneybatter the 'feeling persists
of walking in the middle of an enclosed community'.[3] Similarly,
Deirdre Kelly observed that it still retains a 'quality more like a
country town'.[4] Local people simply refer to their area as 'countrified', 'small townish', and 'villagey', all pridefully expressed.
Their social and psychological detachment from other Dubliners is
unmistakable. They even couch conversation in terms of 'we' and
'they' to denote the difference.

Another trait of village life is community spirit and assisting
others. The tenet that hard times and tragedies 'bring out all that
is best in village life' has been validated by Stoneybatter's social
history.[5] There is no older tradition here than coming to the aid of
a neighbour in need. Ordinary people have always helped to feed,
medically care for, financially assist, and just 'look in on' others
around them. Their oral histories are replete with examples. Evidence may even be found in a current issue of the *Stoneybatter
Community News*:[6]

> Recent events have been a test to the community. Over Christmas and
> during the cold spell, people have demonstrated their mettle. There are
> heartwarming stories. The lady with four children who, finding herself
> without money on Christmas Eve, was presented with a substantial sum
> collected within a local establishment. And the numerous examples of
> the elderly and incapacitated being called upon by their more active
> neighbours, sometimes on entirely unrelated pretexts.

Such charitable acts occur year around, not only at Christmas time.
Apart from individual efforts to assist neighbours, the local shops
and pubs routinely collect donations and hold draws to raise money
for assorted local causes. Mulligan's Pub, for example, holds a
monthly draw, the considerable profits going to help the local elderly
population.

Apart from social characteristics, there are purely visual features
which give Stoneybatter its villagey appearance and rural flavour, setting it off strikingly from the rest of modern Dublin. Old-fashioned
pubs and shopfronts, shopkeepers still living above the premises, and
surviving craftsmen such as a shoemaker, harness-saddle maker,
handcraft tailor and stone carver all tell of small town life. But
surely nothing defines the area so dramatically as its animal life
and horse fairs. Back lanes and alleys harbour horses, ponies, goats
and chickens. And several hundred pigs are still raised in the locality.
Consequently, an enduring village tradition, dating back many cen-

turies, is the annual Blessing of the Animals in Smithfield on the Feast of St. Francis of Assissi. This is performed by a local priest on the cobblestones amid a 'chorus of barking, braying, cackling, neighing, and mewing'.[7] On the first Sunday of each month there is also a raucous horse fair held here with as many as 250 horses and a thousand people in attendance. Like a scene from earlier times, it draws a fascinating array of old cattle drovers, horse dealers, farm people, Tinkers and cattlemen. All this in *inner*-Dublin in the 1980's!

PHYSICAL AND ARCHITECTURAL ENVIRONMENT

'Street names often tell the tale of a town.'

(Patrick Shaffrey, *The Irish Town*, 1975)

'Notice the windows and doors and the care and pride people take in keeping their housefronts and pavements clean.'

(*Stoneybatter Development Plan*, 1985)

If Shaffrey's dictum is true, that the history of a town or village may be deciphered from its street and place names, then Stoneybatter's past may surely be read like some ancient tome. No part of Dublin is so bounteous in colourful historical names — Stoneybatter Street, Queen Street, North King Street, Prussia Street, Manor Street, Grangegorman, Blackhall Place, Arbour Hill, Haymarket, Friary Avenue, Red Cow Lane, Smithfield Market, Thundercut Alley, Chicken Lane, Kirwan Cottages. And, of course, those of Scandinavian origin such as Oxmantown Road, Thor Place, Viking Road, Norseman Place, Finn Street and Olaf Road. Each has its particular history.

It would also be difficult to find another part of the capital with so varied an architectural collection, from primitive white-washed stone cottages to elegant Victorian edifices. Between the two may be found fine examples from the Medieval, seventeenth century and Georgian periods. The most stately Georgian and Victorian structures line the Stoneybatter-Manor-Prussia Street thoroughfare. These larger two and three storey buildings are suited nicely in style and scale to the wider streets they front. Many are embellished by large, handsome front doors, fanlights, artistic ironwork and manicured front gardens. This creates an impressive central vista. Some of the historic pubs along the same course boast fine architecture. A notable example along Stoneybatter Street is Mulligan's Pub,

'Established 1791', with a facade and interior little changed over two centuries. Fifty paces away is Walsh's Pub, of slightly later origin, which served as a coach stop and inn during the early 1800's. At the top of Manor Street is Kavanagh's Pub of Victorian vintage with its rust red brick, crowning turret and decorative interior with dark wood and gleaming brass.

By comparison to the pubs, most shops seem small and poky. But their very simplicity and unpretentiousness imbues them with a charm that is a vital part of Stoneybatter's ambience. Weathered fascias, sagging slate roofs with tufts of green moss, floors sprinkled with sawdust and counter tops worn smooth from generations of hands and elbows rested during good conversation all give the little shops a comfortably aged countenance. Each morning front windows are freshly dressed with displays of fruit, bread, meat and vegetables, while hand-scrawled signs are implanted among them to draw customers' attention to special prices of the day. Nothing fancy here. Everyone likes it that way. Joseph Moore, aged seventy-two and owner of Nolan's, one of the oldest grocers, recognises the appreciation people have for the atmosphere:

> It's an old-fashioned kind of shop. I dress the windows every morning, mostly sausages, bacon, ham, cereals, and jams and fruit. It looks real good. We still hang the bacon and hams on those bars. Very few shops do it now. People smell the bacon and look up in amazement. Even people coming back from England will bring their kids in and show them.

Some shops are matchbox small, like Noel's Family Grocery which still does only counter service and can hold no more than about five patient patrons at a time. Until a few years ago many shops had half-doors. These were practical when cattle were herded down the streets. Closing the bottom half normally kept rambunctious beasts out but sometimes they barged in, creating chaos and disrupting business. 'You'd think you were in a wild west film', remembers Moore, 'Oh, I'd have to get the bacon pole to get 'em out.' Sometimes animals would actually begin to ascend the stairs to the family quarters and have to be dragged out by the tail bellowing. It was great drama for customers and on-lookers.

The 'villagescape' is more than a collection of shops, pubs and historic buildings. It also includes those items collectively known as 'street furniture'. Included are lamp-posts, coal-hole covers, post boxes, boot-scrapers, iron window guards, balcony railings, fences, gates and other decorative paraphernalia. Though seemingly insignificant on their own, they collectively form an important constitu-

13 Joseph Moore, butcher and owner of Nolan's Family Grocery on Stoneybatter Street

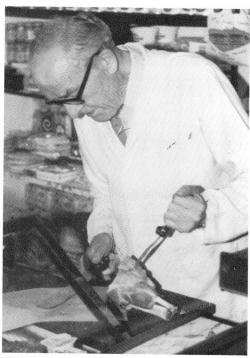

14 Noel's Family Grocer's and local Stoneybatter Post Office on Stoney-batter Street

*15 Delicately decorated shamrock lamp-post in Stoneybatter is one of the
surviving types of street furniture embellishing the old streetscapes*

ent along every streetscape, giving a variety of detail, texture and dimension. Stoneybatter has a bountiful inheritance of quality street furniture. Along major streets may be found delicate shamrock-festooned lamp-posts, harp-shaped boot-scrapers, elaborately sculpted iron gates, railings, window guards and lantern holders. Even remote back streets have interesting brass letter boxes, door knobs and knockers. The artistry and originality of this street furniture, some centuries old, is a visual cornucopia for the careful observer.

It is unmistakably the artisan's dwellings which still give Stoneybatter its distinctive physical form and architectural character. Their linear pattern with intersecting streets creates the maze effect, explaining McLoughlin's observation that one feels almost entrapped in an 'enclosed' community. But for residents it provides a sense of integration and security. Streetscape vistas are orderly and coherent with single or two-storey dwellings uniformly lining each side. One of the most pleasing features of the houses is that they were built to such a human scale. There seems a natural harmony between people and the small houses. Some, like Kirwan Cottages, are so diminutive as to appear more like tiny country bungalows. Built solidly of brick in predominantly red, brown and grey colour, houses typically have two small bedrooms, a parlour and kitchen area. Despite their modest size, these dwellings have traditionally housed large families of ten and more. Annie Muldoon, one of eleven children, remembers with no hint of regret that eighty years ago there were 'six or seven of us in one bed'. Such congestion, however, undeniably caused stress and social problems in some homes. Thomas Linehan witnessed these problems along his street:

> You could get up to fifteen people in a house. I can remember family rows and it must have been the fact that people didn't have enough room to breathe. A very small house and an element of unemployment and a lot of the time it was drink related. Sometimes you'd even have the eldest son and the father coming to blows.

Tenants have a strong tradition of being house-proud. Therefore, although the housing stock is now a century old, it has been extremely well maintained. Roofs, chimneys, brickwork and window frames are regularly patched or replaced. In cases where an occupant is physically or financially incapable of keeping his home in good repair, relatives and neighbours often assume the responsibility. The manager of the local Bank of Ireland affirms that a high proportion of money borrowed goes toward house maintenance. In recent years many people have added extensions at the rear for additional bedroom, bathroom or kitchen space. People also enjoy embellishing their homes. Joseph Treacy, owner of the local decorating shop, understands their motivation:

> People save up to do their house. Putting money into the house has been their pride and joy. Some people wallpaper the living room every year ... feel it gives them a new lease on life. People kept their houses up. It's their *pride*.

Indeed, people seem to be constantly repainting doors and window trim, polishing brass knobs and knockers, scrubbing pavement and sweeping clean the gutters. Testimony to their cleanliness, the Stoneybatter community won first prize in the 1987 Tidy District Competition for the inner-city, sponsored by the Dublin Corporation. Here, too, Stoneybatter stands visually apart from much of the rest of 'dear, dirty Dublin'.

The original criticism that stereotyped streetscapes were drab and boring is today seldom heard. Over the years austere uniformity has given way to highly creative personalisation of facades. Exterior brickwork and doors have been painted a variety of colours, most often red, blue, green, grey, yellow and white. But occasionally the eye is struck (or assaulted) by a glaring purple, pink or turquoise. Many people have also replaced original doors and windows with new ones of varying styles. Widespread, too, has been the addition of window boxes, brass letter boxes, knobs and knockers and decorative ironwork. It is usually in the dressing of housefront windows that the greatest flare and originality are evident. Set off by delicate lace curtains, most windows display artifacts such as religious statues, animal figures, flower pots, vases, family photos, pottery and fascinating curios of every description. The result is a highly variegated, colourful and visually enlivened series of streetscapes.

SOCIAL INTERACTION AND THE 'LIVING' COMMUNITY

> 'The inner-city has a life and spirit of its own.'
>
> (Bairbre Power, *Sunday Independent*, 1981)

> 'Those who love the city recognise that the old streets provide neighbourliness and contact, socially recognizable groups, mutual dependence and responsibility, immediacy of contact with the local shop and pub'.
>
> (Gerry Cahill, *Back to the Street*, 1980)

In his sociological work *New Dubliners* Humphreys concluded that in the burgeoning capital 'urbanization produces a decline in neighbourliness ... city life tends to isolate families that are neighbours and kin'.[8] He found that vigorous social interaction existed almost exclusively in the old, traditional working-class districts little disrupted by external forces. Sadly, twenty-five years after the publication of his study, not much of Dublin fits this description. The living community of Stoneybatter, however, pulsates with buoyant social interaction and neighbourliness. These are especially observable in three spheres of daily life: street activity, the 'neighbouring' custom, and in local shops and pubs. Church and club participation are also important, but periodic and less conspicuous. Generally, women tend to socialise in the home, open doorways, along footpaths, at street corners and in shops; men congregate mostly in pubs, betting offices, pensioner's queues and on park benches.

Before examining the social dynamics of community life, it is important to focus on the elderly population, clearly the most distinguishable group. They form the social bedrock of the community. Dr. Clement Dempsey, a family physician with over forty years of practice in the locality, testifies to the 'disproportionately high number of older people. I have somewhere in the region of 700 patients and, of that, only twenty-four are children.' Publican Gerry Kavanagh puts it less precisely, divulging that 'there are a lot of old-timers here in the mornings because they have nothing else to do. You could call it the geriatric ward there in the bar.'

'Old-timers' are distinguished by more than their age. They represent a past time, values, world view. Having lived through hard economic and political times, they share a special bond that clearly sets them apart from younger generations. To them, the old days were not necessarily the '*good* old days'. Yet most extol the old type religion, morality, family life, honesty, as well as such simple things as good conversation and music in the home. Many live mentally in the past, unable to comprehend the modern world they read about and see on television. Fearing theft and vandalism, they are reluctant to venture from their house after dark; home and neighbours are their security. For the many who live on their own, loneliness can be an enemy. This is especially true for men who are not involved in a daily neighbouring process. Even if they socialise in a shop or pub during the day, a sense of isolation prevails in the deadly quiet of their home. 'Loneliness is a terrible hunger', confides seventy-seven-year-old John Byrne, 'you can die of loneliness.' Local social workers and nurses confirm that this is indeed sometimes the case. It is a sad paradox that many elderly condemn television for the decline of conversation, visitation by friends and family interaction, yet cling to it for their primary company in old age, regarding it as a 'blessing' without seeing the cruel contradiction.

Yet, as a group, the elderly exhibit great spirit and spirituality. Religion has always been the core of their existence and continues to get them through difficult times. Father Brendan Lawless, parish priest, detected their devotion immediately upon his arrival fifteen years ago. 'They have unquestioned faith and love for the Church and priest. They were *born* with it. It's a faith with which they accepted everything they were told by the Church. That type of faith will die out.' Alice Davy, social worker for the Stoneybatter district, concurs — 'their religion is *amazing*. They have very deep faith ... it's a sort of an old-fashioned faith. It helps them cope with loneliness and grief. And many of them are ready to let go (die).' No one in Stoneybatter would deny that it is the elderly who form the real heart of the old community.

STREET LIFE

Urban geographers have documented that the 'physical structuring of a neighbourhood greatly influences social behavior'.[9] This, of course, was the visionary working premise of the DADC a century ago. It has certainly been borne out in Stoneybatter where the small scale, integrated housing structure and inter-connected street pattern generate daily personal contact at street corners and along roadways and footpaths leading to shops and pubs. Some streets seem as busy as beehives at peak times. Cahill, in his book *Back to the Street*, affirms that such 'living streets', as he calls them, are one of the surest signs that a community is socially healthy.[10]

Stoneybatter's street life stirs slowly each morning. Shopkeepers start things off by noisily heaving up metal grates, plunking down awnings and scrubbing the front pavement. Next comes the street cleaner, moseying unhurriedly along, with his bright red cart and long brush in hand. Soon thereafter, the stream of women, many hunched over with age or arthritis, begins as they purposefully push their squeaky trollies and rickety prams down toward the shops. This signals that the day has officially commenced.

Socialisation on the street is both planned and spontaneous. Many people, religiously following the same daily routine, know that they will encounter certain friends at a set time and place. Hence, people meet along the way and stroll together in two's and three's. Street corners draw the largest clusters of perhaps five or six.

Conversational encounters tend to be more personal and substantive than those in greater Dublin where a brief, obligatory greeting or exchange is normally sufficient. Owing to the close-knit nature of the community, there occurs, of course, a fair amount of gossip and exchange of news and information. However, the most serious personal problems and family matters are also discussed in the open air. The high level of expression, animation or solemnity is indicative of the intensity of the conversation. Even light subjects can be drawn out in great detail. It is not uncommon to witness the amusing sight of two women friends carrying on a jovial, uninterrupted and perfectly coherent conversation while walking on opposite sides of the street for several blocks.

By mid-morning, streets are bustling with everyone from children playing to grannies neighbouring. Elderly and unemployed men begin gravitating toward pubs and betting offices. Exuberant children ride bikes, kick soccer balls, hop, skip, chase each other and swing on lamp-posts as in yesteryear, their pitched voices resonating through the bricked streetscapes. On nice days women sit in doorways knitting and sewing, catching a bit of precious summer sun. Toward evening working men return, join in children's play or engage in a card game. Bridget McDonagh grew up along St. Paul's Street and describes the scene:

> It was a lovely street. Seventy-six families and some had nine children. Everybody knew everybody else, like a little community. Children all mixed together and you'd be up at the corner there skipping rope. Everybody had open windows and your mother and father would be sitting there at the window looking out. People all had flower pots in the window and kept nice curtains. In the summer everybody would be sitting out. They'd bring their chairs and there'd be another group on the other side. The men would sit and play cards and play handball at the top of the street. Women would chat, be sewing, knitting. We all left babies out in the prams at the window. If it was a warm night we'd be sitting out late at night talking, until 12:00 or 1:00.

Living streets have been so natural a part of the inner-city that people here cannot imagine life without such invigorating social activity. On the other hand, suburbanites 'may not even suspect that a street life exists'.[11] It simply has not been a part of their experience. Grainne Foy, fourth generation artisan's dweller and now in her late twenties, finds a shocking cultural difference between her inner-city life and that of her suburban friends:

> When I meet people from the suburbs the differences are *unbelievable*.

> I get culture shock. I go out there and I just don't understand it. The whole area is *dead*. Totally dead! ... a totally different culture. Young people I know in the suburbs, they were brought up with no old people around them, apart from their grannies. I think they missed a sense of history. A totally different outlook on life. I wouldn't move out of here ... it's still very much like a village.

An indispensable part of street life (as any real Dubliner knows) are street 'characters'. Dublin has always seemed to breed them in marvellous profusion and variety. Histories of the city make mention of the more famous, from Zozimus to Bang-Bang. These unique individuals are more than mere sources of curiosity and amusement providing the community with frivolity or fodder for gossip. They actually play an important role in the life and history of communities. Because of their eccentric character and unorthodox behaviour, they become prominent figures known by everyone, constantly observed, judged and much discussed. In small conservative communities they provide diversion and comic relief so long as their antics are harmless. They become a sort of icon for the whole community. Ordinary people take a certain perverse pride in their deviant or 'queer' doings. Hence, the proud declaration 'Oh, he's one of our great characters', is an expression commonly heard from locals. It may even be argued that possessing bonafide characters is one measure of a community's individuality and uniqueness. Most street characters never become famous enough to warrant documentation in written form but they become well imprinted in local oral history and urbanlore.

Historically, Stoneybatter has always had a grand galaxy of street characters and comedians. A good number are recounted in the oral histories in this book — individuals like 'Mary Ockey', 'Plush Maggie', 'The Dead Man', 'Carwash Paddy', the neighbourhood drunkard who fuelled his horse on pints of Guinness and rode him up the stairs into the cinema matinee one afternoon, and the frail little French nun who determinedly positioned herself in the midst of rough cattlemen at the market in the dark of early morning soliciting funds for the poor. Stoneybatter still has its village characters who tend to take on legendary stature in their own time. For example, there is the 'bag lady as big as a battleship', as one local describes her, and Billy Arthurs the salty, yet sensitive, newspaper vendor who has been implanted on Hanlon's Corner for over forty years and knows everything that has happened in the area but judiciously keeps a tight tongue.

But none is more famed than Billey Storey, pig raiser and street philosopher, who has been affectionately dubbed 'Lord Mayor of Manor Street', an entitlement he clearly relishes. Twice daily like clockwork the grizzled Billey wends his merry way down the busy centre of Manor and Stoneybatter streets in his pony-drawn float laden with large black barrels of odoriferous swill for his pigs feed. Waving to all along his course, it's a whimsical sight for locals and an exotic one for outsiders. 'I've seen tourists stop their cars in the middle of the road and jump out just to get his picture', says a local grocer. When Billey passes from the scene another classical Dublin character will have been lost, leaving the community socially poorer by his absence.

THE NEIGHBOURING CUSTOM

The custom of 'neighbouring' has always been an important part of life in Ireland's small towns and villages. It has also flourished in Dublin's old inner-city communities. In Stoneybatter it has survived in very observable form. Along streets with as many as eighty adjoining houses, people are placed in extremely close spatial proximity. Because most were born and reared along the same street or in the immediate area they have known each other since childhood and developed close friendships. People know their neighbours well, trust them, assist them, depend upon them. Neighbourly relations can become as close as blood ties.

Neighbouring is essentially a social function of women. Much of it takes place within the home, especially in the kitchen. But the degree of neighbouring which occurs outside within full view is an important indicator of a living community. The two principal nodes for neighbouring are open doorways and frontal footpaths – they become a sort of social extension of the parlour. In warm months front doors are left open as an act of invitation as well as ventilation. Visitation begins about 9:00 in the morning, before shopping and household duties. Normally only two or three women are involved at a time. Like a sacred ritual, some neighbours visit the same friends every morning. If they fail to arrive on schedule someone is sent to see that nothing is awry. Women typically huddle in or beside the front doorway in robes, housecoats, aprons and slippers chatting amiably with teacups sometimes in hand. Conversation here among close friends tends to be quite intimate. Among closest friends virtually every personal fact of life is shared. Father Lawless regards this shared sociability as a vital part of community life:

16 *Engaging in the traditional practice of 'neighbouring' at front doorway*

17 *Lively chat at Smithfield Horse Fair held on first Sunday of each month.
In Stoneybatter the art of conversation is still very much alive*

You'll note the neighbourliness ... a village atmosphere. Go down Oxmantown Road any afternoon, you'll see people standing in doors and talking
in groups having a chat. Ladies out with their aprons on and the hall
doors wide open and two or three from across the road would come over
for a chat on the footpath. It's nice to see this.

More important than social chat, neighbouring provides support
and security during times of difficulty and crisis. When trouble
strikes, many individuals instinctively contact a neighbour friend
before family or clergy. In the event of serious illness or death in
the family word is spread throughout the neighbourhood within a
few hours and neighbours, rather than acting separately, cooperate
to organise a plan of assistance. Over the course of a lifetime everyone becomes both provider and recipient of assistance. Eamonn
O'Brien, a native and now community worker, shares his personal
experience:

There's still very much a rural country atmosphere about the place and
neighbouring is still a part of life here. They've always been great neighbours. People who cared about others. Nobody had very much. Everybody was working-class people and there was a lot of poverty but everybody shared. I can remember the night my father died and I was only
about five years of age. Too young to really appreciate what was happening but I remember neighbours coming in with two or three eggs for my
mother and a half a loaf of bread and a bottle of milk from somebody
else. After my father died my mother had to go to work and I was reared
by neighbours. They made sure that nothing happened to us, that we
were never without a meal. That's the kind of people that tended to live
around the artisan's area because it was a very close-knit community.

SOCIAL MIXING IN SHOPS AND PUBS

'The little neighbourhood shops were meeting places, gossip ex-
changes and re-echoed the heartbeat of the city'.

(John J. Dunne, *Streets Broad and Narrow*, 1982)

Neighbourhood studies reveal that high frequency use of concentrated local establishments promotes 'psychological unity' making
inhabitants feel that they 'belong together and to the area'.[12] In
Stoneybatter, shops and pubs are tightly clustered and act as a
magnet drawing people together in daily spontaneous contact. Along
the east side of Stoneybatter Street within a distance of about fifty
yards are four pubs, three betting offices, a hardware shop, bank,

newsagent and butcher; on the opposite side are three grocers, a pub, butcher, florist, hairdresser and post office. All local life, it seems, converges on this small nexus.

The shops offer spontaneity and variety in social contacts. Even their old-fashioned quality is conducive to familiarity and mixing. Customers chat while selecting goods and waiting in the queue. Conversation is lively but less personal than in more private settings. But the diversity of faces adds to the enjoyment. Local shopping habits reflect the importance of this social experience. Unlike other Dubliners who may efficiently make one or two major excursions each week for groceries and other provisions, people here shop with a higher degree of frequency because of the desirable socialisation involved. In other words, shopping is not just a purchasing act, but a social occasion. Thus, many people deliberately venture down to shops daily to pick up a few items. Local shopkeepers verify that typical transactions are in the amount of five to fifteen pounds, noting that at modern supermarkets they would likely be at least triple that figure.

Equally important as the social interaction among customers is that which occurs between patron and shopkeeper. In many Stoneybatter shops there is a close, quasi-familial bond between the two, built up over many years of regular contact. Moore explains the traditional relationship:

> Most customers, I know them by name and their mothers before them. They been coming in here since they were kids and you seen them growing up and getting married and then you see their kids coming in ... it keeps going on. You call them friends. People trust us, depend on us. You'd have a chat with them about their family and they'll ask me questions too. Now my wife died three years ago and every customer coming into the place brought me a Mass card. Ah, we've got a great relationship.

Shopkeepers here are still highly respected members of the community, as they were in olden days. People view them as possessing a certain integrity and wisdom. Consequently, a strong feeling of trust and confidentiality often exists. As grocer Noel Lynch puts it, 'in a way, a shopkeeper would be looked on as a kind of doctor or priest. Maybe not quite as important, but somebody that they've seen there for years and know that they can confide in.' In turn, the shopkeepers provide customers with a personalised service no longer found in most Dublin establishments. If necessary, credit is still given and in cases where a person is unable to make it down to the shop, goods are delivered to their home. Credit cards are not

used or accepted. There is no modern apparatus for processing them
– 'just a damned nuisance, they'd be', retorted one merchant.
Cheques are accepted but it remains mostly a cash business with
money politely refunded for the slightest of reasons.

Neighbourhood corner stores and sweet shops hold a special place
of nostalgic reverence in Dublin life, probably because of the 'wonderland' aura perceived in childhood memory. Most such shops in
the city have long vanished but in Stoneybatter a few remain as
social institutions. The combination sweetshop-newsagent is still
the busiest of places where wide-eyed children with a few coins
clutched in their palm survey the colourful display of sweet jars
while behind them patiently stand elders. Pat Moylett, proprietor
of the smallest sweet shop along Manor Street, notes its social
importance:

> The sweet shop has always been a contact point, a gathering point, for
> people to come in and have a chat. Some people have been coming in
> here every morning for the past thirty years to buy their newspaper or
> cigarettes. You could nearly set your clock by it. They get to know you.
> In many ways we're sort of confessors for customers, the people who
> come in every day.

Testimony to the importance of the little shops in the personal
lives of people is the manner in which they sentimentally journey
back with children and grandchildren in hand to show them proudly
where they came as a little one. Relates Maura Dixon, owner of
'The Corner Shop' at Red Cow Lane, 'people who have moved away
come back and say they appreciate what you did for them ... and
their children say "Mammy used to tell me all about you".'

The Irish pub, however, is the most intimate forum for socialisation. That Stoneybatter boasts an uncommonly large number is
explained by the traditional male-dominated economy which drew
great numbers of men together in the area. Unlike Dublin's many
cosmopolitan and trendy pubs, these are the quintessential neighbourhood locals. In the five most traditional pubs – Mulligan's,
Walsh's, Hanlon's, O'Dowd's, and Kavanagh's – at least eighty-
five percent of patrons are bonafide habitues, better known as
'regulars'. For many in this old working-class community, the local
pub becomes the most important social element in their lives, taking
precedence over home and family in some cases. It can serve as a
retreat or escape from problems of family or work. Here, men find
unconditional companionship, understanding, support. They readily
confess to being more communicative with pub mates than spouse

or family members. It just seems more natural to them. They rely on their local as a haven of stability in an uncertain world. Publican Thomas O'Dowd observes:

> To the local people, the pub is the centre of the whole neighbourhood. If you did away with neighbourhood pubs where the man comes in after a day's work for a few drinks, where he can relax and chat with his old pals, if you closed down these pubs you'd just have to build mental asylums all over the place.

Elderly publicans say that the local pub scene hasn't changed much in their half century of experience. Flinty old regulars still settle into their coveted seats and the art of conversation is alive and rousing. Gregarious cronies cluster in tight cliques to discuss, dissect and animatedly debate politics, sports, religion, weather, local happenings and the state of the world. All are treated with equal frivolity or solemnity depending upon the prevailing mood of the moment. There may be hushed tones during a serious story, clamorous laughter at a good crack, or roaring oratory amidst political debate. At peak moments a pub can crackle with energised conversation.

More important than the friendly banter and badinage is the strong camaraderie that develops between pub mates. In times of trouble men commonly head first to their local pub for advice and support. In Stoneybatter it is still the custom to help pub friends financially when things are tight, or bail them out of difficult spots in any way possible. Everyone seems to have their turn. 'You develop friends and share the trials and tribulations of life and the joys as well', reveals Jim Higgins, an O'Dowd regular, 'a local pub like here, it's like the pulse of the neighbourhood.' Sometimes the sense of unity and clan is so strong that regulars literally come to regard the local pub as *theirs*. Another O'Dowd regular, Tony Morris, puts it plainly: 'This is *our* pub, the customers, where we come to drink, where we come for our social life. I mean, the publican only *thinks* he owns the pub, but it's *our* pub'.

The uncommonly conservative character of Stoneybatter's pubs is discernible in several forms. For example, the publican's position, similar to his small town counterpart long ago, is that of a local monarch; he is lord and master and his word the law. Such respect is earned only through time and experience. As Higgins discloses, regulars have a clear notion of what makes a good publican. 'In my book a good publican makes the place itself. The personality of the man behind the counter ... a good man, a decent man, a man who will listen, not pry, sympathise, not pity.' Another conservative indicator is the enduring custom of privacy extended to customers. Not only do pubs here retain well-used snugs, but some publicans still refer to certain patrons by a single initial rather than name — such as Mr. 'M' rather than Mr. Murphy. This is a social relic from past times when many men didn't want it known to those in a snug beside them (who may be employers, employees, relatives, or rivals) that they were present.

No feature of local pub life more blatantly exhibits staunch conservatism than the atmosphere of male dominance and exclusivity. Old ways die hard in neighbourhood locals — the last bastion of male supremacy — and in the minds of many men, women simply don't belong. One intransigent regular doubtless spoke for many mates when he proclaimed Walsh's pub the 'Holy Ground', an inviolate male refuge. To be sure, some establishments are more liberated than others. Most men accept women in the lounge or snug but still feel uncomfortable with them in the bar and especially at the counter. They feel that it is an invasion of their privacy and inhibits freedom of expression and behaviour.

If a woman invades their domain, disapproval can be conveyed in various ways, from a deafening silence which falls upon the scene, to surgically scrutinising glares, to hostile words. Walsh's, the most unyielding, has long been viewed by local women of conscience as a dark den of male chauvinism and the regulars a mean pack of sexist neanderthals. Tom Ryan, head barman for the past fifty years, honours the wishes of the majority (of whom he is one) by assigning women strictly to the lounge or snug, but not the bar. Deftly drawing a pint, he assuredly opines, 'it's a male preserve. Men prefer to be on their own. I know this from experience. Women just wouldn't fit in.' In recent years, owing to heightened social consciousness and the rise of the Women's Movement in Dublin, more men have shown enlightenment and toleration. Others, not so mentally pliable, will take both their hatred of the British and righteous sense of male superiority to the grave with them.

18 *Kavanagh's Pub on upper Manor Street — one of Stoneybatter's finest Victorian structures and a local landmark.*

19 *Nicely preserved facade of Mulligan's Pub on Stoneybatter Street, 'Established 1791'*

Chapter 3

Urban Oral History and the Search for Sources

'Many people have much to tell about the Stoneybatter of their youth. Surely such memories should be recorded for future generations'.

(Stoneybatter Development Plan, 1985)

ORAL HISTORY IN IRISH PERSPECTIVE

Oral history may be defined as a 'process of collecting, usually by means of a tape-recorded interview, reminiscences, accounts and interpretations' of past conditions, events, people and personal experiences of historical interest.[1] Like archival data, it is a primary source of information. Through such recollection and verbal expression 'memory becomes history'.[2] Since archives are replete with 'self-serving documents' edited, doctored and drafted 'for the record', Hoffman contends that oral histories are often 'superior to many written records'.[3] Several advantages are indisputable. First, there can be no question as to the correct source. Second, oral histories possess a unique directness and spontaneity. Third, oral interviews typically reveal personal details of daily life not commonly recorded in written form. Fourth, and perhaps most important, oral history captures and preserves the life experiences of individuals who lack the time or literary capability to record their own memories. It thereby creates a 'new kind of history' – not a history of kings, presidents, politicans, business barons, but of *common people.*[4]

Desmond McCourt, noting that in Ireland 'we have the richest oral heritage in Western Europe', laments that so little oral history has been collected.[5] He implores academics and writers to tap this irretrievable resource, arguing that oral history recorded directly from 'live informants' produces knowledge of the past 'barely touched by documentary history'. In recent years several fresh oral historical works have indeed appeared. Three notable examples, all derived from masterful use of the tape recorder, are Henry Glassie's *Passing the Time in Ballymenone* and *Irish Folk History*, and Lawrence Millman's *Our Like Will Not Be There Again*. The problem, however, is that such treatises invariably focus on rural life, folkways and folklore. What of *urban*ways, *urban*lore and *urban* oral history? These terms are scarcely found, much less explored, in the body of Irish literature. An examination of historical sources pertaining to Dublin contained in the prestigious Gilbert Collection (Pearse Street Library) reveals a paucity of information about the city's working classes and common people, and virtually no oral historical documentation.

To redress this omission, in 1980 a one-year Urban Folklore Project was created through University College, Dublin. The avowed objective was to collect 'anecdotal items about how the city has lived, loved and sometimes even died ... before an irretrievable part of our culture is lost forever'.[6] Project Director Seamus O'Cathain particularly noted that in Dublin 'ordinary people have been largely written out of history — not to mention women'. Therefore, students were dispatched throughout greater Dublin to glean information. They tape recorded memories of some elderly, recorded locations of meritorious architecture and street furniture, and photographed old shopfronts — all admirable efforts. But, owing to constraints of time and funding, their findings were modest and fragmented. Furthermore, the project lacked a strong methodological, topical and regional approach. Nonetheless, it did focus attention on the validity of, and urgent need for, the study of urban oral history and urbanlore.

TRACKING AND TAPING

Field research for this book began with several weeks of geographic familiarisation and cultural acclimatisation — casual walking, observing, chatting, inquiring, note-taking. The purpose was to get a feeling for the physical character and social dynamics of the community before seeking individuals for oral history interviewing. The search for the right sources ultimately proved challenging since many old-timers had long faded into oblivion. Tracking down specific cattle drovers, midwives, craftsmen and the like was often a frustrating, sometimes futile, pursuit. Initially, local shopkeepers, publicans, the postmaster and staff workers at old folks centres served as the most reliable sources of information and direction. Pub 'regulars', especially at Mulligan's, O'Dowd's, and Walsh's, eagerly played their part in dispensing leads to the whereabouts of old mates. As it turned out, the pubs, as focal gathering places, became indispensable contact points at which I could meet with individuals or transfer messages. In fact, whenever possible, every person was met on their own 'turf' (shop, home, work place, local pub) where they felt most comfortable. This proved especially conducive to easy rapport and natural conversation. I was rejected only a few times by wary, shy or xenophobic persons.

Success in extracting quality oral history depends in great measure on the relationship between interviewer and respondent. Close collaboration often rests on what Gluck terms the 'cultural likeness' factor.[7] This simply means that if the respondent perceives cultural identity, or some sense of 'kinship', with the interviewer it creates an atmosphere of trust and candour. This concept has great validity in a small, socially cohesive country like Ireland; even more so in a close-knit community such as Stoneybatter. Here, the element of cultural likeness worked discernibly in my favour. That I am Irish-American with a pure Irish name, Roman Catholic, educated by nuns, brothers and priests, have made eighteen previous trips to Ireland, written two books on Dublin, and have friends scattered throughout the inner-city, immeasurably facilitated the establishment of a mood of ease and openness between both parties.

Eliciting oral history is a delicate, exploratory process. Carried to its highest form by a skilled practitioner, it becomes the 'art of oral history'.[8] Probing the mind and heart of a respondent is similar to an archaeologist meticulously uncovering a precious dig site — always there is the element of uncertainty and expectation. Promising prospects can prove to be rich discoveries or vacuums. Therefore, interviews were conducted in a deliberately casual, informal manner but with certain sets of questions in mind. Questions were phrased in such a way as to trigger recollections or insights but not so narrowly framed as to inhibit discussion of extraneous matters. Respondents were always allowed the freedom to mentally travel in terms of time, place and subject. Subtle guidance was used to re-focus thoughts on salient points. Their words ranged from nostalgic ruminations to passionate protestations. The bond of trust was especially evident during the revelation of personal traumas such as infant loss, death of parents or spouse, debilitating illness, or the anguish caused by alcoholism or repressive Church dictums. Taping sessions typically lasted from one to three hours, though some extended to twice that. A number of individuals were re-visited and taped again the following summer to better distill some relevant point or elaborate on a dangling theme. Finally, transcriptions were condensed and arranged sequentially to create coherence and a natural flow. But the respondents words, expressions and intonations were not tampered with in any manner.

FADING LIFEWAYS AND LORE

People in Stoneybatter of every social order proved highly responsive and cooperative. But the elderly clearly constituted the most valuable 'memory bank'. Because they feel close to their roots, have been a part of history, and now have an abundance of free time in which to chat and reminisce, they were unfailingly receptive. It became apparent, however, that there was another reason for their cooperative spirit – a strong consensus that the oral history, urban-lore, customs and traditions of Stoneybatter are fading away at an accelerated rate and that they should be recorded and preserved before they vanish. They base this conclusion on a number of observable trends which surface with unanimity and repetition throughout their oral narratives. Most commonly, they cite family fragmentation, the 'generation gap', decline in religion and morals, growing materialism, and the disruptive impact of television on family life and conversation as the causes. Very simply, in the 'old days' families remained close, shared values, and grandparents and parents related their life experiences to upcoming generations. This is how oral history and tradition survived here. Today, the heartfelt lament is that 'nobody cares, nobody listens'. Mary Bolton, aged seventy-eight, remembers wistfully how her home was jammed every night of the week with family and friends sharing music, dancing and lively conversation. 'People got more out of life then. But when television came in the whole body seemed to go out of it. It changed the whole atmosphere. Television was the *ruination* of the world.'

Their collective affirmation that local oral history and lore should be recorded and preserved in book form before it is lost, was, for me, a comforting confirmation of my belief in the value of my research project.

*20 Chris Carr, a 'Grande Dame' and near-legendary figure in
Stoneybatter community*

Chapter 4

Grandes Dames

CHRIS CARR — AGED 90

I t seems that everyone in Stoneybatter either knows Chris or knows of her. She is commonly lauded as a 'grand old lady'. At ninety, her life has spanned the momentous events of this century. During the Rising her father was a part of the Movement, acting as a gun-runner at Howth. He hid a gun in the home and paid Chris two pence to clean it with a rod and vaseline. In such an environment she became highly politicised, joining one of the first Cumann na mBan formed during the Hostilities early in the century. It is rumoured that she is to receive a special honour from the Fianna Fail Party.

She lives along Blackhall Place and enjoys remarkably good health. Every day, without fail, she goes out for walks, visits and a bit of shopping. For such outings she likes to wear a prim hat and proper dress. She can scarcely go a few paces without encountering a friend and engaging in chat. Everyone is openly fond of her. Sprightly in manner, her mind and memory are tack sharp. Events surrounding the struggle for independence are still fresh in her mind and hanging prominently on her wall is a large photograph of DeValera. 'He was a God in this house.'

'My father was a hide classer, as they called it. The butchers would bring in their skins from the abattoir and my father would look through them. There was first, second and third-class hides and they would go off to England to be made into leather. My father's job wasn't a bad job at that time. His money was two pounds a week and that was supposed to be good wages. We managed. My father was very jolly, always in the best of humour. He was a lovely step dancer. Never idle as long as I can remember. Me mother was very gentle. There were ten of us, seven girls and three boys. Twins were the first but they died in a fortnight. My sister Ann when she was six she was out playing with papers and she was burned and died. I'm the last of the family to be here.

'I couldn't help my mother enough in those days when there were hardships, really terrible hardships. My God, our mothers had a hard

71

time and we never realised it. Parents tried to cover children from
the worries. Mothers never told their children about conditions,
about money, they bore it all themselves. That's why the children
in those days were so happy. They didn't realise what was going
on at all. Women would be going from 7:00 in the morning to 12:00
at night mending, sewing, knitting. And washing all day every day
because we hadn't any change. Me mother, after all her work she'd
be sitting in that chair mending our clothes ... a very hard life.

'People were poor and hungry. There was no handouts in those
days. You could die of hunger. Only a neighbour would share with
you, that's all. That's the only thing that kept them alive. People
would give children bread and jam. We used to buy oxtails down
at the butchers, only two shillings. And there were things called pot
herbs — thyme, parsley onions — they would boil and simmer for
hours and that was the most beautiful oxtail soup you ever tasted.
You got real nourishment. And there was a family down from us
with fourteen children and the husband had a little plot to raise his
potatoes. He'd bring them down and my mother had a big oval pot
that would go on the big fire with open grates. And she'd have a
pot of cabbage. We'd get loads of potatoes and cabbage. She'd put
them on the table in a huge dish and all the children would be
around with their plates.

'In those times poverty was there all the time. There was no
charity of any kind. I saw children in my school in the depths of
winter in barefoot. The teacher used to have them warm their feet
before the fire. And people weren't getting proper nourishment.
There was sickness. And contamination. To call a doctor you'd
actually have to be on your last. I really don't remember doctors
coming to the house because there were no dispensaries in those
times. See, we were under British rule and their idea was "let them
die". The more Irish that died, the better. When our Government
got in, they started up things like open dispensaries and gave the
poor free milk. And the Church was very poor because the people
hadn't the money to give to the Church. It was two pence a week
the men would throw in when the plate would go around. That's
all they could afford. People used to repair the priest's vestments
because they couldn't afford to buy them.

'People, they had their own cures. They cured pneumonia with
linseed meal which used to be sold in chemist's shops. That would
be put in boiling water and they'd get a cloth and double it over and
put it on their back. After two hours that would be changed and
they never died, they always got better. Now they're dying of pneumonia and there's doctors all around them! I'll never understand

*21 Collecting sheepskins fresh from the slaughter house down an alley
off Stoneybatter Street*

it. And for chest trouble my mother used to get brown paper and a tallow candle, melt that and rub it all around on my chest and then put a piece of red flannel on the chest and I'd be up in a couple of days. My father had kidney trouble and a neighbour told him to get this flannel and double it over and tie that around the kidneys and wear it for a month. The idea was that the heat would cure it. Even slept with it on. Pure flannel. And he was cured. No doubt about it, they were genuine cures.

'We used to hold wakes with the dead person laid out on a snow white bed. Both my parents were waked in that way upstairs. You always kept a white – snow white – sheet and pillow case and they were never used, only for a death. And you would loan them to the poor people if anyone died, cause they wouldn't have them. You'd get them back and put them in the laundry again. Neighbours would wash up the dead for you and put a habit on them. They wouldn't let you do anything because you wouldn't be in the mood. There'd be a little table at the end of the bed with the loan of candlesticks from the Church. Candles were lighted and there was a dish of Holy Water. Anyone who would go up to see them would kneel down and say a prayer. That would go on all night and people would sit up all night with you. There was great sadness. And a child's death in a family at that time was something terrible. Heart-breaking. But you'd be making up sandwiches and you'd come in a get a drink or cup of tea and chat. The next day all the men would carry the coffin down to the Church and then they'd go to the undertakers. That was the custom.

'We used to make up marvellous games. Each street played in their own way. There was a thing called "Hopping-cock-a-rooshee" where you'd go hopping on one leg and another thing, the "Honey Pot", where girls go around in a circle and the leader would run in and out and she had a follower going after her. Boys used to play "cap-on-the-back" where one boy would take his cap off and put his head against the wall and the others would make a run and jump on his back. Then another and another. Suddenly the whole lot would fall on the ground. In our home we used to chalk the wall. You had wallpaper half way at the top because you couldn't paper down to the ground with children. The bottom of the walls would be green paint and it would wash off very easy.

'Every Saturday we'd get tuppence from me father. A penny would go for a matinee at the picture house and the other penny would go for Nutty Favourites. You'd get eight of them for a penny. They were little balls with coconut on them. They'd keep you going the whole time at the picture house chewing them. And we'd get what was called "Swanky Creme", pink and white bars. It was lovely coconut. They were a penny a bar. Now around the corner from the blacksmith's was a little shop selling Indian Ale at a penny a glass. It was a teetotaller's drink. It was brown and had a queer taste. You'd turn the little handle on the wooden barrel. In the summer two of us would give a ha'penny each and divide the glass between us because we were thirsty.

'There were a lot of crazy people around. There was Mary ... "Mary Ockey" we used to call her. Don't know what her name was. She was knocking around with a cane and a little black straw hat. Every day she'd leave this little can with a little handle on it at a public house on Queen Street. The publican would put a glass of porter in it and she'd collect it. She had a belt with a hook and she'd hang it on the belt and her coat would cover it on her way home. But one evening, one of the fellas took the can and made a little hole in it. Off went poor Mary and, of course, it leaked all the way and when she got home there was none in it. The next evening she was back, on her knees with her hands upraised, and she was cursing all the curses that ever was. Fellas would go by on their bike and jeer at her, "Mary Ockey, you're an idiot". They'd laugh at the poor creature.

'There was another person we used to call "Plush Maggie". She wore a long cape, all plush, a red one, and very tall and thin. She used to be going around picking up scraps. My friend and me was on the step with a big piece of cake you'd get for a penny. Maggie came along and said "you're not to eat that, throw it away". *She* would have eaten it. And I said, "we are throwing it away, we're throwing it down our throats". I shouldn't have said that ... that was rude. Then there was another fella used to play the concertina. He used to wear an Inverness jacket with the cape around the shoulders, like that nifty fella on the telly, Dr. Watson, the detective. He used to play at the public houses and he'd sing the song, "Squeeze her gently around the waist, promise you'll buy her a new suit dress, squeeze her tight, press her light, and her sides will be all right in the morning".

'This was an area where the IRA was getting information. There were barracks all around here with the British soliders. And the Black and Tans were stationed up here near Richmond Hospital. They were conscripted from prisons in England. They never served as a soldier. They weren't in the army, they were a bunch of their own kind. They murdered an awful lot. They used to come out at night when curfew would start. They were desperate. They used to raid public houses and come out with bottles of whiskey and they'd drink it and then they'd raid a house. And when they raided your home they *raided* it. They'd come and rap on your door at 4:00 in the morning with their gun. They'd pull everything out of the wall and throw it around the place and put bayonets through the cushions.

'They went around breaking into shops and robbing and terrorising everybody. The shops would have to give them whatever they wanted. They were drunk and could do what they liked because there was no control. Anyway, the IRA got word about them, got tipped off, and watched them down on the quay where there was a fish and chip shop. Five of them went in and ordered fish and chips and didn't pay for them. The man, of course, was afraid to open his mouth. They were drunk. Anyhow, the IRA walked in behind them and had guns at their back. But they didn't use their guns, they used their hands on them. They beat them like a man, you know? Left them lying there, all five of them.

'My father was in the Movement. Now we didn't know it at the time. That was all hid from us. My father's rifle was hid in the wardrobe and I was given tuppence to keep it clean with a rod and vaseline. Eventually, thank God, a man came to take the gun away before my mother's nerves gave in entirely. And my two cousins were on the run. They couldn't go to their home, of course, cause they'd find you at a relatives. When men would be on the run they'd hide out, sleep out, in the Dublin mountains. But Easter Week one of them got word that his mother was very ill and he came out of the Customs House and was arrested and sent away to England. Someone must have gave him away.

'My father was in on the Howth gunrunning. I remember that he was at Howth Head waiting for the gunrunning ship, the "Asgard", to dock. That boat was coming and and that man, Erskine Childers, he was arrested and executed. He brought in the boat to Howth and he had German arms on it for the IRA. The men went out there and they were unloading the rifles. Of course, the British didn't know anything about this, God forbid. There were Boy Scouts here at that time attached to the Volunteers and they went out with small handcarts and they were supposed to be selling something but they had the rifles covered up in those handcarts. They wheeled them along and brought them up to the hall around there. My father gave his overcoat, a new overcoat, to hide some of them. He never got it back.

'My sister joined the women's nurses for the IRA and they really helped the wounded, making bandages for them. When they'd be going out on a job they'd make a little pack with iodine, pad and bandages. See, the men used to be going out to attack the British lorries and when a man was wounded they'd have to take him away cause if they got him he'd be hanged. They used to be brought to Jervis Street and there was a basement hospital where a doctor, who was one of the boys himself, was there with stuff waiting for them. Doctors who were part of the Movement would look after them and dress them.

'When Independence came there was great excitement, I needn't tell you. The soldiers all marched out of the barracks down to their boats. They were laughing and singing "A Long Way to Tipperary". Some of them were all right, you know. Can't be all bad. Now the crowd down on the quays gave them plenty of clapping and plenty of boo's, I can assure you. And I gave them a few boo's as well.'

MARY ROCHE – AGED 90

At ninety, she is now blind and lives alone in a housing complex just behind Queen Street where she grew up. A visiting nun checks on her regularly but she prepares meals for herself and is generally self-sufficient in her cloistered little world. As a young girl her mother died and she had to take over the household responsibilities for her father and four brothers. She grew up fast and there was little time for childhood delights. 'I never went to a dance in me life'.

'I was born in 1899. I think I'm the oldest of the living in my neighbourhood. There were five children. I was the only girl. At twelve, my mother died and I took over for me father and brothers. I was never out a lot, always something to do. My mother had taught me to bake and I had to do the cleaning as well. Had to do all the cooking and sweeping for them. But the neighbours were very good and used to come in and help and see if we were all right.

'I lived on Queen Street, a marvellous street, with the Haymarket and Smithfield around that neighbourhood. We'd play at skipping, ring-a-rosie and making swings on lamp-posts. But when the horses got loose they'd run down the street and everyone had to clear out of the way. Go mad the horses would. Now where I was living on Queen Street on the corner there was an old lady in the shop and she was sitting behind the counter and the horse come through the window and everything went out into the street. The window was full of stuff and the horse had to be shot in there. He was all cut, his head. Couldn't be saved.

'Stoneybatter was a lovely town but very poor at that time. People were very poor ... very poor times they were. There was food but no money to spend. We hadn't got nothing. You could leave your door open and go out and no one would ever come in the door. There was no money to be taken. We used to go to the Daisy Market to get shoes. There'd be loads of shoes in stalls there and you'd have to look for them. And in those days the pawnbroker was very important. We'd make up a parcel of shirts and get two shillings and you could get some bread, butter, tea and sugar. At the end of the week when you'd get the money you had to go down to the pawn and collect the shirts and air them out for the men to wear.

'At that time you could stop school any time you liked. I stopped at twelve. Very simple lessons. Spell "cat" and "dog" and that kind of thing. You wouldn't be asked any hard questions. And the day the priest would be coming in to examine you, asking questions, me mother'd wash me frock. We loved the priest. Great respect for him. We'd try to beat each other out to bow and say "God Bless you, Father". And we'd all want to be able to answer the questions. He'd often give us a copper or maybe sweets.

'People were very poor but they were happy days. Halloween was a lovely time. At church there'd be a party with apples and nuts and all. And the Halloween party at our place used to be game playing in the home. Maybe our mothers would make a brack and put a little brass ring into it that you'd get in the shop for a ha'penny, or maybe put a ha'penny into it and we'd all be trying to get the cut with the ha'penny in it. At Christmas there'd be a ham and maybe you'd get a bit of roast as well on a poker over the fire. We had the Christmas candle on the table and the family around and we'd sing Christmas songs. We used to hang up stockings and you might get a sugar stick in it. Very seldom we'd get presents. Little rag dolls, that's all we'd get, with china heads. Me mother'd buy them at a place down at the Haymarket for two pence. Ah, the children were delighted with them. I miss those days ... I'd like to have them back again.

'People were living in big tenement houses along Queen Street. Very old places. There was ten and twelve children in rooms. No place for them. When I was only seven this tenement house was so old that it collapsed, fell and took the other house with it. There was a child killed and a man and woman killed. It was early in the day when it collapsed. People were out in the daytime and the children were at school. If it had happened in the night the whole lot of them would have been gone. Well, we went over there and Oh, My God, the rubble. They were digging for weeks trying to get the people out.

22 *Surviving stone cottages in Chicken Lane which were originally thatched*

23 *Brass door knockers are one of the most attractive and conspicuous features of highly personalised house fronts in the artisan's dwellings*

'We were in a bad state when the British were here. When the
Rebellion broke out the Black and Tans, they'd go around to houses
and you were put down in the cellar and they took any food we
had. The Black and Tans took over our rooms and we were only
young and lying down in the cellar on straw. There was sniping on
the roofs and bullet marks everywhere in the homes all over the
place ... and there were three or four or five of the neighbours shot.'

ELLEN DUFFY – AGED 87

S he is known simply as 'Miss Ellie' to everyone. For the past sixty-
six years she has lived in Chicken Lane in a three-hundred-year-
old stone cottage that once was a forge. Today the old pleasant sounds
of animals and children romping about the lane have been replaced by
the raspy noise of engines from a car-repair shop.
    As her children tell it, 'Mammy had a hard life.' The cruelty and
deprivation of her childhood under a mean-spirited step-grandmother is
like something out of a dark Dickens' tale. Having survived a long life
of hardship, she now finds great peace and joy in the attentiveness of
her children.

'I was born in Donegal. My mother, she was a Dublin woman and
she was trained as a maternity nurse. The first district she got was
up in Donegal. She met my father there and I was born eighty-seven
years ago. My mother died when I was two years old. She was going
out on a case and in those days they drove on hackney cars and
the horse took fright and she was thrown out and killed. I had one
brother but we were separated. I was sent to live with my mother's
people and he was with my father's people in Donegal. My brother,
he was pampered by three aunts. Had everything he wanted. Everything was at his beck and call. I never knew a happy childhood ...
never had it.
    'When my mother was dying she asked my Aunt Lilly, a nun,
"will you look after Ellie?". My aunt took me over to England and
I was reared over there in a convent. The years in the convent, those
were happy days because you had pals there. And Auntie was very
good to me. Now my grandfather, who I adored, his first wife died
– my mother's mother. He remarried but his second wife was hard
and hadn't much time for me. My Auntie wanted to educate me
but my step-grandmother, who had control, said "No. She'll be
handy at home." She thought I'd be useful at home up on Prussia
Street because they had a hotel, a beautiful house and garden with

ten bedrooms, two receptions, and two kitchens. I was only about ten. My Auntie, she didn't want me to go back.

'You have no idea how she treated me. I was the outsider. I was only a slave. Anything that was hard work, I had to do it. I was the pawn and I'd do all the dirty work for them. When I'd come home from school at 3.00 I'd be told to go upstairs in the bedrooms and wash every chamber pot and all the basins. And I'd have to clean the knives with the old-fashioned emery board. Then I had to go and feed the pigs. I was never let outside, straight in after school. I never did speak up because I'd be punished and get a wallop. And my grandfather, he was very quiet and kept away. She took the run of the place and it was handy for me to do the slaving. I had no friends. I wasn't allowed to mix with anybody. I had no pals. Wouldn't be allowed sweets. I never got a toy in me life! No friends, no one to talk to. I used to see children passing by and they were happy. I always used to say, "why did God take my Mammy?". I didn't even know my brother.

'There was two maids in the house and they got jealous of me. And what did they do? They started stealing stuff. Stole my grandfather's gold watch and he had a big silver cup and they stole that. And I got blamed. I was brought upstairs to my bedroom and my hands were tied. I never forgot it. I was up in the room for about a week. The maids would hand up meals to me. You have no idea what I went through. To the maids, I was only in the way. They got jealous. And I had *nothing*. I was innocent. I didn't know what was going on. I hadn't the sense to know. I wondered how could anybody be so wicked to children. And I still say it. It made a terrible impression on me to see how anybody could be so cruel.

'When my step-grandmother started to get sick she was lying in bed and when the time came she'd hold my hand and wouldn't let go. It was just saying that she was sorry for the way she had treated me. She died in 1921, the time of the Troubles, and was laid out and it was a beautiful room. An old-fashioned brass bed and beautiful white marble dressing table. In the corner of the bedroom there was a hole dug in the floor and there was a black box in it and it was full of money. All sovereigns and half sovereigns. All covered up with the wood floorboards and then the carpet was over that. She left me a hundred pounds.

'I was married and had my first child in 1923. My wedding was in the paper and my brother wrote to me. That was the first time I ever heard from him. He made himself known to me and asked would I like to come to Donegal to visit him? So one day when we were out in the car (in Donegal) I heard one aunt say to another,

"I see the man in grey up there". I didn't pass any remark the first time. But the next time I heard it, says I, "Who is the man in grey?" And I was told nice and gentle, "that was your father". He was standing along the edge of the road with another man and I just got a slight look at him and I said, "He's no father". I was *disgusted*. From the time I was put on the train in Donegal town at two years of age with a label around my neck and my name on it, to be met at Amien Station, my father never bothered to inquire about me. He *never* inquired. After all those years he never put pen to paper to know was I dead or alive. He was a drunkard.

'I moved to Chicken Lane when I was married. The lane was very poor. There were three thatched cottages out there. There was chickens, goats, hens, ducks, cows – everything. It was a country lane. Dirt road. Pigs next to me. This was my husband's family's home. When I moved in it was a pigsty. There wasn't a floorboard in the place. It was all earth. Muck! This used to be a forge. It's three hundred years old. The floor had to be dug up and put floorboards down. I had no money. Had to do it by degrees. I had to make sure that I had beds and a table and enough food. That was the basics.

'When we had children we had to have everything ready for the midwife when she came. Basins of water and clothes ready. She would always carry a little leather bag with all her instruments. The midwife, Mrs. O'Shea, was a wonderful woman. A real lady. I paid her three guineas. She was very good. Now it was very serious for me on the first. When Paddy was born I remember seeing Mrs. O'Shea getting him by the ankles and twisting him around to get the life back into him. I got septicemia. Every bit of skin on my body, from the top of my head to my toes, fell off. And me hair fell out. The doctor sat beside me and said, "You haven't much hope". It was only touch and go. I was anointed and all. I was six weeks in bed. But God spared the baby to me.

'When you lived in Chicken Lane long ago you were an outcast. This was always counted as poor. You were beneath. There was hunger and poor people were trying to get a living. On Monday mornings the women would be queued up to pawn their husbands' suits for to get enough money to keep them through the week. The husbands at that time used to drink the money and give their wife nothing. They went to the pubs and that was all that mattered. Men, they could get away with murder. Sure the men would beat the women and they'd have black eyes. In a little cottage up there one night I heard shouting and looked out and here was this poor little girl and the fella beating her and she was lying on the street.

I could see the husband and the son beating her up on the street. There was a place down on Queen Street they called "Little Hell". It was a tenement house and every Saturday night there'd be murder in it with the husband beating up the wife. When I was a kid I'd love to run down and see that, the murder and the police would be there. Oh, it was rough times then.

'I had a hard life because my husband got delicate. He was on night work at Guinness's. He got paralysis. I've six children. Then I had to go out to work meself in Guinness's. I was a cleaner for thirty years. I'd get up at half past four and I had to be in by six. They were very strict. Had to punch the clock and I worked until nine. Had to work there for thirty years to rear up my family. I done without meself to give to them, to educate my children. I always tried to make Christmas special. There was a little shop over off Thomas Street where you could pay off toys, a little each week. My children have been good to me. "Mammy had a hard life", my children all say, "Nothing's too good for Mammy". I have their love and affection. That's all I want. I think I'm living on borrowed time now.'

MOLLY BAKER – AGED 91

Born in 1898, she has now outlived most friends. She lives in a small brick row house on Blackhall Place where in mid-August she sits huddled before a fire with a shawl around her shoulders due to hypothermia. In recalling her long life she feels both nostalgia and sadness. She was told by her parents as a young girl that she was 'homely' and would 'never marry'. She never did. But her life has been rich in family and friends.

With most friends now passed away, and confined to her home by poor health, the telephone and television are now her most faithful companions. She likes music and news but has little use for comedy and action shows. As night falls she becomes fearful of the crime she constantly hears about. One Sunday morning when her door was ajar her handbag was brazenly snatched, a traumatising personal violation.

She is devoutly religious and despite life's disappointments feels that God has been good to her. She is especially thankful to still be able to bathe and feed herself rather than having to live in an institution. On nice days she can usually be seen sitting in her open doorway enjoying the fresh air and watching curiously the new generations passing by.

'I was born on Queen Street, the first of eight. I nursed me father and mother here. Both of those, thank God, didn't live to see the world as it is today. Oh, they'd be shocked because they were very simple people, had no money. When I was young my father told me that this place was once a forest with Robin Hood and his merry men.

'We never went hungry. God was very good to us. But around Arbour Hill there was very poor people. People would just have soup. We had plenty of potatoes, fresh butter, eggs and milk. Children were in their bare feet and there was a boot fund every year for them. There were men from the country who would come up to the North Dublin Union and take poor unwanted children to do farm work. They were orphans. Farmers took them to do work for them and it was miserable conditions. The boys would work for them for the season. Now my father was a male nurse and one time he went down in the country to see them and he said that some of the boys were made slaves.

'Stoneybatter was a flourishing area. People made their money through the British. They had money to blow and we were kept down because England never intended to give us anything. They wanted to keep their thumb on us. British officers would buy up the fruit. But country people would bring in potatoes, eggs and butter and they'd barter the stuff and get their tea and sugar and wants. The turf men, they'd bring turf to the door in a little pony and cart. We had an old turf man and he'd come to Smithfield on a Thursday night and spread a sack under the cart and sleep on it all night. Ah, a lot of people slept in the streets and beggars would come to the door. And there was Jack-the-Tumbler and he'd get a couple of pence. And people coming around selling fish and to mend umbrellas.

'Back then very few people were educated. I wasn't that bright and I was dying to get out of school. The nuns were hard and you'd be put up on the stool with the dunce's cap. I wanted to stay home. Children used to play hopscotch, skipping rope and playing in the streets with a rope around lamp-posts. But I wouldn't go through Thundercut Alley if you paid me. I'd be afraid. I didn't like any enclosures and there was a bend in it. Ah, t'wasn't a nice place. I heard a joke about it one time about a big Sister at the convent who was colossally big with big skirts, a big woman, and she said to a fella she met, "Can you tell me, could I get through there?" And he said, "If you can fit through there it'll be a great day for Ireland." He said that for a lark.

'We were only humble people but I have old memories. We saved to buy this piano, had a half crown a week to spare. And we thought we'd never get it home. My father was music mad though he didn't know anything about it. We often had two fellas playing it together.

Me mother'd make up a bunch of scones and we'd have a night of it. Many an evening here we'd be up till ten o'clock and children would be told, "Now don't be telling your parents that I kept you out gallivanting about." That piano would be going with Irish music and me father loved that. The memory of that, those would be my most pleasant memories.

'In 1916 you didn't go near a window. You dare not open a door. You'd pull the blinds and get inside. My father was a Redmondite, always looking for Home Rule for Ireland. I was young then. When there was curfew everyone was in fear. There was a terrific lot of shooting privately. We'd hear rumours of people being shot at night and things being taken from their homes. You could be knocked up at night and your house ransacked and you questioned. We had friends along this terrace whose sons had to be dragged out. They were fighting for Ireland. There was an old chap in Manor Street there, a rebel, a *real* Fenian, he was taken out of his bed and shot by the Black and Tans. You'd hear of people being taken out and even women. There was a terrible lot of atrocities during that period.

'I have old memories ... and I have me crosses ... sickness and one thing or another. I was never married. Couldn't see the point. I was very homely as even my father and mother said, God rest them. "Molly, you'll never marry. You'll never get what you're looking for." I'd be looking for too much in human nature and I'd no experience. I was living in a fool's paradise. Now I had a couple of friends but I never felt that I'd like to go away with them. I never met anybody that I could say touched that cord within me. But God has been very good to me with regards to friends.

'I don't have long to live. There's people around here living to be 103 and 104. I think that's very sad, living to be that old. I wouldn't like that, God willing. Because you'd become a nuisance for everyone else. I like to wash every morning and as long as I'm able to do that, thank God, I'm grateful to him. I can't get out so I ring a friend. I have a phone and appreciate it. So if you be down and out you can ring. I'll tell you one thing, I'm very worried when it comes to night. At night I fear all the things I read about in the paper.'

ANASTASIA BARRY – AGED 90

All of her ninety years she has thought of herself as an orphan. From the age of three when her father died tragically, she and her sister and brother were cast like 'waifs' into a cruel world of loneliness and struggle. Life in orphanages did little to prepare her for a happy, fulfilling existence in the outside world. Frail, timid, only four feet, eight

24 *Anastasia Barry, aged ninety, is one of the community's 'Grandes Dames'*

25 *Surviving row of small stone cottages at top of Arbour Hill*

inches in stature, and barely able to read and write, she had to content herself with menial domestic work. Pride and pay were scant.

Her only joy in life came from being reunited with her sister and sharing her companionship since 1919. The little single room they shared for the past quarter century in St. Bricin's at the top of Arbour Hill was the 'only real home we ever knew.' Her sister's death two weeks ago has left her terribly sad and lonely. 'I wouldn't care if God called me tomorrow', she quietly confides.

'My own life was a sad one. My father was killed when I was only about three. He was in the building line and he was up on the scaffolding and fell down and he was killed. He lived for seven days before he died. But I don't remember him. My life was a sad one after that because in them days, that was in 1903, there was no such thing as help of any sort if mothers be left without a husband. She had three children, a boy and two girls. I was the youngest of the lot. Our mother had to go out and look for work and we had to be put into orphanages. We were just like waifs.

'All three of us were separated. My sister was put into the Marian Convent and my brother was put into Artane and I was put into the Sacred Heart Home in Drumcondra. At that time there were no nuns in the home and they were extremely kind and good and did everything in their possible power to help us all. I knew no other home and I was very happy in it. In 1912 I was sent to the New Ross Convent with the Good Shepherd Nuns and that was very different from the Sacred Heart Home. I was there to 1918. No matter what your health was you had to go through a course of training. Now I was very small anyway. We had to do laundry work and cooking and milking cows and baking the bread. The baking of the bread was really beyond all human nature for young children. There was a great big table the length of this room and we had the flour from one end to the other and it'd be wet with yeast and we had to mix it all up and try to get the dough heaved up. It didn't matter if you were able or not. We had to do it. Our stomachs and systems wouldn't stand up to that treatment but this was never known outside. I strained me insides severely at them stages, lifting, heaving the dough. Ah, I'll never forget it.

'There was no one taking an interest in us. You couldn't write to your mother and tell her these things because the letters were censored by the nuns before they went out. But my mother would write occasionally and she was really attentive. She really had affection for us but her circumstances didn't allow for any means of supporting us. Our mother's mind seems to have gone vacant from the time our father was killed ... but she never forgot our birthdays. And my mother came to New Ross to see me once there. It was on a bank holiday in August time and the children were out playing, picking blackberries. They said that there was a visitor for me and I remember running in the door. And when I seen her my mother says, "Oh, that's not my Annie." "Oh, yes mother, I *am*", says I. Cause I had remembered her from visiting me in the Sacred Heart Home. I knew her but she didn't know me. "Oh", my mother says, "she was kept so beautiful in the other home. She wasn't kept like *that*." See, we were running wild out in the fields. You can imagine. The nun sent me off to get washed and cleaned up. Then we went to Benediction and had a cup of tea and that was all. She died of bronchial asthma and heart trouble in 1926.

'We were poorly educated at New Ross. I only got to fourth standard. That was nothing. Only barely enough to read and write. I started work in 1918. Cook, housekeeper, or kitchen maid, that's all we were ever able to get. My sister was a cook and did housework as well. I was nineteen before I seen my sister. We had a very happy reunion. From 1919 we never parted. Separated in jobs, of course, but we used to visit each other on our off days. But our life was a sad one because you had to go from job to job. I considered marrying. I had a boyfriend who worked for a tea company. I was about thirty-five. But he got T.B. from all the wettings, making deliveries, and died. So that was the end of that. Never bothered anymore.

'In 1938 I was spring cleaning in a lady's house and strained me back. And I was on the sick list ever since. Only worked twenty years me whole life doing domestic service. I was on the National Health Insurance. It was a very hard life looking for furnished lodgings, going from one room to another. My sister used to get part-time jobs and we made up our minds to get a room together. The rent was ten shillings. There'd be very little to live on after that. Being trained to knit and sew and cook and do things, we managed some way. From the time we started living together we never parted. She's only two weeks dead. This is the longest place we ever lived, the first we called real home. We managed the best we could on what little we had. Never in debt for anything. Never owed a penny. Nobody could ever say that we owed them anything or ever done them a wrong. Never.

'I just live from day to day. With the way life is going at present I wouldn't care if God called me tomorrow. I'm quite happy and free. I know I'd have no regrets leaving behind me. I have no regrets or remorse or conscience for anything I've done in me life. Whatever the Lord wills, I'm satisfied.'

Chapter 5

Grocers and Butchers

ROBERT PAYNE – BUTCHER, AGED 66

One can peer into the open front door of Payne's Butcher and Sausage Maker Shop on Stoneybatter Street and see a half dozen full sides of pigs hanging from hooks. Beside them dangle long sausage chains. Customers queue up next to the fleshy pink pigs which are out-stretched as long as they are tall.

It's the oldest butcher shop in the neighbourhood and has remained basically unchanged for the past seventy years. The wall tiles with inlaid pigs faces are always shiny clean. When Robert was a boy his father was struck and killed by a car during a snowstorm directly outside the shop. From that day on, he had to take over the business. It is a well-known fact that over the years he has helped out the needy with meat scraps but he declines to discuss it – 'We just don't talk about those things.'

'Around the turn of the century all this pork business was run by Germans here in Dublin and any native people who picked it up, picked it up from the Germans. My father was one of those. He started serving his time with a German over in Baggot Street. When the War started in 1916 they interned all the Germans or they had to leave the country and sell their businesses and that's how my father bought this shop in 1916. The German's name was Anger and my father's name was Payne, so they used to say around here that, "First there was Anger and then there was Payne".

'When my father took over this shop it was a little poky place, very antiquated. We used to live upstairs and had a pony and cart for deliveries. All up around Prussia Street there were cattle and pig yards. You could buy your pigs from these dealers live and drive them up to the abattoir and kill them. That's what we used to do. We never done anything else here, only pork. My father used to say that you could sell pork on the top of a mountain. You're dealing with three or four generations of people that are used to what their parents got for them. My father was killed in a motor accident right

*26 Pork butcher and sausage maker, Robert Payne at his shop on
Stoneybatter Street*

here in the street one snowy day. He was knocked down by a car crossing the road. I was only sixteen and I had to start learning the trade. I had no option, really.

'Sausages were always popular here. We'd make sausages from the remnants of the pig. We don't have any waste, that's the beauty of the business. My father used to say in making sausages, "You can use everything but the squeal." We used our own formula and when I was young you could have a choice of peppers from different parts of the world. In those days we just had blocks of ice to cool a room down on warm days. Then we were one of the first places in the country to get refrigeration.

'After the War there was the "Emergency", a time of scarcity of fuel and everything. You could only buy about eighty percent of what you needed. But we managed to keep going. Every morning there'd be queues outside the shop ... like a cinema. Could be up to fifty people waiting for the shop to open. It would be "first come, first serve" and we had to ration some things. People had to buy cheaper bits of meat to make stews and bones to make soup from. Now a pig's head, what we called a pig's cheek, we sold an enormous amount of those. And pig's feet. We used to buy them in bagfulls and we'd boil them and sell them hot. Now Saturday evening there's be a barrel of cooked pig's feet, steaming hot, and the drinking people were very fond of them. They'd buy them and take them off to their drinking places and have them with their pints. They sold for about sixpence. They'd line up to get them and on a Saturday night here the doors were often open till 12:00 at night. Ah, you couldn't shut the place.

'Small businesses like this are going out of business. A small man can't compete with a big firm now. People are going to supermarkets and quality doesn't mean so much anymore. They'll buy anything for convenience. Younger people aren't keen on cooking and some probably don't even know what a good piece of meat tastes like. A lot of the pork shops have diversified, taking on chickens and beef. I've been tempted to do it for economics, but I really don't want to. I want to stay with tradition ... and I feel you lose your identity too. You become just another shop. We're known for pork and nothing else. The business has been good to me but I have no sons or daughters coming into the business ... I'm the last.'

TOM MURRAY — GROCER, AGED 65

Murray's Grocer's on Stoneybatter Street can be spotted blocks away because of its bright red and white striped awning beneath which is a colourful display of fruits and vegetables. It's also a handy place to seek shelter during a sudden rainstorm.

Tom is stocky, bespectacled, and always wears a white shirt and tie beneath his soiled apron. When speaking, his eyebrows seem intractably arched. Apart from the customary meats, breads, vegetables, and canned goods, he has recently added a few wines. It's a cosmopolitan touch, a small sign that he's not to be outdone by the fancy new supermarkets up on Prussia Street. In the old tradition, he lives above the shop and has a beautifully flowered rear garden where he putters around, reads the newspaper and sips coffee. Suburban living holds no lure for him.

'I left school when I was sixteen to serve me time learning the business from the bottom up and I've always worked in the grocery trade. I've had this shop and lived above it since 1948. It was a grocer's shop at that time. I can't tell you much about who lived in it before that but during the Troubled Times the man who lived here was shot downstairs.

'There's a distinctive look about this place, like a small town in the centre of Dublin. This is a very old part of Dublin. It's where the Danes settled. People living around here go back generations. When I came here there were horses and carts. The Dublin cattle market was up there on Prussia Street and the buyers would come in from England on the boat and they created a lot of business. See, after the War food was scarce in England and they'd come over and buy plenty of bacon and stuff off you. They would drive a couple of hundred cattle at a time down to the boats and the streets were full of cattle manure and the smell of cattle but you lived with it, got used to it. It was money, it meant money. Cattle would come into the shop and I remember this one time one of them coming up the stairs. And all those cattle jobbers and characters … ah, they were colourful times.

'It was all counter service at that time. We had bacon, sausages, our own bakery. We cooked all our own meats. Everything was out in the open. Nothing pre-wrapped. Our floors were bare concrete with sawdust on them to keep them dry. No tiles then. You had to dress a provision window and a grocery window, especially at Christmas when you'd put little lights about and mixed fruit and cherries … very attractive. I worked for years seven days a week.

'Ah, this was really O'Casey's Dublin. There used to be such wit. But those old fellas, the characters, they've gone. But you've got

Billey Storey, the pig raiser, up the street here and he even has goats. Pigs and goats in Dublin, it's *unbelievable*! Now there's no other city in the world that would have that. If I have a bottle fly in my shop I'll be prosecuted and he's up there raising all sorts of animals. The law can't touch him because of some bye-laws going back to the time of Queen Bess.

'They're very friendly people around here. I know all my customers by name. You'd know exactly when Mrs. so-and-so was coming in. And years ago we worked on credit but it was a nuisance because you had to make up those bills and get them ready every week for the people. That died out with supermarkets. Small grocers had to gear themselves to compete with the modern supermarket and a lot of them went by the board. I survived ... can't tell you how. It was a do-or-die effort to keep it. It was the only thing I knew.'

LEONARD LIFFELY — BUTCHER, AGED 70

His shop on upper Prussia Street is uncomfortably close to the new supermarket. Competition has taken a heavy toll. Business has declined by seventy percent since the 1930's when the shop was surrounded by houses jam-packed with huge families and clusters of bed-and-breakfast establishments for cattle buyers. Though fast-food places and changing family eating habits have further chiselled away at his profits, he is philosophical rather than resentful. Today the shop has officially been turned over to his son but he still spends four or five hours a day helping out. It combats boredom.

'My father made a start of it in 1932. I was going to school but he says, "You're going into the shop." I was thirteen. I didn't like the idea. But they were hard days and so he put me to work driving the cattle to the slaughter house and doing everything in general. I'd go on me own and drive them in from Chapelizod to the abattoir at the top of Aughrim Street. Sometimes I'd have three animals, sometimes eight. Just walk them in and they were killed with a pole axe. And if you didn't strike them right the first time then you had to go again the second time. It was terrible. I didn't ever do that because I didn't like that game. Then I'd bring the offal and the head down to the shop on a big bike with a big basket and I'd serve in the shop the rest of the day.

'In the 1930's we trimmed nothing and sold it with the bone. They loved fat in those days. If the sirloin didn't have that much fat on it they wouldn't buy it ... a half inch or more. Oh, they wouldn't touch it, honestly. They thought it gave you extra flavour. Ah, no flavour on thin beef. Today you trim everything, take every bit of the fat off nearly.

'When I started, odd pieces of lean meat was only four pence a pound. That would come available when cutting up a beast. You see, you have a lot of stew about a beast. If a beast weighs 480 pounds, that's about the average weight, you'll only cut about 360 pounds of beef out of it. We get fifty-eight pounds of sirloin and about thirty-two pounds of round and the rest is moreless stew and casserole steak and whatnot. The rest is fat, bone, gristle and so on. It used to be that they'd buy their stew and soup meat and all. Now people don't worry about making stews and soups much anymore. No, that's very hard. Eating habits have changed.

'Our trade has gone to the devil. It's gone down by three-quarters. When the cattle market was on, there was fifteen bed-and-breakfast places on this street. I supplied them all. And there were houses with good families in them, four or five, up to eight children. Houses got knocked down and the people all got old and died. That's done a lot of harm. Beef and lamb was our chief things. Once I was doing five cattle and twelve sheep a week. Now we're doing only one beast and three or four lambs. Years ago people was great judges of meat. The younger generation, it's all the same to them. Today people eat a lot of things out of these take-aways. The Kentucky Fried Chicken does a terrible trade and McDonald's is packed all day. It's real meat, no doubt about that, but I like my own better ... I know exactly what's in mine.'

NOEL LYNCH – GROCER, AGED 53

Noel's Family Grocery' is nestled just beside the Post Office on Stoneybatter Street, a handy location. It's a modest shop even by neighbourhood standards; there is only room for a handful of customers at one time. It is still a counter-type grocery rather than self-service. The front window is always kept crystal clear and the bright colours of cereal and detergent boxes, biscuit packages, and canned goods sparkle in the sunlight. Each sign is hand-drawn. A fresh sample reads, 'Electric bulbs below usual prices.' No hard sell here.

A religious man, he takes his family to Knock Shrine regularly. On his counter are assorted charity containers. His slight frame, fair hair, and pink cheeks match his quiet, sincere manner. He's quite content behind his own little counter and one cannot imagine him in an aggressive business setting. Yet, in a moment of candour he confides, 'The street cleaner takes home more pay at the end of the week than me ... and he has his pension as well'.

'Our family has been in the grocery business since 1895. My grandfather started at Summerhill and all his children were born behind the shop where he lived. He maintained that he was the first dry grocer in Dublin. He didn't sell spirits. He just sold groceries. Before that, groceries were sold in a section of a public house. There was a section where they served drinks and another section where they sold basics like tea, sugar, butter. The first job I had in the grocery was weighing up vinegar out of a barrel into bottles. I must have been about ten.

'My father took over this place thirty years ago. It was a very busy place because of the cattle market, packed with people and animals. You could hardly cross the road there with the animals going up and down. In the morning the messenger boy would go out with his notebook to different customer's houses. He'd write down what they wanted, come back and make it up, and then deliver it to them on his bicycle. We used to give credit and have a monthly account.

'We'd buy loose and weigh our sugar, flakemeal, flour, washing soap, salt. All that was weighed by hand, and biscuits the same. "Give me a quarter pound of that and a half pound of that", and so on. And butter and cheese were cut off a block. And I can remember people who would come in with a cup to buy two old pence worth of jam because they couldn't afford the six penny jar. We used to get jam in big tins and give them a cupful or a penny's worth. Same with tea. You'd weigh out tea in two ounces. There was poverty but people had their pride.

'Now packaging of foods has been an improvement, easier to handle. But it's not as interesting. When you walked into a shop you got a wonderful smell that was a mixture of everything, a beautiful smell. When I'd open the door in the morning we'd get a smell from the mixture of sacks of sugar, tea, spices, pepper and the aroma was floating around the place. But now that has gone and you wouldn't get the same kind of atmosphere about a shop.

'In a way, a shopkeeper would be looked on as a kind of doctor or priest. Maybe not quite as important, but somebody that they've seen there for years and they know they can confide in. They've seen you and your father before you and maybe your grandfather as well. They know that what they tell you won't go any farther than that. They come in and have a chat. It's more listening than asking questions ... and you have to be patient. Some very amusing

27 Butcher Peadar Casey in doorway of his tiny shop on Aughrim Street

things come up. There about ten days ago this old lady, she's about eighty-three, came in to me and looked to see that no one was coming, and she said, she whispered, "I been thinkin' of diverting my kidneys. How would I go about that?" So, I wasn't too sure what she had in mind. So, I said, "Now when were you thinking of doing that?" "Oh, after I die." "*Oh*", I said, "I *know* what you mean. Ah, yes." They do tell you little things like that.

'When the big supermarket opened up I was a bit worried, all right. Our sales dropped about thirty percent in the first week. About ten or fifteen percent of that gradually came back. Trade could go quieter but there will always be a place for a small shop. Being a local shop we're able to help them, cheer them up. I'd like to keep the shop up even though there's very little money in it. The business is in my blood, like the gypsies or itinerants. And there's family pride here because my sons would be fourth generation in the business.'

PEADAR CASEY — BUTCHER, AGED 63

For thirty-five years the little butcher's shop on Aughrim Street provided a fair livelihood but now times are hard. The sparkling new supermarket over on Prussia Street has severely hurt business. It's mostly the old faithful customers who come in now. These days he can only carry a sparse selection of meat but it's as fresh and lean as ever. Quality and pride have survived.

He frets openly over the Dublin Corporation menacing his little shop and admits to losing sleep over it. A street-widening scheme threatens to demolish the premises. The small man, he notes, has no chance against the Government. There is much anger mixed in his sadness.

'I'm Dublin. Born on Malachi Road. I was one of eight, with two bedrooms and one big kitchen and a little place to wash. I have a lady who comes into my shop now and she always recalls how she used to get a penny off my mother to wheel me up and down the road in the pram when visitors would come to the house. See, there'd be no room. My father was in butchering all his life and I went into the trade at eighteen. It was a job. Half crown a week and ten shillings during apprenticeship. At that time you were in the union and if you ever done anything wrong the boss would threaten the union on you. "I'll report you to the union!" You were always threatened. The fear was always there. And I remember one time I was trying to cut a steak and I done a bad job of it. The boss, he called the office girl out and said, "Show him how to cut a steak." That was really demeaning.

'I was very lucky starting off with me shop. I was cycling down Aughrim Street one day and it started to rain and I sheltered in the porchway of this empty shop. It was To Let. I went home sopping wet and told a friend about it and he said, "I've ten pounds I'll lend you." Now I've got nothing, not a shilling meself. But my mother got a loan of 200 pounds. The shop cost four pounds a week to rent and I bought some stock — cattle and sheep — and that's what we started on. From day one I never looked back. It's not a big business — a family business. My father came in to help me and we were happy. We mainly sold beef and lamb.

'We sold sheep's heads at that time. Many's a good family was reared on sheep's heads. They'd make soup out of it. The whole head. We'd take the skin off it and take the eyes out and then crack it down in two or four pieces and they'd put it in a pot. And maybe carrots or onions. Sheep's heads cost about six pence. And we used to sell offal, that's the bones and the fat. There was fat merchants and bone merchants who used to go around and collect. From fat they'd make drippings for frying, like lard. And the bones, I'm not sure what they done with the bones. I think they sent a lot of them up to the zoo for the animals. Mind you, it was nice money you were getting for that. It was the creme. So, too, with the hides of the animal. We'd get the cheque each week from the hide company and that was a little perk.

'You'd help the poor people out. The Little Sisters of the Poor would come on Friday mornings with buckets and you'd hand them stew meats. There was one little French nun, a very old nun, and she used to stand in the market at 4:00 in the morning. She knew *everyone* in that market, collecting alms from them for the poor. She'd collect money and you'd want to be hard as nails not to give her something. One day someone offered her a drink ... he was calling her bluff. But she said, "Thanks", and went into the public house with this man and when the drink was handed to her she said to the barman, "Would you put it in an empty bottle?" She put it under her cloak and brought it back to the convent. She never drank it ... it was for the poor.

'The Corporation, they're going to take my shop. They're going to knock it down. I appealed it but I got nowhere. For five years this has been going on and I've had approximately a year's sleepless nights ... genuine worried about what's going to happen. I feel that it's completely and utterly unfair that they can walk in and close a man up. When I retire I'd love to go down in the country. Out in Connemara. The old bog road. I love nature. I love to go into a field and listen to the grass growing. Peace. I love peace and tranquility.'

Chapter 6

Shopkeepers

MAISIE DALY – FRUIT-VEGETABLE SHOP OWNER, AGED 77

Her tiny fruit and vegetable shop at the corner of Chicken Lane and Stoneybatter Street was a grand neighbourhood meeting spot. Probably the most unpretentious shop in the area, it had a bright blue facade, crudely-painted fascia, and an old-fashioned wooden half-door. In front were colourful fruit and vegetable displays and a few sturdy boxes on which the local men would sit and chat every day. Maisie always took special pride in decorating the front window with pretty pictures, a thoughtful verse or poem, or perhaps a favourite prayer. As she puts it, the shop was a 'landmark'.

Maisie was no less famous than her shop. Every morning for nearly fifty years she could be seen pushing her pram through the streets heaped with produce from the fruit and vegetable markets. After nearly sixty years living above the shop, it became dilapidated and she was evicted by the owner. It was terribly traumatic. Today she lives in an old folks housing estate atop Arbour Hill surrounded by a collection of old 'teddies' she has collected along life's way. The shop, though forlorn and empty, is still standing. Each day she is compelled to pass by and put her hand upon it. It's her way of holding on to the past. But she knows that one morning when she passes by, it will be a demolition heap. One senses that she would prefer to be the first to go.

'"Maisie", that's a pet name. I was really christened Ann Margaret. But my aunt said, "Oh, that's very straight-laced, I'm going to call her 'Maisie'." Oh, dear, Oh, dear.

'I lived in Amien Street as a baby and then we came to live in famous Stoneybatter when I was only two or three. I know that my father carried me there. My father came out of the British army and got the little vegetable shop. In the beginning we sold everything to try and earn a living ... a bit of fish, soaps, powders. Started from scratch and in those days it was tough going. We were over sixty years there. My father and mother, they were very happy. My father loved his home, his pipe at night, and a bottle of stout.

99

28 Maisie Daly beside her now-dilapidated little family fruit and vegetable shop on Stoneybatter Street

And, ah, my mother would give you her heart if she could take it out. So good natured.

'Stoneybatter was lovely, like a little country village. At the top of Chicken Lane was beautiful cottages and chickens and pigs and an old-fashioned dairy. I thought I was in the country. Mr. O'Toole used to deliver the milk with a lovely horse and churns all shining and gleaming. Mr. Lennon, a famous old Dublin cabbie, had a horse-drawn cab and we used to love to have a nice little ride as far as we could till he'd crack his whip and we'd get off and run away. And Daddy Duke, an old-fashioned shoemaker, we'd sit and watch him fascinated doing all the waxing and making the shoes. We'd some great times, happy times.

'In the Troubles of the Twenties, my mother was worried about me, afraid to let me go very far away in case of sniping and firing. So I went to a little private school in Manor Street. We were beautifully taught there by two ladies, two sisters. Only ten or twelve of us. It was very nice, very select. It was in the drawing room of their home and we could go out in the garden for lessons if it was fine. We were taught refinement and manners and music, and a great love and respect for older people. That is not with us today. I was a great reader. I love books. Old history books and books on Irish life and autobiographies. Books are my life. I love them. And I love nature ... trees, flowers, plants, birds. It was a beautiful education.

'Now that shop of ours, it was a landmark. It was a famous old corner. There was only the gas light. Everything was discussed in the old corner shop. Ah, I loved talking. Could talk till the cows came home. We used to have a great crowd used to stand and chat and talk and smoke. Great men they were. Nice days. Looking back on it, there wasn't much argument or fighting. Poor Jack Costello up the street, he used to drink and get a bit rowdy and start a bit of a row. There was an old box there and men, women and children would sit on that. They'd sit there on good days and bad days. They'd tell you about Confirmation, Holy Communion, the marriages. Everything was discussed.

'We had a lavender man we loved. He'd come with the little sachets to sell. You'd put them by your clothes and the perfume of the lavender would come back on the liner. And we had another lovely little old lady, a small, fat little old lady with a funny little hat, and she'd sing outside the door, God love her. She'd sing "Mick McGilligan's Daughter, Mary Ann", and then come in for a few pence. Ah, we loved her to come along. And we had a lot of mouth organ players. They'd play outside and then come in and you'd give them something.

'My mother was a terrific, a Wexford woman. A real Irish woman. Now there was a few boards outside the door to display vegetables. This day, my mother had put out a lovely lot of spring cabbage and the Tans came down and one of the Tans happened to sit on top of this cabbage. My father was looking out and said nothing. He was very quiet, conservative, and all for peace. But my mother, she said, "Now I don't intend to have that at all", and she went out and just told him, "Up on your feet now, Sonny, stand up and don't sit on the bit of greens and press them." She was great. She was terrific. "All right, mother", he said. Some of them were all right I guess.

'My shop window used to be lovely. I'd buy little flower plants and cacti plants and display a verse or a poem or a special prayer and put it in the window. I loved it so much I wanted to share it with everyone. And pretty pictures I'd get, like pretty postcards of Ireland, I'd get hardboards and paste my picture on it and put shellwork around that and varnish it. I'd arrange that in the window. People would read those lovely poems and enjoy those lovely things. The corner became recognised. I got great joy out of that. I was charmed that they found so much joy in it. It was great happiness.

'I didn't marry. But my mother was from Wexford and there I met the only man I ever would have married. I went there for my holidays. We gathered at the crossroads at night and danced and sang. They'd come over from the mountains with violins and we'd dance till all hours of the morning. I'd lovely days there. I'd be eighteen or nineteen when I met him. Joseph Dunbar was his name, a Wexford man, and he was lovely. We'd meet together at the little stile, a lover's seat where trees had intertwined to form an arch and there was a seat in it. It was very refined. You'd sit there talking and Joe – I could hear his voice now – he'd always call me by my Irish name "Moira". He was a mad Irish speaker. Loved everything Irish. And we'd walk home. I loved him very much but it wasn't to be, perhaps. He was the last of his family and they were all married and they were anxious for him to remain where he was with his mother and father. So he remained on to look after his mother and father and we parted and that was that. It was a lovely love affair, Joe and I. But after that, he married a very nice girl and had a very big family. As a matter of fact, he invited me to his home ... but I didn't go.

'Now I'll tell you what happened to the shop. It fell into decay and the pipes were giving out and I had a burst and leakage. I was only a tenant and with no backing I couldn't do anything. Wet was coming through and I could no longer carry on business. Even though I had nothing in my shop, everyone came into me and chatted. When I closed the doors I was very, very sad. Oh, they still remember me. People stop me on the street and say, "Oh, Miss Daly, we're delighted to see you. We remember your little shop so well." My old home, I still put my hand on it every day I pass it.

'I've no regrets, thank God. None in the world. I had none of the world's riches but I had something that you just couldn't explain. A sad life, a lonely life after my father's death, but a nice life. I still have a few good friends, thank God. God has been very good to me. I've got the greatest faith. The smaller things in life have given me great joy. For instance, if I go out there in the garden now and see a flower growing, a rose or another that I've planted, to me, that's Heaven. And the other night I looked out there and saw that sky and it was beautiful. It was amethyst, silver, gold. And I said, "Thank you, God, no artist will ever capture that." I can't explain it, but that's the way I am.'

PAT MOYLETT – SWEET SHOP PROPRIETOR, AGED 41

It's the smallest sweet shop in Stoneybatter – only about ten by twelve feet – and, as Pat puts it, has been there 'for donkey's years'. Owned by his aunt, it is situated on Manor Street next to the old cinema. As a child, he was brought into the shop by his father. It was a grand gallimaufry of sights and delights. Today he runs the shop for his aunt. Since the neighbourhood sweet shop has always been a local meeting place, he has learned a lot about human nature from his perch behind the counter.

'My granduncle left the west of Ireland before the turn of the century to go to work as an apprentice at Harrod's in London. Then, in the 1920's, he had one of the first Irish-owned sweets companies down in number fifty-seven Bolton Street. At that time, around Independence, it was unusual for an Irish man to own a factory but he was a great success. He made a famous sweet called "B-B Toffees" which older people still remember. Now my father came to Dublin from Mayo when he was fifteen years of age and served his time as a sugar boiler in this factory. Then my father went into the sweet wholesale business.

'This shop has been in the family since 1940. It was my aunt and uncle's shop. And it was a sweet shop before that. When I was about four or five years old I would come in here with my father to deliver sweets. It was a *wonderland*, an *Aladdin's Cave* for a small boy. I can remember coming to stay here for a fortnight when I was about six. You could read all the comics you could read — two at a time — and get all the chocolate biscuits and drink all the lemonade you could get into you. My aunt and uncle had no children of their own and I always wanted to be in the shop. When I got older I'd go for messages for them around the city on my bicycle.

'This shop would have been big by the standards of the 1940's when most shops would have been huxter shops. See, in every area there were houses that were set up in the front room in a tenement building. They were higgledy-piggledy places and they'd sell everything — bread, sugar, tea, the whole shooting gallery. And they'd give credit. Now in this shop the counters were very nice mahogany wood and there were two scales for weighing out the sweets, one at each end of the counter. One is there today, the original scale. Behind the counter there was probably twenty different drawers and we had everything — pencils, school supplies, nibs, rubbers, jam pot covers, Holy pictures, a wide range of stuff. We prided ourselves on people coming in and asking for the most oddish thing and we'd have it. Unfortunately, those things wouldn't contribute to the success of the business. And to my aunt and uncle, cleanliness was next to Godliness. In keeping a shop, that wouldn't have been the norm in those days. They made a great display of having the girls wear white shop coats, which was virtually unheard of. In fact, they spent more time cleaning stuff than selling it.

'My mother and sister were killed in an accident when I was fifteen and I came to live here. My uncle died and my aunt sort of got old and couldn't manage the shop on her own. We sold milk, tea, sugar, bread, butter. And we'd get a box of a hundred Player's cigarettes and make those up into a little packet of fives. We'd sell loads of cigarettes in fives ... a sign of the times. And we'd sell single cigarettes. And on the back shelves there used to be nearly a hundred different jars of sweets. Sold a lot of penny sweets. In those days people would buy only two ounces of weighed sweets. You could get six sweets for a penny. You had "Honeybee Sweets" made down on Richmond Road. They were in a box with a picture of a bee on it and stripes. And "Circus Toffee" made by Milroy's which was one of the best companies with a factory down behind Mountjoy Gaol.

'You had a number of small sweet factories around Dublin which specialised in penny toffees maybe four to six inches long. They made penny bars with various names. There was "Giftie's Toffee", a "Sailor's Chew" which had toffee with coconut, a "Cough-No-More" which was black toffee with a licorice through it. And they had a two penny bar which was known locally as the "Two Penny Honey Cap", a penny bar covered in chocolate and wrapped in silver paper. Now that was a luxury if you had two pence for that. See, the main thing for children back then was how long they'd *last*. And Sundays used to be good for business because children would have three pence when their grandparents came to visit them.

'The sweet shop has always been a contact point, a gathering point, for people to come in and have a chat. We used to have a library here at one time. People would rent out a book for a week. All that died out when television came in. Some people have been coming in here every morning for the past thirty years to buy their newspaper or cigarettes. You could nearly set your clock by it. In many ways we were sort of confessors for customers, the people who used to come in every day. They got to know you. We used to have one character lodged in the house across there and we called him "Who Flung Dung" because he was always coming in with cow dung on him and he smelled a mile off. I like children and have purposely made it a policy of everybody in the shop to be as courteous as possible to children. I always insisted that if a child comes in before an adult, the child is served before the adult. And at Christmas time I'll give them maybe a box of jellies.

'Now I've often seen from behind the counter the biggest contradictions in Irish life. One thing that surprises me is the very great number of elderly people – the most respectable people – who'll come in and buy an English paper like the *Star* or the *Sun* with a naked woman on the inside of it. And they'd buy it on their way down from Mass! On Sunday morning I'd get a great laugh out of the people who'd buy the *News of the World* where they'd have naked women, divorce cases, sex scandals, homosexuality, lesbianism, all that explicit stuff, and they'd buy it and fold an Irish paper like the *Irish Press* or *Irish Independent* around it. My perverse sense of humour would be that I would purposely fold the *Press* inside the *News of the World* and watch them reverse the thing before they left the shop. Another contradiction about Irish life is that all we ever had to do was get a magazine with the British Royal Family on the front and it was the first thing that would sell.

'There has been a revolution in retailing. People now are used to going into a huge supermarket which probably costs two or three million pounds, set up with the very latest of everything. This shop now is really too small because you can only take in a certain number of pounds for each square foot you have. It's really a battle nowadays. But people will still come in who have been out of the area for maybe thirty or forty years, or who have emigrated, and they'll

29 Annie Muldoon's little fish and poultry shop on North King Street. Though the shop is now closed, she still lives there where she was born and reared

30 Simply dressed shopfront window typically giving Stoneybatter its unpretentious shopping atmosphere

come in and stand there with fond memories and talk about how many sweets they got for a penny.'

ANNIE MULDOON — FISHMONGER, AGED 82

She lives alone above her antiquated fishmonger's shop on North King Street. There is no television, fridge, washing machine, or other modern appliance. The shop has been empty for years but a row of colourful flower pots adorns the front window and religious artifacts hang on every wall. One of eleven children, she devoted her life to looking after younger brothers and sisters and caring for aged parents whom she worshipped. It was, she firmly believes, the Good Lord's plan that she 'wasn't meant to marry', though there were 'plenty of chances.'

Alone and lonely, she now lives in a kind of dreamy world of the past, dwelling on love of her parents and talking transcendentally about Heaven and being reunited with them in the world beyond. She seems ready to be called.

'I come here when I was four years old and I'm here ever since. This was me father and mother's place. It must be over 200 years old. It was a fish shop. We were all reared here, all eleven of us. Six or seven of us in one bed. We'd no sink, no hot water, no fridge, no nothing. Only bare knuckles. Me mother, ah, she was a dinger ... a great woman. Six o'clock every morning, hail, rain and snow, down to Mass. She'd be working away washing, cleaning, baking, making shirts, darning socks.

'Me father was the *best*. He never missed Mass and he never drank. And that man, he never hit one of us. Ah, fathers here years ago used to murder the poor little kids. They'd come in, some of those old fellas, with drink. And you'd see some of the women getting beatings. I remember once he said to me mother, "Any man that goes in and stands up at a public house and drinks and neglects his children, that bastard will never see the face of God." Those poor litle kids. At night me father used to play the fiddle and we were as happy as Larry because you had your mother and father. I loved them. They were so *good*. God, when I'd come in and see me mother and father sitting there it was half me life. The closeness of the family, that's what kept us together.

'We worked at the shop here from 8:00 till 11:00 at night. People had nothing. Rabbits was food for everyone. Three for two shillings. Ah, we often sold two hundred here on a Saturday. People loved them. Did you ever eat a rabbit? Ah, me mother used to stuff them and roast them and sometimes make a rabbit pie out of them.

31 Scene at the old 'Corner Shop' in Smithfield at corner of Red Cow Lane

Ah, the back of a rabbit and a bit of streaky bacon ... you couldn't beat it. And people used to be queueing up for the fish ... cod, mackerel, herring, kippers, smoked fish. Women in their shawls would be coming in for hens and chickens. You'd get an old boiling hen and you'd have it for a week in the pot. Fish now is not the same. Fish has no flavour. They're polluting the rivers. And now when you get a chicken you can't eat them cause they have them forced all in cages. See, they should be out picking on the dung hills. Nature. Out in the fields. That's where all the cancer has come from, out of these deep freezes and fridges. There were no fridges in our days and you'd never hear of anyone dying of cancer. And I wouldn't eat meat now because they have the cattle all injected. That's not natural. It's there in the Book — the Lord made the sun and the rain and the grass. But that's all done away with.

'We were all wild when we were young. Running into the church and up the lamps. "Ah, Mrs. Muldoon", they'd say, "You have a very wild bunch." But I'll always remember my mother said, "The wild flower is beautiful but the hot-house one is of no use." Ah, she was a lady. But you'd have to be in at 11:00. Me father used to say that you'll see nothing good on the street after 11:00. I had plenty of fellas in me time. I was a devil. Going out to the road houses and all. The fellas, put your arms around them and give them a kiss. I could have got married. I'd plenty of opportunities when I was young. I've no regrets. Me mother always said that when you come into this world everything is laid out for you. She said there was a number on your back when you'll die.

'I suppose it's God's holy will that I had to look after them. So I did. I loved them. They were so *good*. I loved the ground they walked on. I remember when the ambulance come up for me father. He was seventy-six. He only lasted three days. Me God! I'm still heartbroken. But what can I do? I have to carry on, haven't I? I'll be with him, please God. I'll have me place up there with him.

'Me mother lived to be eighty-four. She wouldn't have died at eighty-four only me father died a few years before that and she lasted seven years. What you call a broken heart. From the day he was gone she was not the same. She used to want to go there and hit her head off the railing. She never rested. Seven years. "Where's your father?", she'd say. I used to bring the doctor and he says, "Can't do anything for her, Annie. You can't mend a broken heart." Doctors wanted to put her into a nursing home but I wouldn't let her outside that door. "You don't come inside that door", I told them, "I know what's wrong with me mother. She's only heart-broken and you can't blame her. Look at the man she lost." I minded me mother to the last. She died in my arms and she kept seeing a "Lady" all night. "There she is ... she's beautiful", she'd say. And the priest came and said, "She's gone. The Lady came for her." I loved her.

'All them grand people are gone. Them God-loving, Christian people. And what have you today? Dirty, rotten divorces, separations, unmarried mothers, people living with one another. It's no wonder I always say that God is angry with the world. Sure, it's there in the Bible that the world is in labour, same as a woman expecting a baby. You can *see* it. There's no summers. Here, long ago, God bless us, the summers ... the butterflies ... the bees. You had everything. It was beautiful. It was too good to last.'

JOSEPH TREACY – DECORATING, AGED IN SIXTIES

For seventy years his family's shop on Stoneybatter Street has furnished most of the wallpaper and paint for the surrounding artisan's dwellings. Thanks to the strong house-proud tradition in the community, business has been prosperous over the years. Customers can still count on the same personalised service extended to their grandparents.

As a young apprentice in the trade, Joseph carried out much redecoration on artisan's houses and has great fondness for them. He takes a personal interest in their upkeep and preservation. New wallpaper or fresh paint, he professes, dispels visual boredom, transforms one's living environment, and even revives the human spirit.

'We're a village kind of shop. My family has been here for seventy years. I was born above the shop and our family lived there until 1960. It's a pity that you didn't come here three years ago. My mother would have been here and she has seen generations. Mothers and grandmothers used to bring their children in by the hand to meet my mother, she was here that long. She was eighty-nine but couldn't stay home. I knew that she was slowly breaking down and I'd sometimes send her home and she'd say, "Now don't do that." She shouldn't have been working but it's what she wanted. Her mind was perfect to the end but her body was breaking down. The doctor said that she would die behind the counter ... and she did. Took a stroke.

'When my mother came here in 1916 the British garrisons left a lot of money here. Seemingly, they were very nice people to deal with. They were a decent sort. We used to supply all the stuff to the officers' quarters – good quality wallpaper and paint. We used to bring it all in from Liverpool then by boat. There wasn't much manufacturing in Ireland then. We hadn't got our wallpaper and paint factories. Most of the people here were tradesmen. A lot worked in Guinness's, Jameson's, Player's, and other factories. They reared big families — seven, eight, nine children.

'The old stock of people kept their houses up. The buildings are well built but they're old walls and unfortunately they haven't got a damp course. In other words, there was always trouble with damp-ness with the result that it takes more to keep them going. They break down quicker, the walls do, which is good for business. And twenty or thirty years ago they burned coal and turf and the smoke, that's why they had to do the room over. Even a man smoking a pipe for a year in one of those rooms can do dreadful damage. And in three or four years the outside paint would be breaking down.

'I'm sure that there are doors up there that were never burned off, never stripped. I remember when I was an apprentice, going back forty years, burning off an odd one, stripping it down, and it was a dreadful job. And you'd be getting all the different colours. Could have thirty or forty layers of paint. Years ago when the Artisan's Company owned the houses they painted them outside and you might have a whole row done one colour. It used to be dark green, dark brown, and dark red. One row green and the next row red. The Irish used to be dull. Now people are going for brighter colours. And brighter clothes.

'People save up to do their house. Putting money into the house has been their pride and joy. Some people wallpaper the living room every year. Some feel that by decorating their room it gives them a new lease on life. The way they look at it, eight rolls of paper at two or three pounds is like a woman years ago who would buy a hat. See, we've a damp climate seventy-five percent of the time and like a cheerful paper does wonders. Even people in the tenements on Queen Street decorated every year, some of them. A woman with maybe a crowd of little children around and a husband who was working hard and unfortunately — typically Irish — he used to drink a lot. And no holidays. To have her walls papered, a room decorated, it did her good ... it was like a holiday.

'I'd say eighty percent of our customers are regulars. The old people, they all like a bit of advice. Having a chat is part of the business. It's old fashioned but it's good. Pensioners take good care of their homes. What else would they spend their money on? They're too old to travel far and they don't drink much, don't entertain much. It's monotonous up and about in one atmosphere for a couple of years. And with the coming of television they spend more time at home. So if you do up a room it does you good. And it's their pride.'

PAT KEARNS – PAWNBROKER, AGED IN FORTIES

Kearns' Pawnbroker's on Queen Street can be spotted at some distance because of its three gleaming brass balls. Pawnbroking has been the family business for more than a century. It is one of only four remaining pawnshops in Dublin. The shop occupies a dilapidated brick Georgian building. Surrounding tenements of the same vintage have been demolished. Very simply, the pawnshop has survived because there is still a need for it in Stoneybatter.

Pat has a warm, understanding face which puts customers at ease. Most people are regulars and all the older residents have a very personal acquaintance with the shop. During times of hardship it served as their last resort. Pat, keenly aware of local history and tradition, is proud of the role the family business has played in the life of the community.

'My granduncle had this place and it was a pawnbroker's before that. It goes back at least one hundred years. In 1930 there were nearly fifty pawnshops in Dublin. They're a part of the history of the city. The pawnbroker is still the small man's banker. Years ago people used to bring in different things, mostly clothing and shoes, on Mondays and take them out on Saturdays. They'd be queued down the street. Today there's no market for second-hand clothes. Men's suits, you can't give them away. There are few people today really destitute, unless through their own fault, like drink. Today anybody can get fifty pounds as social assistance.

'I imagine I get in about 1,000 customers a week. We get all classes of people here. And nowadays they're no longer just women. I'd say it's about fifty-fifty. Most customers are regulars. People who just can't manage their money. People live beyond their means. Then they need money for mortage payments, car payments, car insurance, the ESB (Electricity Supply Board) bill. That *has* to be paid, especially in winter time, or you'd be cut off. You know the week the ESB bill comes up because you're busy that week.

'Today it's the middle class people really who are more stuck. Banks will gamble on bigger business but they won't deal with the small person. Banks today are not very givish with loans. If you have no security a bank won't give you a loan. The small people rarely have a chance. A couple of years ago when the depression come (1970's) a lot of middle-class people that were used to good jobs and company cars and a couple of hundred pounds a week lost their jobs and they were down to dole. They couldn't handle it. Didn't know what to do. If they go into a bank most of them have nothing. But here they have collateral, something of value to put in ... so they have their *pride*. There's not so much of a social stigma attached with coming into a pawnshop as there was years ago.

'The best things for us are small with high value, easily stored, and easily disposed of. Anything in jewellery fits into that. But we do a lot in televisions, videos, tools, bicycles. We get billiard cues and fishing rods. We wouldn't take in false teeth and some things from the old days. We used to take pianos here. We even took cars at one stage. Years ago you had to go up to the top of the house with clothes or to get somebody's suit and that took a few minutes. Today we get a lot of rings and jewellery. It's easier and faster. Now you just take the ring out of the drawer and they're gone. We give people the second-hand retail value. We get our two percent from volume. An item has to be unclaimed for four months before we can auction it off. But you'd give regular customers more time. I've seen stuff stuck here for years.

'We wouldn't want to encourage someone who needed the money for drinking. It's hard to know what they really want it for. We use our own judgement. If a person were drunk you'd know where the money was going but with gambling you wouldn't know. Children will even be sent in by their parents with a note. You have to use your own discretion whether people are telling you the truth or lies. They'll tell you sad stories to get a little bit more money. Then you might see them later on the corner with a bottle in their hand. Maybe he drank the money and the kids at home haven't had a bite. Sometimes if you refused him the wife would come in and thank us.

'Without us here, the people in this neighbourhood, if they needed money, would have to sell their stuff with no chance of getting it back. I think we're a very fair system. Most people are appreciative. They might say, "I was really stuck that day and I was grateful for what you did for me." It makes you feel very good. We once got a letter from a doctor that used to live in this area when he was a medical student and he had passed his exams and he said, "Without the help of this place I couldn't have made it through".'

MARY KILMARTIN – FLORIST, AGED 72

She is the owner of Kane's Florist (her grandmother's name) on Stoneybatter Street. The family shop, dating back nearly a century, has served the neighbourhood faithfully on its most special occasions – Christmas, Easter, birthdays, weddings and funerals. Flowers and fruit have cheered up the homes of Stoneybatter for generations and in this she takes obvious pride. She still lives above the shop in handsomely-furnished quarters and intends to live out the rest of her life there.

'The shop goes back to 1897. I was born in 1918 and my father was born here. It was the family business. My grandmother's name was Kilmartin but when my grandfather died she married again and her name was Kane. She was one of the characters of the neighbourhood — interesting and funny and amusing. She was a very big woman weighing twenty stone but only about five foot two. You can imagine how big she was. Even the children when they were in school and doing needlework and they'd make something that was big they'd say, "That would fit Mrs. Kane!"

'When I left school I came into the shop straight away. Back then we had two shops, this and the one next door there. This was the fruit shop and when my grandmother was alive the other shop was a vegetable shop. But we sold a few flowers at Christmas and things like that in the fruit shop. Then when I came in I started with the flowers. From the time I was a child I used to love flowers. The fruit became more important than the vegetables and we gave those up. Then the flowers became more important than the fruit.

'There's always been competition. I've seen some shops change hands ten or twelve times. We've survived because we're here so long and we're so well known. I never got a lesson on flowers in my life. I went to London and bought all the flower books and from there I found my way of doing things. During the War years we had flowers but no fruit. It was difficult because we had a big family here, four brothers and two sisters, so times were bad during the War years.

'About half our business is for special occasions. We always do a lot of work for Christmas and Valentine's Day and, of course, Mother's Day. It used to be that there was no such thing. Before that, it was mostly Christmas and Easter and Church holidays. And now we do quite a number of weddings. The whole style of weddings has changed. They're all big weddings now. Years ago they used to be ordinary weddings. You'd get married in the morning and go off on your honeymoon by boat to England and there would only be corsages. Today there's bride's bouquets and bridesmaid's bouquets plus church flowers.

'At funerals they use more small flowers than they did. They'd put in the church and taken to the cemetery ... and round wreaths and crosses. The artificial wreaths on grave sites, what we call shades, now thirty or forty years ago they were china flowers and they were expensive. I haven't seen anything like that for years. We sell a lot of the plastic ones now. Some people always want something special that will keep. But some of the older people would only want fresh flowers. Some wouldn't touch artificial flowers. If anybody put artificial flowers on me I think I'd get up and go away!

'Men are buying more flowers for their women today. Thirty years ago a man wouldn't carry a bunch of flowers. You'd have to wrap them up to look like a sweeping brush or something like that, cover them completely. They were just embarrassed to be seen carrying flowers. The Irish men are very bad that way. They'd actually say to me, "Would you cover them up? I don't want anyone to see me carrying flowers." But now on Mother's Day you have all the young boys coming in for flowers for their mother and Valentine's Day they're all in for roses for their girlfriends. Today I have some men who come in and arrange their own flowers and they're twice as fussy as women.'

32 Collecting the morning milk and newspaper at the corner shop on Sitric Road

33 Leslie Foy, signwriting craftsman and local preservationist

34 Shamrock-festooned iron window guard. Relic of cattle market days. Such street furniture serves to visually embellish the streetscape

Chapter 7

Craftsmen

One of Dublin's last handcraft signwriters, he has etched the character lines into the face of Stoneybatter by writing many of its shop fascias and facades. The elaborate lettering and ornamentation of Walsh's and Kavanagh's pubs and Muldoon's Fishmonger's is testimony to his skill and creativity. He has lived his whole life and raised nine children in the same house on Kirwan Street. Ruggedly handsome, he bears an uncanny resemblance to actor Robert Mitchum. His wife claims that everyone takes note of it. He doesn't seem displeased with the comparison.

Having spent the past forty years contributing to the visual beauty of Dublin, a city he unabashedly loves, he is saddened and angry at the defacing and destruction that has occurred. In condemning this, he is passionate and articulate. Indeed, one senses rage. He exhibits a fierce attitude of protection toward *his* Stoneybatter, believing that if it were threatened by unscrupulous developers, local residents would rise up in unison against the 'enemy'. He leaves no doubt that he would be in the forefront of such a movement.

'I was born in this house. I know who my people were. Going back generations I know everybody on my mother's and father's side. I know all about them. I've got a genealogical brain on that. My kids, they say, "Dad, write this down for us so that when you go we'll have a record of all your family, what they have done and who they were". And I'll do it and it'll be there for them. For example, this area right here, this very house, was built on a famine graveyard. This ground was owned by Dr. Kirwan who had an orphanage at the top of Prussia Street. It was an orphanage for Protestant girls and boys. Originally, it was an orchard. But it was used during the famine in 1848 to bury the dead because of typhus and all.

'This is a very historic part of the city. It has a village atmosphere, very unique. Other Dublin people didn't know where this was. People would say, "Stoneybatter? I've never heard of that place".

117

Nobody knew about it. It's been a nice secret, like a country town. There was no development. Time here stood still. So people around here have a sense of history that you wouldn't find in other parts of the city. It's something that's part of you. People born and reared here never feel out of place. The woman down the street, her grand-mother and my grandmother were brides here together in this street. All the people in and around here were born and reared with me or before me. I *belong* here.

'I started my seven-year apprenticeship as a boy, about sixteen. There weren't many really good signwriters in Dublin. There was an elite group of no more than twenty of these men. And they never advertised, just lived by reputation, word of mouth. As a young man, you were sent out on jobs with a highly skilled craftsman and you watched them and asked them questions and learned the tricks of the trade and from that you developed your own technique. But some of the old signwriters were very secretive about sharing their knowledge with you. The masters held their cards very close to their chest. They'd do things behind your back, especially the tricky bits. The reason was that there was so much unemployment and if they showed you, it could mean their jobs. It was a threat to their jobs and this was universally accepted. So you had to figure much of it out for yourself by trial and error and experience and just watching other people work.

'In the business there was what they called letterwriters and sign painters and signwriters. A signwriter was the highest form of the art. The signwriter was artistic. He could do all styles of lettering – Roman, Old English, Gothic, Germanic, even Egyptian. And I could do gold gilding on glass or wood and imitate wood graining and marble. Lettering should have an artistic flow about it. So it has life instead of looking stamped, rigid. Some is very elaborate three-dimensional work with highlights and shadows. That requires great skill and forethought. I've done a couple hundred pubs in my life all over this city. And a lot of places around here. A lot of work on shopfronts.

'People would stop and watch you working on a job. It would distract you when you were young, starting out, but after a while it's part and parcel of what you're doing. And signwriters always wore their ordinary clothes. Never knew any signwriter to wear overalls or a uniform. But I've had people standing around at the bottom of the plank looking up. I think it's a compliment. And maybe sometimes I'll play to the gallery. Dublin people are great critics and they'll come out of a pub and give their expert critique. I like it when people recognize the artistic value of what I'm doing.

'Dublin used to be a more beautiful city, a more personalised city, when shopfronts were done by hand. Each individual shop had a particular type of lettering that was peculiar to them. Every sign-writer tried to give the customer something individual and they almost always achieved it. You could have forty shopfronts on a street and not two of them written the same way or same style. That was amazing. Shop owners used to be more proud of their shopfronts. Very much so. Because shops were owned by the people who ran them and many lived overhead. If you look along Stoney-batter and Manor Street you'll notice that all the shops are built into houses which housed the family overhead.

'I love this city. I have a great affinity for this town. Everything I do regards my trade is a reflection of how I perceive my town. I wouldn't do anything that would be a discredit to it. If your work maintains a certain standard of excellence you contribute to the overall well-being of the town which you love. That's why I'm sorry to see the plastic fronts. In the late Fifties and early Sixties it started to come in. Whole streets became taken over with plastic, like Capel Street ... plastic alley from one end to the other. Totally plastic. It's terrible. Capel Street was one of the nicest streets for signwriting in the city. A lot of good work on that street by good men. Plastic has become over-dosed. A gigantic sales job. So many beautiful shopfronts, so many beautiful buildings destroyed because somebody had to sell plastic. O'Connell Street was *destroyed*. Here was the main thoroughfare of an old city and they allowed that to happen. A very historic street destroyed, turned into a canteen, literally into a fast-food consortium on both sides. It's one of the finest examples in Western Europe of institutionalised vandalism. Dublin is a *sleazy* place now.

'Nobody with the name of a Dublin man was responsible for that. Our city centre was destroyed by people who weren't born and reared here. They were men in the Government from other parts of Ireland. Our administrators and civil servants, architects, town planners, builders, people who can produce laws or stop laws or cir-cumvent laws, they're all country people and they've converged on Dublin. They're not Dubliners. No Dublin people with a heart would stand by in Government and commit that monstrosity that's called O'Connell Street. That was done by people with no feeling for Dublin. As a matter of fact, they had animosity toward Dublin. People from the outside have a very high degree of animosity toward Dublin. We don't inflict anything on our rural cousins but they can inflict great harm here, and have done so. They live in the suburbs and they'll protect their beautiful places. But they don't care what they do with *my city*. Look at O'Connell Street. Look at Capel Street. That was *allowed* to happen. Devastating.

'Developers just grab the money. "Give me the money. Give me the money". That's all they want. Look what they did to Molesworth Street. It was a beautiful street, beautiful Georgian and Victorian buildings. When the "Save Dublin Society" objected, they just got their bulldozers out on a Sunday morning and bulldozed half the street down and it was a *fait accompli*. It was gone! You could object all you liked after that. The people who put up the new buildings were from Cork and Tipperary and Limerick. That's where the TDs come from. You try to explain to people who were born and reared in the country not to destroy *my* city and you may as well be talking to a wall. They have an ingrown hatred of Dublin and all it means. It's "progress" because they love the money they can make out of it. They'll legally tear this whole place down and put up something ugly. We have the ugliest buildings in Europe in this city. That has been documented. And what we knocked down to put up those buildings ... it's sinful. No other country would have done it.

'The Corporation will come along and tear down a street and put the people out. Put them out in Coolock, in Tallaght, Crumlin, Ballyfermot. Uprooted people. Moved them out. That's what happened to so many Dublin people. They died of broken hearts. They just gave up. They vegetated. Their hearts never left Sean McDermott Street, Marlboro Street, where their houses were ripped down. And all the old people, when they died they're all taken back to the church on Dominick Street and Marlboro Street and Gardiner Street. Brought back all the way across the city to the church where they were christened, where they were married. They made their children promise ... "When I die, you bring me *back* and lay me out down there. I'll be buried in that church". They never left it. They've torn the heart out of the city. The city is dying now and the people's hearts are dying.

'I'm worried about the future of Stoneybatter. This is such a great historic part of Dublin. One of the last districts of its kind left in Dublin almost untouched. If a speculator gets his paws on it, he'll destroy it. They'll be whittling away at the edges trying to get bits and pieces of it to break the planning and zoning laws. People here have to be like watchdogs and not allow this to happen. Any attempt to come in and steamroll this area, bulldoze it, I'd say there would be a dramatic response to that. A speculator couldn't come in here and ride roughshod over what is beautiful and replace it with what is ugly. We're always watching for this type of thing, a sudden surge by the enemy. They wouldn't allow that to happen here. I'd certainly be in the forefront of that. Constant vigilance.'

DAVID O'DONNELL – COOPER, AGED 70

H e was born in a brick row house on Blackhall Place in 1920 during politically turbulent times. The Black and Tans, detecting light seeping through the upstairs curtain where his mother was giving birth, ascended the stairs and burst into the room. They were firmly ordered to leave by the attending midwife. That's how he came into the world.

Following in his father's footsteps, he became a cooper and worked at Guinness's. There was great job security and camaraderie. Coopers thought themselves indispensable to the brewery. But in the late Forties the shift to metal casks, known derogatorily as 'iron lungs' and 'depth charges', threatened the cooper's livelihood. A decade later wooden barrels were obsolete. When Guinness's closed their cooperage, in the prime of his working life, David was dispirited and despondent. He took to driving a taxi but found the inactivity and boredom numbing. An accomplished artist, he today spends much of his time sketching and painting local scenes around Stoneybatter.

'I was born in Blackhall Place. During a raid, actually. It was curfew and there was light showing in the room I was born in and the Black and Tans came in. There was heavy fighting in this area and there was a curfew on. My mother once saw a machine gun mounted opposite of where her old mother was staying and she went out anyway to warn her. Actually, my mother was more for the British side of it and my father was exactly the opposite. He had a photograph of Robert Emmet, who was executed, over the mantelpiece. But most people around here were pro-Treaty.

'This part of Dublin has a villagey atmosphere. I remember saddlers, wheelrights, blacksmiths, bootmakers, tailors, tobacconists, bakers. They all did a great business. On Sunday mornings you'd hear all the church bells. There were buskers and music and dancing. They played the ukulele and concertina and melodion. A violinist would walk around from house to house playing very beautiful music and people would give him pennies. Life was better back then.

'I remember my father. He was a cooper as well. He always wore a bowler hat and had his boots polished in the morning and always used to wear a white stiff front with a flannel shirt underneath. He died when I was very young. I did my apprenticeship at Guinness's. Served me time to a man named Jones who you said "Mr." to. We were always called "boys", the apprentices. There were nearly three hundred coopers in Guinness's in my time. Many from around here and the Liberties. Coopers were well paid craftsmen. Your master was responsible for you and he paid me eleven shillings a week the first year. After five years you came out of your time and had your test, making a barrel. Then you got your certificate and could work as a journeyman.

'The thing that I noticed from the first day was the *smell*, the oak timber, which has a very distinctive smell. It was the first thing that'd hit you, a very pleasant smell. And there was tremendous noise all the time because of the banging of the hoops. Quite a lot of men would go deaf in one ear. We were on piecework. You made so much for each cask. You could go in to work whenever you liked and go home whenever you wanted, provided that you could make your week's wages. But there was this thing that when you made a cask you wouldn't think about the money, you always wanted to make a *good* cask. Have a good look at it and get pride out of it. Reputations were important. You wouldn't get a good name making a bad cask. I was a *master cooper*.

'I'd be in by eight making my casks. You'd have to light fires for blazing heads for casks, set your tools out, and have your staves cut to measurement. Each man had his own berth with his tool box there. Tools were handed down from father to son. I inherited my father's tools. Tools were very, very important. They would come to fit your hand. And nobody would loan a tool to anybody else. Now on piecework some men would be exceptionally fast. You'd be perspiring all the time. All the hard work encouraged drinking. See, we had our beer every day. Porter it was. Our allowance was one in the morning and one in the afternoon but you could manage to get as many as you liked. A man could put away six or more pints in a day and it wouldn't make you tipsy, not when you're working in the shop.

'And, ah, your hands would crack like a horse's foot. At the end of the day there'd be just solid welts. Usually in the winter time I'd get a crack down along here and it would be quite deep. I often stitched it up with a piece of thread when it would become really open. It was like leather. You wouldn't feel a thing. Then when I came home I'd put tallow or goose grease on my hands. I'd do it in front of the fire because that's what my father used to do.

'Guinness's was a good employer. You could have breakfast there in the morning, a full breakfast for nine pence, and that was subsidised by Guinness's. You could have a wash, shower and shave. You could have your lunch there and your tea. We had an athletic ground and there was a bar on the grounds where you could get a pint for seven pence. You had newspapers in the reading unit or you could read a book in the library. And if you wanted to go over there in the evening there was billiards and card tables. Guinness's even had this burial society where you'd put so much into it, you know, on your burial. The fellas nicknamed it the "Bury Yourself Society".

'When metal casks started coming in we weren't so worried because we had a strong guild, the Dublin Cooper's Society. I first saw a metal cask after the War and thought it would be a failure. Many coopers felt that beer shouldn't be in metal, that beer or spirits should be matured in wood. See, there's a happier relationship between wood and the beer and the oak breathes. When there was a change from wooden barrels to metal a lot of people felt the taste changed, that it was a tinny taste. More synthetic. They pressurised it. It's *not* the same pint by any manner.

'The younger coopers were the first to go. Some of them just out of their time. They went to bottling or elsewhere in the factory. I finished out making garden seats and miniature barrels. It was sad because we were just killing time, really. We had to clock-in at 8:00 and clock-out at 5:00. I remember a foreman coming over to me when I was making garden seats and saying, "For God's sake, take your time in making those things ... cause we've nothing to do." I was very disappointed at the end of coopering because I had visions of my son going to the craft.

'I was still young enough to do something else, so I put a taxi on the road. But I had been used to action all the time and I'd sit in the taxi and was irritated, maybe sitting the whole day waiting for a fare. I just couldn't understand sitting down the whole day.'

JOHN CRUITE – SADDLER AND HARNESS MAKER, AGED 68

One of the only two saddlers and harness makers left in Dublin, his tiny cubicle shop is in Smithfield next to Red Cow Lane. On the front of the dusky saddlery shop it reads 'Established 1890' and he has occupied the premise for nearly four decades. His heavily striated workbench faces out into the cobblestoned market place which was once packed with horses, cattle, pigs, drovers, farmers, and Tinkers. Things now are much quieter — and considerably less interesting. Occasionally, a horse and cart clatters by, evoking memories of bygone days. And on the first Sunday of every month a lively horse fair is still held.

The scent of leather from his shop wafts out into the street sometimes inticing passers-by to peer in or maybe enter to have a chat. He welcomes the company. He still uses the same tools and techniques of

his ancient predecessors. The last of a breed, he openly laments that the
life he has long led is nearing its end. But there is still an unmistakable
glow of pride in the old craftsman when he shows off a saddle or harness
made completely by hand.

'I got into the craft because my brother was at it. It was really very
hard work. I worked from 8:00 in the morning until 6:00 at night.
You only got Sunday off and there was no half days then. First of
all, you learned how to make wax ends, hemp with wax on it with
a fine end on it for sewing. It takes a strong man to be a harness
maker and saddler, to take a big heavy needle and rise your stitch.
Believe me, it's hard work and the perspiration would come through.
A hard, dirty job and I like to take a drink. I find it does me good.
But two pints and I'm finished. I was never drunk in me life. Don't
know what it is to be drunk. When I started it was five shillings a
week but I was happy at it.

'I remember all the old men, the old harness makers. They were
all fantastic ... exceptionally good craftsmen. They were genius's
at their job, the old men. They learned me a lot. The majority of
old harness makers, well, they were a set all to themselves. They had
their own peculiar ways. If you went in to see them working and
they thought you're looking at them, they'd nearly cover up their
work. Didn't want you to see what they were doing. Very selective
some of them. But the majority would show you what to do.

'After I finished my apprenticeship with my brother I travelled
the country wide as a journeyman. Used to go to different shops
to work. I was a journeyman for twelve years. You'd only have to
carry about a half dozen tools with you and that would be sufficient.
You'd carry very little clothes packed in an ordinary little case. I
had a bicycle so I cycled. It was lovely to be out. You'd see all the
little rivers and streams. I seen a lot of the country and slept in
boarding houses. It was a great experience travelling all around and
meeting all the different journeymen. I worked one time in Offaly
and I was staying in digs and there was about twelve craftsmen there,
the whole lot. We had a great time. I stayed in a job for a couple
of weeks and would move on again in fine weather.

'When I came to Smithfield it was all cobblestones. And it was
all a family community. There were at least twenty saddlers in
Dublin at that time. There were four harness makers just in Smithfield. I had three men working with me. It was fantastic. It was
completely different years ago, people bringing in their stuff and
taking it out every day. You know, firms like dairies had sixty and
seventy horses. And every Monday evening you would see nothing

out there, only loads of horses and hay. Horses would all come from County Meath, Kildare, Louth, all over, and there was always a sale of hay on Tuesday morning. They used to park their loads of hay there and stable their horses and go in and have a couple of drinks and come out and sleep on the hay. It was very warm, you know. Then there'd be a horse fair here on Wednesday and there would be hundreds of horses running up and down. I seen horses running away and they do a lot of damage.

'I always specialised in harness making. But you don't like being at one thing all the time. So I did both. Making a harness and a saddle is a completely different ballgame. And there's a different style of harness in the city. No comparison between the city harness and the country harness. The city harness was all double harness, double stitching, much bigger and all that brass. In the country on the farm they never bothered much about brass. Then there was the van harness, what they used for brakes and milk vans. Very few firms in the country used van harnesses. See, city harnesses had to be heavier and stronger because in the city if a horse broke away it could kill people.

'The majority of people who come in say, "Well, you're carrying on the old trade and it's nice to see it." They love the smell of the leather. I usually have a chat with them. It's just like the old blacksmith's, that's where you went to get all your news. But it's not like years ago. They're all in a hurry now. Years ago people weren't in a hurry. Little children love to come in to see the old harnesses and old collars and old saddles, the things that their grandfather used to have. And lots of old men still come around, men in their eighties some of them. They'll have a chat about the old times and the horses. It's sad, you know, to see everything gone. It's a lost art ... but I have a great love for my work and I'll never retire. I'll keep working until I'm not able to do it.'

PETER CROWE – STONECARVER, AGED 48

As one passes by Oxmantown Lane, the monotonous thudding sound of mallet on chisel can be heard. Inside a small stone shed, chipping away contentedly at a block of stone, is Peter Crowe, one of Dublin's last stonecarvers. The shed and open yard are littered with chunks of marble, granite, and limestone of varying size. Scattered about are old tools inherited from his father. Everything is covered with a layer of white dust looking like freshly fallen snow.

Peter did a six-year apprenticeship under the old rigorous system. He

learned all the skills of the old masters. Thirty years ago he busily carved
Celtic crosses, ornate statues, and stately monuments. But stonecarving
is now a dying craft and he is reduced by modern economics and changing public tastes to making mostly machine-inscribed headstones. It has
been a humbling decline for the prideful craftsman. He relishes the creativity in the few handcrafted jobs he gets these days and fantasises about
having time in his later years to return to the purity of artistic carving.

'I started in this business when I was fourteen. My father was a
stonecarver and my grandfather was a stone mason. I served my
six-year apprenticeship up at Farrell's at Glasnevin. I did Celtic
crosses with interlacing and monuments and headstones. The money
was dreadful and the craft was dying out but I didn't have any
choice. It was really the only thing open to me at the time and I
was going to make the most of it. The men were very good and
would teach you in good faith anything they felt you should know.

'In the winter we used to work inside the workshops and in the
summer, or fine days, we'd prefer to work outside because of the
dust. Men used to like to swill the dust down with a pint of Guinness. There were some pretty hard drinkers among men I knew.
My father was a heavy drinker in his younger days. He used to tell
me that it didn't interfere with his work but I think it did. He really
loved the old mallet and chisel and the dust and putting on his apron,
making tea at 10:00 in the billy can over the fire.

'Tools were passed down from father to son. I inherited them
from my father and they could be a hundred years old. When I was
serving my time I used to sharpen my tools on a forge. We were
allowed two hours a week for sharpening. If the chisel was blunt
you'd put it in the forge and keep working the bellows to get the
fire hot. Then when it was really red hot you'd take it out on the
anvil and beat out a nice point on it. Then you'd put it back in the
fire, take it out red hot and put it into a bucket of water to get the
right temper. You'd see almost the colours of the rainbow in the
tool when it was hot, but the right temper would be yellow. Then
you'd clean it up with carburundum and you had a nice sharp tool.

'There's great pleasure in working with stone. I could tell just by
looking at a piece of stone, by the colour and the feel of it, whether
it was going to be a very hard, brittle piece or a nice soft piece. I
enjoyed working on Irish limestone more than any other material,
as opposed to granite or imported marble. Irish limestone is a bluey-
grey. I think it's more natural looking than the polished granite.
Now around the Sixties the Celtic crosses were dying out. Employers
felt that more simple, straight-forward monuments were quicker

and suited the machines better. It was a quicker turnover. See, with Celtic crosses there was quite a lot of handwork. Men could spend *weeks* doing interlaced panels by hand. It was *time pressure*, really, because labour costs were rising. Hence, the machines. And people today can't really tell the difference between a hand job and a machine job.

'Today I do both handcarved and machined headstones. A lot of my business comes from around this neighbourhood. There's such an elderly population up around Manor Street and Oxmantown Road. Families keep coming back because they like to deal with somebody they know. I don't advertise in newspapers or anything like that. It's just word of mouth. If a person contacts me about a stone I visit them at their house, go to the cemetery with them to have a look at the grave, walk around and talk to them about the stone. Very personal service. It's comforting to the older people and to their sons and daughters as well. Now the bigger firms couldn't do that.

'I put a headstone on the wrong grave once. I made a blunder and that was it. The man went out and looked at the stone and was pleased with it but he rang me that evening and said, "Peter, the stone looks very well but there's only one snag ... you put it on the wrong grave! You made a 'monumental blunder'!" He had a sense of humour about it. Now to put a name on a headstone that's already there I go out and cut it by hand. It can be a difficult job if the stone is very low. You have to actually dig a hole in the grave and get down to ground level. Oh, it's dreadful in winter, all right. In the summertime graveyards are quite nice in the fresh air but in Ireland January, February and March are ferocious months weather-wise. I try to put my clients off till spring.

'It happens about once a year that I misspell something. Usually the person's name. Most inscriptions tend to be identical — "In Loving Memory of My Dear Husband". But sometimes people like to have verses on the stones. I must say that I don't care much for them. They're not very good verses. I like poetry myself and I think that's why I look at some of these things and think they're dread-ful. But I do it if that's what they want. You have to be very tactful because they're upset and emotional. It's meaningful to them and I try to do the best job I can.

'I recognize my own handcraft in a cemetery. The other day I was in Glasnevin Cemetery and I looked at a small stone with hand-carving on it that I did in 1960. I felt a bit sad, really. There was a sadness seeing that handcarving and I thought, "God, I'd love to have the time to get a block of stone in the rough, square it and chisel it, rub it down with carburundum, carve it and get a great satisfaction." I would never like to lose the touch because I think of my apprenticeship and all I went through to acquire it. I'm very proud of being a *craftsman*. I love to walk around old churchyard cemeteries in the country and look at crosses and think in my mind of the men who did that work and how they lived. It's quite sad, quite nostalgic, really ... to think that I'm part of that tradition ... the last of a breed.'

RICHARD PENDER – HANDCRAFT TAILOR, AGED 65

O ne of the last handcraft 'Bespoke' tailors in Dublin, he can proudly trace his heritage back to the Norsemen. Tailoring goes back generations in his family. He did his apprenticeship under a strict and demanding father but learned the craft well. He unabashedly terms himself a 'skilful master tailor with full qualifications'. His expertise in making military and police uniforms is known throughout the country.

He is the stereotypical finicky tailor – precise in cutting, sewing, and even speech. He still puts in long hours at his shop on Manor Street. People in Stoneybatter look up to him as a leading figure and he is conspicuously the best dressed man in the neighbourhood.

'My great grandfather was a tailor, my grandfather was a tailor and my father was a tailor. I was one of seven and the rule in our family was that everybody worked. In those days an apprentice got ten shillings a week. You started off by sweeping the floor and you picked up the rags and sorted the wool from the cotton and put them in separate bags. The Jewman came once a month and you gave them to him and if you got seven and six off him you thought you were great, which was good money in those days.

'At that time we had eight men in the workroom. They were hard times. Tailoring, weaving, and footwear were always deprived trades. Workers were exploited. As an apprentice you were bound to the master for seven years and you were a *slave*. The master was the boss and the men hated the masters. My father roared more than he hit but he gave us a statement. He wasn't educated in book knowledge but he was educated in other things. Now my grandfather, he signed his name with an "X". In those days our workroom was small, we had outside toilets and you worked until you were finished. I took all the menial jobs I was given and I said, "I'll be bloody well good at it." I can remember trying to sew at first and trying to cut a straight line. But the job that was worst in the workroom when I came in was to sew on the buttons. It was a challenge. And today I sew on buttons better than anyone.

'My father was a master tailor and cutter. He did a cross-section of the tailoring trade. He did uniforms, ladies wear, gents wear, wedding wear. The only tragedy was that he forgot to make money. But he was a born gentleman. He didn't know how to use bad language. Bad language would not be tolerated and the other thing you would dare not do was to throw a scissors to anybody ... disgusting that anybody would throw a scissors. First, it was ignorant. Second, it was dangerous. We were instilled with this respect for each other. On Monday morning you usually discussed the football matches played on Sunday and who shouldn't have won and who did win. And politics would come in very strong because in Ireland everybody has political feelings. But you wouldn't speak ill of anybody. We had this code of decency among us. Respectability at all costs.

'Back in the 1930's and 1940's most Irish still bought tailor-made suits. They generally had one suit that they were married in and they were buried in the same one. They'd make sure it didn't wear out because they'd only wear it on Sunday. Only took it out to go to Mass. And they let it out if they got fat.

'Now a tailor, he'd make all the clothes for his family. If a man was able to, he would save pieces of cloth from his work to make a small boy's trousers or other items for his family. Whatever a man had left over from the piece of cloth given him, that was legally his. That's what we call "cabbage". This cabbage would be accepted as his property. It wouldn't be considered pilfering. It's always been accepted in the trade that you're entitled to cabbage but you are not entitled to skimp to get it. If you skimped, that's robbery. So a tailor could make trousers for his little nipper and skirts for the girls and a costume for his wife. For his own suit he'd aim at picking up a piece of cloth and the colour wouldn't matter.

'I term myself a civil and military tailor. My forte is military uniforms. The army and police have to have their uniforms made specially. We work with officers, the higher echelon. Now the term "bespoke" means that the customer has bespoken his request, has told you what he wants. But basically, a tailor, he's ninety-percent psychologist. He sees a fella with a hump on his back and he has to convince that man that he hasn't got it. He puts on a jacket and says to him, "Oh yes, I can improve that." Or if a man comes in to you and he's an athletic type of fella there's no good in tightening him into a shape suit. And if a fella comes in and he's slouchy, he's got to have room in his suit. You've got to know people but you can't tell him his faults. A customer has no faults. And a tailor was not good enough to drink with. The attitude of the customers is that "He's my *employee*, he makes my clothes." No, you never drank with your tailor.

'We're a dying breed. There are very few of us left. I'm sad to see it happen but I feel it was inevitable. We had neither the ability or the foresight to keep up with progress. In the Fifties my father was charging twelve pounds and ten shillings for a suit. I charge 130 pounds now for the same suit. By 1959 the tailoring trade was on its knees. The big tailoring firms in Dublin, they would have twelve tailors working in the place and they would meet and greet the people ... but that's all dead. Things changed. There are no apprentices coming into the trade. As a consequence, our craft is being choked out. I feel very proud that I succeeded. Until four years ago I worked constantly for ten hours a day, six days a week. I'm proud of my heritage.'

JAMES DONNEGAN – SHOEMAKER, AGED 58

He is one of only four handcraft shoemakers left in Dublin. His little shop is wedged in a small space along Aughrim Street. The strong smell of leather and dyes is inticing. The neighbourhood shoemaker's shop, like the local forge, has traditionally been a gathering place for idle folks. He is cordial, but pesky, lingering visitors impede his work. In such cases he is tactful but direct.

Contrasting with his thin frame are strong, heavily veined arms. There is an intensity in his eyes as he stitches away uninterruptedly as the tape recorder listens to his words. Repairing shoes consumes most of his time these days but he still delights in the creativity of producing a handmade pair. He grouses about the spread of fast fix-it shoe repair shops in Dublin. 'Staples and glue, that's what they use.' He is a craftsman to the core.

'I was at the craft since I was twelve years old. My father was a shoemaker before me and I did my apprenticeship under him. At that time it was seven years apprenticeship. My father was a journeyman, travelled around the country. I remember journeymen coming into my father's shop in Kildare when I was a kid. Years ago my father told me that shoemakers were the best dressed tradesmen, years and years ago. And they were called "Dons". I don't know whether it was the way they dressed or where they got it from. And they were called "waxies" from using the wax threads. Shoemakers were also known as big drinkers and they were never open on Mondays. Always drinking in the pub on Mondays. They all had eight or nine children as well. That would have had something to do with their drinking.

'The shoemaker's shop is like the old forge in that people will stand there and chat away. You get people saying they love the smell of the leather and that. Old people will stand there all day for a chat, they've nothing else to do. They'll talk about the weather, the state of the country ... which needs an awful lot of talking about. But I don't encourage anyone coming in every day of the week and sitting there and talking away.

'A lot of people call me "cobbler". It's a term I don't like. Because a cobbler, to me, it's like what they call a "cowboy", it's not a tradesman, not a qualified tradesman in other words. Years ago I think cobbler was a term for a man who done it in his own house on his family shoes, but he was certainly never a handmaker, that's for sure.

'Handmaking now is nearly a thing of the past and you can't get the tools anymore. There's only about four men in all of Dublin that's doing any handmaking anymore and they're all older than me. I'm the last shoemaker in this area, on this side of the river anyway. A lot of the old people grew up with handmade shoes. Years ago every second man had handmade shoes, even ordinary tradesmen. Times have changed. We're not doing the same amount of work we done in me father's time.

'Professional people — doctors, dentists, solicitors and publicans — people with money, have their shoes handmade today. My cost is about 130 pounds for a handmade pair. The factory shoe now, they'll cost forty pounds. They're a lot of plastic and rubber. It takes me roughly fourteen hours to make a pair of handmade shoes and make them correctly and I'd say that thirty-five to forty pounds would go to materials. I've known a good pair to last for fifteen years. But the ordinary man in the street wouldn't be paying 130 pounds for shoes. I make any kind of shoe but mostly orthopaedic stuff. There will always be orthopaedic work as long as you have motor cars and motor cycles and accidents.

'You have to work all hours in this trade to make a living at it. It's not like taking something off a shelf and selling it. It never was an easy trade. You don't find too many millionaire shoemakers ... even in America. I work six days a week every week of the year. I'm often here from 9:00 to 9:00. There are enough repairs to keep me busy. And I take great pride in the job I do. That's what's missing in most of the shoe repair shops in Dublin today. They just don't care. Young kids seventeen and eighteen are doing it. They do their training in a month and they put them into big, flashy, lovely looking shops. But if they can't do the job what's the point? They're glueing it and using staple guns! I still use the nails and old things just like it was done a hundred years ago. And they charge more than me for doing an inferior job. Doesn't make sense, does it?

'The old trades are dying out completely. When I was around fourteen there were around sixteen handmade shoemakers in this town. Now when I go and the few others, there won't be any left. It was a very highly respected trade at one time. The older generation appreciates craftsmen but younger people today are not worried about good work. They wouldn't know whether it was done right or wrong. I had an old man once, always used a cane, never walked right. I made him a pair of shoes and he started walking right ... so I must be doing something right.'

35 One of the last of the old Dublin corner shops – on Sitric Road

Chapter 8

Animal Handlers

BOBBY WALSH – DROVER, AGED 85

I'm the oldest drover still alive.' That's how Bobby greeted me at the door of his one-room flat in St. Bricin's old folks housing estate. 'I'll be glad to have a chat with you next Monday if I'm still around.'

From age ten to seventy-three he drove cattle and sheep, earning a reputation as one of the best. Wages were meagre and conditions rough; existence was always on a day to day basis. And, as he tells it, drovers were treated as the lowest human beings. Always a loner, he lives by himself in a small, stark room, barren of furniture, poorly lit, and in want of a good scrubbing. He has no teeth, is nearly blind and deaf, and appears painfully thin. One wonders how often he bothers to have a meal. 'I'm just skin and bone now.' He is the last of a breed in what was once the 'wild west' of Dublin.

'I was born on the south side of the city. My father was a baker and we come over here to the "buildings" when I was four, up there around the cattle market. I'd never been a drover, only for that. I'd have never seen cattle at all. I started to walk them down when I was only seven or eight, a fella giving me a penny to help bringing them in. I never went to school. I went a couple of weeks, in and out, but I couldn't content meself in it. I'd have to get out to help milk the cows. A couple of times I was brought to the court and the magistrate told me mother that I'd have to go back to school. Ah, I hated it. The headmaster told me mother "He'll never learn anything. Might only learn to spell 'cat' or 'dog'. Teach him yourself." The master couldn't get any good out of me and I'd get four of five slaps with the big cane. You weren't supposed to be a drover then till you were eighteen but I was doing it at ten and eleven.

'It was all a begging job. You had to go up to the corner (Hanlon's Corner) and look for a shilling. Stand there to see if a man would come along with a couple of cattle and say, "Come here and give me a hand." And he'd give you a couple of coppers. There was

36 Bobby Walsh, Dublin's oldest surviving cattle drover

*37 Centuries-old Smithfield Market, still cobblestoned and the site of a
monthly horse fair*

only about twenty constant drovers and they lived in a house at the yard. The rest was all casual drovers ... you know, a fella from the corner. It was mostly casual jobs I done. A good drover, he took to the job. It was in his heart. He wouldn't go to anything else. I never went to anything else. Ah, I was gifted at the game. They said that I was one of the best drovers up there at the cattle market.

'You had to know how to drive cattle and sheep and lambs. It was always a rushing job. They would hire you for one or two days, the day before the market and market day. I was paid two shillings for bringing them down from the railway and putting them into the yard. The Cabra Railway they called it. Then there was another railway beside it called the Liffey Junction where cattle come out of the west of Ireland. You used to have an ash plant. We used to put a screw into it and file off the head, make it sharp for prodding them. Instead of hitting them, we'd spur them. It was better for the cattle. But some fellas, they'd be hitting and prodding the cattle. But you'd lose more time that way. The more kind to them you were, the better. Especially rubbing them under their neck or behind their leg, what we called the "cod". Scratch them and you'd drive them quicker. If you'd rub their neck or their back it would make them more used to you, more content. But some of the drovers were very rough. Fellas would come along and hit them. They used to get terrible treatment.

'Every second drover had a dog. Ah, you'd want a dog, especially with sheep. Sheep was worse than cattle altogether. Ah, they were stubborn. With sheep you'd think you were walking into a river – not a shadow on the ground. Sheep have bad eye sight and you have to catch them and maybe pull them the length of the bloody market trying to put them into pens. Now I had three or four dogs. One I called "Bob" after meself. They were half collies and had terrier in them. "Short hairs" we called them. You had to get their two big teeth broke cause they'd be ripping the sheep's legs. They were wicked on sheep. Get the top of the two big teeth cut off or the dog might rip the sheep's leg or maybe tear their ears off them. I got me dog's teeth cut so they couldn't bleed sheep anymore. Matter of fact, some men put a ring in their nose, like a pig ring, the type you see in pigs. If he pushed against sheep it would hurt and he wouldn't bite them. *Couldn't* bite them.

'At that time there were trams and we'd be going down with the cattle and sheep and the tram would come behind you and there was a bell that'd go "ding, ding, ding" and you had to try and get the cattle and sheep apart to let him pass. And in a few minutes more a tram would be coming the other way. So the old dogs, when the tram would be coming, we'd send them over and they'd bark. Ah, there was some good dogs in Dublin.

'We were out in all weather, that was the worst of it. In the summer we'd have to go out in the fields because the animals would be on the land, not in the yard. Cattle lands was all around Ashtown, Blanchardstown, Finglas, Castleknock … three or seven or eight miles back. And you'd get a wet shirt sweating, feeding the cattle with pulp and turnips and getting oats and barley and hay and carrying buckets to feed them. And we used to lay in the hay. Now wet weather in the wintertime was the worst. But you'd always be warm because it was a galloping game. And you had to keep the dung off you. We had a long cloth coat, yellow it was, and old rubber boots cause you were always in wet and dung splashing.

'Now cattle and sheep used to get mixed up. Drovers would have to get in between them and separate them all out. Ah, I got a few kicks off them and was knocked down a couple of times and got up again. I was lucky. I seen contrary bulls coming that would go for you and knock you down. And I could throw a rope on them and tie them. Now you might have ten men trying to look at brands on them and that would last the whole morning trying to draw them apart. And you'd see rows over fellas getting mixed up with sheep and cattle. Some of them was bad tempered, you know. There was a lot of them poor and no education and no savvy at all. There would always be a row at Hanlon's or Conroy's (pubs). You'd see them throw off their coat out there and fight. Some of the fellas would give you a cut with a stick. You'd see a fella getting a lick of a stick and knocked down. They'd let them fight it out and they forgot about it then in maybe a week or two. They had to work together, you know. I was never a fighting man.

'Ah, drovers were big drinkers. That's all they lived for at that time. They'd be around the pubs in the morning waiting for them to open at 6:00. The drovers would run over and would be sweating and wet and they'd have a glass of hot coffee with whiskey in it. That was a great drink. The hot coffee would be mixed with treacle. It would be really sweet, like honey sort of stuff. They'd mix that all up in the pub the night before and have it when they opened. Mix it up, put whiskey in it and give you a hot glass. They'd put boiling water in the glass to warm it up. Ah, you'd drink four or five of those and you'd be mad to go back to work then. They were cheap at the time, about fourpence or sixpence. God, I'd like to be getting them now.

'It was a rough life. You'd no money. It was all pennies and coppers you were working for. You were half starved. Pig's cheek and

38 Pig raiser and 'local character', Billey Storey, with his pony along Manor Street

cabbage and potatoes and corned beef. And there was no thanks
for you, no matter what you done for the men that owned the
cattle. Once they paid you a few bob they didn't want to see you
till next time. People would pass you by and wouldn't say hello to
you. It annoyed you. Being a drover had a very bad name. People
always looked down on them. Once an old judge or magistrate on
the courts heard you were a drover he'd nearly give you a month
before he asked you what happened. A lot of drovers were illiterate,
couldn't read or write. They were put down as a very illiterate
crowd of people. They wasn't recognized as much of people at all.
But they was decent, honest, hard-working people.

   'I often heard old drovers say, forty or fifty years ago, "This place
will come to an end some day", and their word was right because
it's gone now. There's houses all built on the market now. We were
all sad about it ... but I was getting a bit old. The old drovers now,
they've all died. All dead and gone. And I knew them all. But I
don't mind being on me own. I was never much fond of company.
Everyone has to go. Oh, God, I don't think I'll live much longer.'

BILLEY STOREY – PIG RAISER, AGED 70

His piggery, up a side alley about fifty yards off Manor Street, con-
sists of an open yard, white-washed stone sheds (once cottages)
several hundred years old, and a wooden stall in which he keeps a pony
and goat. Dubbed the 'Lord Mayor of Manor Street' by locals, Billey is
a real Dublin character in the best tradition. There are few like him left
around today. Pig raiser, street philosopher, self-proclaimed social pundit,
his mind flutters wildly from subject to unrelated subject. He has a gift
for covering a galaxy of topics in a single inflated utterance. Strong
opinions on the weather, politics, pig market, drinking, women's rights,
crime and breakdown of the Irish family are all congealed in passionate
outbursts. Only an unflinching tape recorder could hope to capture all
his words and thoughts. His weathered visage and scruffy manner belie
a gentle character and pensive mind. He believes that pigs are like people
in many ways – better in some.

'We're 150 years here, to me great grandfather. And he had milk
cows as well. I was ten years old when me father would have me
sweeping out and carrying the feed in buckets. At that time a boy
did what his father told him. Today they call their father by their
first name because the father thinks it's making him younger. Oh,
I wouldn't have done that. Me father'd break me jaw. My father
was eighty-five when he died, working every day.

'Now this is the only city in the Common Market that has pigs. This time last year I had 170 pigs but I've only thirty-five now. Years ago when I was a school boy we had pigs in our kitchen. They'd come in and trail you around. They're very intelligent, you know, easily trained. Pigs are like human beings. Pigs, hanging up, are built the same way. The heart and all is the same formation. Very delicate animals. They're very allergic to heart ailments. And they don't castrate pigs anymore. I have boars in there and in hot weather it's like the human being ... they get sexed. Now I'm sorry to say that, but it's true. Warm weather affects them sexually just like a human being. And they might be rearing up in the cell.

'The ordinary, ignorant person thinks that a pig will eat anything, but he will not. Pigs are very stubborn and pig-feeding is a full-time job. I start at 7:00 in the morning to collect feed from hotels and hospitals. I collect in the mornings and sometimes in the afternoons. My pony knows where he has to go. He's only six years old but he's quiet in the traffic. Sometimes my pigs get too much swill. They gulp it, like if you'd start drinking and you couldn't get enough of it. Sometimes with pigs it's like an alcoholic when he goes into a hospital and has to be drained off the whiskey.

'I have a sister with bronchitis and she's on a lot of tablets. I got that goat there for my sister's milk. I milk the goat every morning. It's helping her breathing but it's like everything else ... when you get old, like an old car, you can only patch it and next thing it falls apart. Same thing with a human. When I was young I'd suck the milk out of the cow and it never did me any harm. The milk you buy today is only water. Now on a Saturday night I often drank eight or nine large bottles of stout. But, you see, a great cure if you're going out on a booze like that, you drink a pint of milk first and that puts a coating on the stomach. See, your body carries between three and three and a half gallons of fluid. Now just imagine eight or nine pints of that going into your body. Your heart is there floating and it's a terrible sensation. It's going to bed with the weight of it on you. You're lucky to get up the next morning.

'Ah, things are all wrong. Well, the world is all right ... it's the *people* that's in it. I look around and see the drink that these women consume ... and smoking. Now this is what's going on. All the wives now is working and they say to their husbands, "Here you are, Jack, I'm going out to meet Mary and you look after the children. Here's a pound, go up and get some potato crisps or something." It keeps them happy and they see no home life. This is the cause of *crime*. Like they call this a Catholic city and you can't even keep your windows open. And a woman can't carry a handbag, it's strip-

39 Luke Nugent, an old cattleman, having his morning pint at Walsh's Pub on Stoneybatter Street

ped off her. See, the world is being overpopulated. And electricity is on the way up and there's no manpower. I think work is great. An idle mind must be a terrible thing. I'll never retire. *Everybody* knows me. I should be well known, the way I'm going around with my pony and float and all. People will even be taking my photograph. They call me the "Lord Mayor of Manor Street".'

LUKE NUGENT – CATTLEMAN, AGED 78

Luke perfectly fits the image of a crusty, old cattleman. He might well be an elderly version of the 'Marlboro Man' of cigarette fame. As a young lad he would ride horseback beside his father for many miles in the chill and darkness of early morning to arrive at the cattle market when it opened. Before long he was sitting with other cattlemen in the pub each morning sipping hard whiskeys to start off the day. After more than a half century of handling unruly 'beasts', the cattle market closed and his whole way of life came to an abrupt end. Now, most mornings 'Old Lukie', as he is affectionately known, can be found in one of Stoneybatter's pubs chatting with cronies about the old days – and still drinking the same hard whiskeys.

'My father was a cattle dealer all his life. Used to come to the market all the time. I used to beg him to bring me and we'd get up at about 2:00 and we'd be here about 4:00. We'd come on a good horse. I was about twelve when I started. There was nothing but cattle everywhere you went. And there were pigs, calves, horses and goats. The goats, they'd be kept for luck and they used to keep the cattle quiet. So they'd bring goats to the cattle market and then they'd be brought back. Women and kids used to go up with a can and milk the cows and get free milk. You could drink it fresh out of the cow in the morning if you were thirsty. See, a man with a cow, he'd be stuck with it and the milk would be flowing out. Some of the men would put glue on the animal to make it look bigger. It would be very uncomfortable for the animal.

'When I was twelve I'd be with my father and watching everything he done. He might give me a bit of a lecture to make you more cautious. Finally, he'd send you away on your own two feet with his money to buy cattle. I was about fifteen. I'd go to fairs all over Ireland and buy the cattle. Now there was no scales. I'd tell their weight by feeling their flesh with my thumb, and I'd know by their coat as well. And I'd be right most of the time. At that time you could buy champion cattle for twenty-five or thirty pounds, cattle you wouldn't buy today for 1,000 pounds. We wined and dined on the best, slept in good hotels, plenty of steak, and you met interesting people.

'People were honest and most deals were made in cash. Some of these dealers could have up to five thousand pounds on them — in cash! When deals were made between men they'd spit in their hand and give a slap. You could pull out thousands of pounds in the market and no one would ever take a pound. You wouldn't show a fiver today! There were ten banks up the street there and never robbed because there were two policemen who walked up and down, watched the whole thing. They'd be in civvie clothes, but they'd be more times in the pub than be watching the banks.

'There were trams running on North Circular Road then. Now the abattoir was on the far side of the road and instead of taking animals on the road in front of the trams you could take them through a tunnel underground to it. A man got killed there one time, crushed in the tunnel. There was places you could stand in (to let the animals pass), but unfortunately he wasn't near one of them when the cattle were coming and he got crushed. Now at the abattoir they used an axe, like a sledge hammer, and they'd hit him in the forehead and down he'd go. Then they'd get a stick and put it in the hole and stir up his brains and you'd see him kicking on the ground. You'd see his nerves and skin going. Some of the men were geniuses at killing animals.

'Drovers came from all over Dublin. There were some great drovers and some very bad ones. And a good dog would take the place of a drover, or two or three or ten. If it was a bad night or morning with rain on market day they'd be cursing. They used to say that it rained every Thursday, that it was the curse of the cattle drovers. There was no such thing as protective clothing, no rain coats and no rubber boots at that time. Drovers would just put an old sack over their shoulders to keep out the wet. Now if you had property along the street it was up to you to protect it with iron bars on the windows. You see, if a beast would be walking by a window and he sees himself in it, he'll walk through it because he thinks it's another animal. So people would bar their windows. And animals could come in the doorway if it was open.

'There were characters around then. You had musicians and women sold fruit and sold matches and there was men selling ash plants for driving the cattle. They'd cut them to maybe three or four feet and they'd be sold to the drovers and cattle dealers. And there was bootblacks, used to polish our boots. They had their little box and when you'd be finished in the market you'd put your foot up. They'd use an old sack and water to get the cow dung off and then they'd dry them and put polish on. They'd shine them up for sixpence. At one time there were about ten of them but they died out when the market went. And there were Tinkers – itinerants – around then. They were tinsmiths and a lot of them went in for chimney sweeping. And great horse dealers! They had a language of their own and if they didn't want you or anybody else to know the price of a horse they'd just use their own language. And they were great fortune tellers. One time I had this woman tell my fortune for a half crown. She said that I'd become very wealthy and I'd go across water and I'd be in love with two girls. And I said to her, "They're all lies ... I'm married!"

'Now the pubs opened at 6:00 in the morning. But to get a drink you had to be a cattle drover or a buyer or a butcher or connected in some way with livestock. You could even have a woman coming in herself selling pigs or a couple of sheep. Sometimes the men would question the women coming in for a drink to see if they were associated with the market. She was allowed to come into the pub until 10:00 when there was a proper opening. Anyway, if it was a cold morning you could get hot whiskey and a few cloves and that would warm you up. See, the cloves would heat it up, burning like pepper. It would heat your whole insides. The men, they all drank whiskey or brandy. The floor was all sawdust and there was spittoons you could spit into. And there'd be ten or twelve dogs – in the pub. They were acceptable.

'Women was different than now. The farmer would come in on market day in the pony and trap, or maybe a donkey and cart, selling butter or eggs or something they'd made. Well, the farmer would go into the pub and he'd drink. But the woman, when she had her shopping done, she was never brought into the pub. Never allowed inside. All she could do was put her head inside and say she was finished shopping. And he would say, "Go out and tackle the pony, yoke it up." She might have to sit outside there for hours. And if the husband got too well jarred ... well. Then when she comes home she might have to milk the cows or feed the calves and maybe the pigs and she'd have to fix his tea. She was moreless a slave. Ah, but no one ever questioned it. He was the boss. The husband was the boss. Whatever he said, that was law in the house. And if there was ten children, what your father'd tell you to do, *you'd do*. Now you'll never see them times again. But they were the good old days. Women were happy ... you see, they were contented with what they were doing. Everyone seemed to be more contented.

'Ah, it was sad when the market closed. A different life altogether. It took me a hell of a long time to get used to it. You see, they done away with a lot of the old customs. Ah, they were great times and you never wanted. There was no such thing as being afraid to go outside the door with a couple of pounds on you. If anyone saw you drunk, well, they'd pick you up and bring you home and put you to bed. But today they'd knock you down, give you a bang with a bottle or knife, and take it off you.'

PAT COOPER – HORSE DEALER, AGED 63

He stops me along Manor Street – 'I hear you're writing a book about the place. Are you interested in horses? We were the biggest horse dealers in Dublin ... in Ireland ... in all the world!'

Horse dealing in the Cooper clan goes back more than a century and, indeed, his family did dominate in the buying and selling of work horses in Dublin for generations. From boyhood he travelled all Ireland with his father attending horse fairs and learning the tricks of the trade. To hear him tell it, there was no one shrewder. His tan, weathered face, sharp squinting eyes, and cautious choice of words certainly conform to the image of a tough and canny horse trader.

'The business goes back four generations in the family. I started at thirteen. My father trained us. We'd be out to fairs every day. We had three or four uncles working for us and two other brothers and me father. In me father's time they had to bring the horses two hundred miles by road, forty miles a day. One man could bring ten or twelve tied together, riding on one's back. There were no cars on the road then.

'We were the only ones in the working horse business. Had a monopoly of the whole business. We'd keep seventy or a hundred or even two hundred horses at the stables on Queen Street. We had one acre of land there. My grandfather bought tenements there. We were the grand landlord. We owned the tenement property. My grandfather bought the houses, four storey houses, for ten pounds. There was five and six in a room and the rent was only about a shilling a week. Queen Street was a very good locality a hundred or two hundred years ago and then it came to be a slum area. Front doors open all the time and very bad conditions. Only one toilet for the whole lot. It was a terrible rough locality. There'd be fighting and arguing every night between the men the minute the pubs would close. Tough as could be ... no tougher street in this town.

'We got the horses at fairs all over Ireland. It was a hard life. We were away at fairs every day. If it was seventy or eighty miles outside of Dublin I'd leave at maybe 3:00 in the morning. If I went to fairs in west Cork I could be away for a week. Ah, it was all business, hard work. We were never finished. Now the fairs in Ireland wouldn't start unless we were there. If they didn't sell to Cooper they didn't get enough money. People used to say that they heard of horse dealers being rogues and robbers but they never met a decenter man than Mr. Cooper of Queen Street.

'At fairs a farmer could ask any price. Farmers would try to get as much as they could. But they didn't know the value. They'd ask for a town and have to take a village. Ask a hundred and fifty pounds in the morning for a horse and then take a hundred an hour later. We could give twenty or thirty pounds more for a horse than anyone. It was all a cash business. We made the deals in the bars of the little hotels in the towns. And if I paid a farmer a hundred and fifty pounds for his horse he'd give me one pound back and say, "That's for luck." And when you'd buy the horse you'd just get a scissors and put a little mark, a little clip, on him to identify him. So another dealer wouldn't go near him knowing that he'd been bought. See, a farmer could keep selling away but he couldn't sell him when he had a mark.

'You had to know horses. At a fair like at Ballinasloe there'd be maybe 3,000 horses showing up for sale. We'd buy five or six year old horses. A younger horse would be too young for Dublin. They had to be mature. And when we'd bring horses from the country we'd have to make them used to the trams. Anyway, you had to know if a horse was right. Sound and correct. You'd want to know if there's steady bones, bad ones, splints ... there's many faults they can have. We never had a vet. We were vets ourselves. We knew more than the vet knew. A vet only knew what he was reading out of a book. We had the practical experience. If a horse got colic, that was the main thing. It's a twisted gut. We'd give them colic bottles ourselves whereas others would have to go and call a vet.

'There was a terrible big population of horses. We supplied horses to CIE. They kept roughly 400 horses. Kennedy's, the big bakers on Parnell Street, they had a hundred horses. Great Northern Railways had another hundred. You had Johnston-Mooneys, the bakers, with 150 horses. And we supplied Guinness's with roughly 350 horses. And we used to supply a terrible lot of dairies. At that time a horse would be sold for about 130 or 140 pounds. When we'd sell a horse he'd be put on a month's trial. We wouldn't be paid for a month. We had the reputation that you'd keep that horse for a month and if he was right you'd come in and pay. It was a fair policy. You couldn't do that today but at that time it was a different generation. At that time you wouldn't be done for a penny.

'Now a horse in the quiet part of the country, he'd stand there all day. But with trams passing and everything they might walk away. If a horse wasn't right, traffic-wise, he wouldn't stand. Now there were horses that might work for fifteen and twenty years. And when a horse had been working in Dublin for, say, ten years we'd take him back. We called them caste horses and after working in Dublin for years they'd go in the legs. So we'd sell them to the farmers and they'd come right working on the land. They were all right to work on the land. You'd have to put him on a cart, put him on a mowing machine or a plough.

'We'd get a terrible lot of horse hair. Horse hair was very dear and they used to make brushes out of that. They'd come to us with big tails and we'd cut them and trim them. We'd have a big quantity and we sold that all for making brushes. And we had people twenty miles out in the country who'd collect manure from us, ten shillings for a big cartload, to use for vegetables. We had to clean it out anyway.

'Now in the war years there were no cars, only pony and traps around here. See, there was no petrol here and tractors were laying idle and they were coming into our place same as a supermarket looking for horses. Then when petrol came back the country was flooded with horses and we started to export horses in the Fifties. We were exporting to Belgium, France, Holland. We were shipping boatloads of working horses and breeding mares to France. And sending pit ponies to Belgium and Holland to go down into the pits for mining. And we were sending riding horses to England. Some of the exported horses were killed for human consumption in the butcher shops. In Ireland here they just couldn't get the taste for it. Now there was a factory in Limerick and he opened a shop in Limerick and Cork and Dublin selling horse meat, about thirty years ago, and it never took off. Just because it was a horse and that's it. You wouldn't know the different between horse meat and beef. Do you know the difference between horse meat and beef? People say that it's dark in colour. I know different. There's two steaks and no one can tell the difference. The only difference how you can tell is to render down the fat and the fat of a horse is like the fat off a chicken, a liquid, where off the heffer beast it's a solid fat.

'The last firm in Dublin to keep horses was Dublin Dairies. They went into the late Sixties. They kept cutting down. They went down from about two hundred to only four or five. They were the last. In a couple of years you'll hear children say, "Oh, there's a horse, Mammy, there's a horse, Daddy", and that day is coming very fast. I'd say in two or three years you won't see a horse in Dublin.'

PADDY DOYLE – PIG RAISER, AGED 53

Paddy is a lean, friendly chap with an unruly shock of black hair. He happily wades around the muck of his piggery on Oxmantown Lane in a pair of worn high boots and wears an ever-present smile despite the apparent unpleasantness of his task. Pigs have been his life. Same with his father and grandfather. But he is the last of the clan – no doubt about that.

Down to only seven animals now, he must wait for the Dublin Corporation to arrive one day soon and demolish the old stone shed in which they are kept. It's in their plans. But life goes on and he's always amused when curious passers-by amble down the narrow lane and discover the smells and squeals. 'I'm just tending my pigs', he explains.

'All me life, from me grandfather and father, pigs were always part and parcel of the family. It's in the blood so to speak. My grandfather came from Arbour Lane but I've been in this lane for thirty-eight years now. Normally we kept about forty pigs here. I have only seven now. Raising pigs in the city is dying out, no doubt about that. Years ago people would tolerate pigs on their front door, but not now. The problem now is the manure. You can't wash it down or it'd be polluting so you have to take it away to dumps. Very few places now in the world where you'd get pigs in the city.

'Pigs, they're not easy to keep fed. People get the impression that pigs would eat anything but it's very much the opposite. They're very fussy animals. I have contracts from hospitals and restaurants and old people's homes. Wherever there's a congregation of people using a fair amount of food there's a fair amount of waste out of it. I go each day and collect that. Some just want to get rid of it but in most cases you have to pay for it. You have to be careful, especially with small pigs. You have to nurse them like babies. It's watered down like giving a baby a bottle and as the baby gets older it goes on to solids. Most losses occur in the first three or four weeks when they get a change of feeding. They'd get up to fifteen stone and that's when they'd be sold. For me, they're not company, it's a business. But down in the country some old maid would be keeping two or three little pigs and she'd have names on them. I remember going to a convent a few years ago and taking two pigs out, they were selling them to me, and the Sister blessed them as they were going out the gate.

'Seven or eight years ago children down here broke open the gate and let the pigs out. It was Halloween night. They lit a bonfire and broke the shoulder of one of the pigs and were trying to get him up on the bonfire. Trying to put him on there alive. And they put

40 Pig raiser Paddy Doyle cleaning his piggery on Oxmantown Lane

my trailer on the bonfire as well and that was burned out. Ah, they weren't children, they were savages! Since then, every Halloween night I have to sit down here.

'People come down the lane and they can't believe there's still pigs here. I'd hate the life to go because, as I said, it's part and parcel of your life. I have a routine where I get up and work and do this and that. You get into a happy habit. It keeps a few bob together. I have six children, five sons, and not one of them has taken after me. None of my fellas were ever interested. Actually, I wouldn't want them to because there's not much future in it now with the Corporation coming down and all. The Corporation can come down any day now and take away the lane. That'd be the end for me because there'd be nowhere for me to go. The writing is on the wall for that.'

41 Arriving at Smithfield Market for the monthly horse fair

Chapter 9

Women Folk

MAUREEN GRANT — THEATRE DOYEN, AGED 60

The daughter of a cattle drover, she rose from humble beginnings in Queen Street tenements to know the likes of Sir Laurence Olivier, Tyrone Power, Laurel and Hardy, and countless other luminaries. After more than four decades behind the bar, she has become known affectionately as 'The Mother of the Olympia Theatre'. She is one of Dublin's best known and most loved 'commoners'. Stoneybatter has always been her home and today she lives in a new housing estate along Prussia Street on the old cattle market site.

'I was born on Arran Quay but we moved to Queen Street when I was twelve months old. My mother came from England when she was a girl and went into domestic work. She met my father who was forty-two and they married within a year. She was sixteen! They went up the aisle and people thought it was his little daughter. He went up the aisle on crutches. He was an invalid. His hip was blown away in the Boer War. They got married and had eleven children ... so age didn't make any difference. I was the eldest. Ten girls and I've one brother. Thirteen of us lived in one room. Living conditions was very bad. Seven of us used to have to pile into the one bed and there were armchairs at night. Parents had no privacy whatsoever. I don't know how they managed to have such big families. We were very innocent and never noticed anything.

'My father was a cattle drover and we used to go up to the abattoir for the killing. We'd be sent up to the market there with two billy cans and we'd get them full of hot milk when the beasts were milked. And on a Thursday the butchers would throw my father lumps of meat into a sack and we could count on that. Then he was clear and he could enjoy his few pints. My father was very fond of the drink and if he fell he'd have to stay where he'd fall and sleep there because he hadn't the power to get up. My father used to say, "I'll

42 Maureen Grant, who rose from humble tenements on Queen Street to become the beloved 'Mother of the Olympia Theatre'

43 Cobblestone pattern at Smithfield adds an aesthetic quality

drink it out of an old boot." And he would, too. I think it was him that frightened me from ever taking a drink.

'My mother had only one good hand. She was born with a hand with only three thumbs and it was much shorter than the other. But she would make you *ashamed*. She did everything a woman with her two hands would do. And more! She got down and done her scrubbing, got her floor cloth around her little hand. And she rode a bicycle. She was fantastic. But she was kind of a young woman to accept such a big family and when I started to grow up it was kind of put onto me. I had to be up at 6:00 in the morning, make all the breakfasts, get the children out to school and then out and do a bit of shopping. She'd get up then and have her bath. I never had time to have a bath then. So, from the time I was twelve I had to start in knowing how to run a home.

'Queen Street was a great place going back a long time ago. A very poor kind of street. Kids, we went around in our bare feet most of the time. But families were close and neighbours would help out. If they had a drop of soup, any bread left over, it would be brought over. People never let their dignity go. They didn't work all that much around Queen Street because there wasn't that much work. Even if they did, the money was so very small. A man would come home and he'd hand up his wage. Then he'd go off and have his beers with his friends. But the woman is up at six in the morning.

'Women on Queen Street, they'd have the big black shawls wrapped around them. Now they'd come outside the pub and if a woman went for the jill, or half a jill, she'd give a shilling to a man and he'd come out (of the pub) with it in a little can for under her shawl. And when they went home they'd be singing their heads off. Then maybe somebody'd come out with an accordian or a mouth organ and the next thing you'd see were the skirts going up and the big boots they used to wear. Ah, they were good times, all right. Of course, we always thought it was very funny and we'd be jeering them. Oh, and you'd get a slap across the face with a shawl.

'On Queen Street when somebody died the wake would last three days and there was a hooley every night. They'd have all the sand-wiches and all the drink, everybody sat around and got piddled-out-of-their-mind drunk. Eat, get up and put on the old record, and the corpse is in the bed there and they're up doing the Highland Fling. They made a complete week's party out of it. People would kiss them and everything. This was a death years ago. It was some-thing to be remembered.

'I hated school. It was a very bad experience. If you only sneezed you got a slapping. So I done about three or four years schooling and that's all. I mitched most of the time. I used to go all around the Phoenix Park till school was over. One evening, when it was getting dark very early, I was coming home and I saw this old lady – the banshee – sitting up on the window sill with a big head of white hair and she was combing her hair and she was howling. I actually saw the banshee! I run all the way home into Queen Street and I was very upset. And I got a smack across the face to get me out of the state I was in. I said what I had seen and my mother says, "You've done something and that's a warning of some kind." I didn't do much more mitching.

'When I was fifteen I just collapsed in the chapel yard. When I woke up it was nine months later. I was in the hospital. It was acute meningitis I had. Nine months I was unconscious and they didn't think I would ever walk again. The first person I saw when I opened my eyes was my father coming up the ward on crutches and he was crying. Then I started to come around a bit. But I was two years there and I took epileptic fits. I found it very hard to get out and mix with people. I'd get panicky to get home.

'I used to get seven and sixpence relief money but my mother used to take it all the time. So I just decided that I'd get out and get a job. I told lies about me age and told lies that I was a professional barmaid and went into the theatre, at the Olympia. And I got married to a lad from Paul's Street. I really had it hard. By the time I was twenty-four I had eight children. I was working in the theatre … I managed. But they never knew at work that I was pregnant. Never knew that I had them children. I never got big. I'd always say that I had a cold and I'd go out for two weeks holidays. I got away with that for seven of my children.

'See, I'd know when I was going to work that something was wrong. So, I'd leave the bed ready and in them times all you used was newspapers. I used to save all the newspapers and spread them all over the mattress. You didn't have sheets and all to spare. So I'd spread the sheets of paper before I'd leave for work. It meant when I come home only getting into the bed. But I'd get into work and get halfway through the labour – actually more than half way. Then I'd have to crawl along the quays and you'd have all these guys bothering you and shaking their money at you. Oh, it was *desperate* in them years. And I'd get home anyway and the baby would be born. And I'd be back on duty in two weeks. When I was expecting Mary, who was the eighth one, I worked upstairs in the Circle and I stood on a cork and I fell and was taken away to the hospital. That was the first time they found out cause the baby was born in the hospital.

'The Olympia Theatre ... Oh, that's my life. I go in there and it's a different world altogether. At the Olympia I'd work every night and be happy at what I do. I met everybody ... Laurel and Hardy, Broderick Crawford and Tyrone Power. He was beautiful. And I met Laurence Olivier eighteen years ago. I just seem to hit it off with everybody. I'd never retire. Never. Most of my family has been in the theatre, too. One time there was eight of us here. It was like a family theatre. Jimmy is the manager there now, Alice is there, and my daughter-in-law is in the box office. So when I go there'll be somebody else to carry on.'

MARY KINANE — WIDOW, AGED 72

Her father opened the neighbourhood men's hairdresser's shop on Stoneybatter Street in the late 1800's. For over a century her father and brother kept local men and visiting country folk trim and well-groomed. The family lived above the shop. As a child, she would peer from her bedroom window and observe the frenzy of activity as herds of animals were driven directly below her safe perch. Farmers clattered by in their horse carts heaped with produce. It was great drama.

She was allowed to be around the shop so long as she didn't interfere with men's conversation and was watchful of the straight razors. She can still recall vividly the scents of shaving cream and hair tonics. The shop was closed two years ago due to her brother's illness. After her husband's death she moved back into the family home above the shop. Gone are the cattle and horses and carts, but the view out of her front window remains surprisingly the same as when she was a young, wide-eyed girl.

'A hundred and six years my family was here. I was born in this house seventy-two years ago. My father was fifty-seven when I was born and my mother was thirty-eight. The business was my father's. He was very young when he started, only in his teens. Country people came in here from all parts of Ireland because you had the cattle market. They all came in here to shop with their horse and gig. It's always been kind of a small country town. The cattle men would be knocking on the door of the shop about 7:00 in the morning. My father would be working until 9:00 at night and on weekends until 10:00. All the shops stayed open till late at night.

'As a child I was supposed to be upstairs in bed but I'd rather be looking out the window and I'd see the pork shop on the opposite side there and they'd be open and you'd see a lot of the poorer people coming along for pig's foot and they'd be sold cooked, always on a Saturday night, and for tripe. And every morning early you'd see horses and carts bringing in all the vegetables, piled up with cabbages and potatoes and carrots. They used to be brought in fresh every day. The men might have a young son with them and you'd often see the boys on top of the vegetables fast asleep.

'There used to be a big, long striped pole outside and gas lighting in the shop at that time. My father had five men working in the shop. There was three chairs in the back and three in the front. When my father was starting out some of the men lived here in rooms. There was always a housekeeper who would have breakfast for them. There was a fireplace in the back shop and front shop and we used coal. They were always kept going from morning to night and people had to wait their turn. I think then it was tuppence for a haircut and a penny for a shave. My father also used to do wig-making. That was a specialty for him. I remember he had a shaped head and as children we were playing with it.

'There was just a standard cut — short back and sides — that was the usual. And they'd put Brilliantine on their hair at that time. A lot of shaving went on at that time and men had their own mugs with "Harry" or "Jack" or "Pat" on them. I remember easily seeing seventy or eighty on shelves. Mugs and brushes were always washed and cleaned and put away for the next time they'd come in. And you had the open razor and I'd be told as a child not to go near them. But you would ... and I got cut on my hand and had to go to Richmond Hospital.

'Men never liked it if the odd woman came in and waited for her husband. Conversation was always horses, horses, horses. They were race mad. And we had the army barracks up here on Arbour Hill and there was always an awful lot of British army all around here. They were customers in the shop but no distinction was made. My father got on all right with them. The "Tommies" we called them. Never minded British soldiers in the shop. But the Black and Tans, they were a different type altogether. Mr. O'Carroll up here on Manor Street, a great friend of my father's, the Tans came late one evening looking for his sons and they shot him on the doorstep.

'Customers were all regulars. There was a Mr. Fitzpatrick, very posh, always had a rose in his button hole, and dapper. When he used to come to get his haircut he always brought a small bottle of first-shot whiskey. It's like potcheen. And he always got it rubbed into the back of his neck, to avoid getting colds. That was his own idea and he always got that done. You'd always know when he was in because you'd smell the whiskey. And the Stoneybatter Inn up there, that used to belong to people named Keogh's and old Mister

Keogh was Lord Mayor of Dublin at one time. They were very big publicans here, very wealthy. And he'd always come into the shop and lift me up on the seat when I was a child and he'd ask me to put this rose in his button hole and he gave me two shillings, which was an awful lot of money at that time.

'When my father died suddenly in 1930 of a heart attack my mother kept on the business and my eldest brother gave up his schooling and took it over. He carried it on until a couple of years ago when he got very ill. But I still see some of them today (old customers) and they say, "Do you know that your shop was the first shop I ever got a haircut in when my father brought me in when I was only a little boy?" '

BRIDGET McDONAGH – STREET SURVIVOR, AGED 57

I t's one of the saddest sights in Stoneybatter. St. Paul's Street, once alive with seventy-six families, hundreds of frolicking children, and a strong sense of community, has been reduced by demolition to an ugly rubble heap of bricks. From all appearances, it could well be a war zone. The few houses still standing have been ravaged by vandals and squatters.

Standing in the front doorway of her home, one of only three still occupied, is Bridget McDonagh. She was born and reared in the house directly across the street, now her sister's. In melancholy mood, she recounts the joys of childhood along the cobblestoned street and details the circumstances of its appalling current condition. Simply put, the Dublin Corporation condemned the street to death. Against their wishes – even pleas – residents have been evicted and transplanted in sterile housing estates. Once empty, their houses were speedily bulldozed.

Bridget and her sister, along with a few others, have bravely resisted the Corporation's evacuation plan, enduring intimidation and coercion. Despite the cruel inevitability of the outcome, she remains defiant, determined, and stoic. Yet she is conspicuously frightened, suffering anxiety and anguish. To her, the moral cause is as important as the personal struggle for survival. 'I'll stick to my guns.' Her story is an all-too-common one in inner-Dublin.

'I was born just across the road at fifty-eight Paul's Street. My sister, she's still in my mother's house. When I got married I got the place over here. My husband was a lamplighter but I'm a widow thirty years. I was left with four children and had to go to work up at the Garda Headquarters in Phoenix Park.

'It was a lovely street. Seventy-six families and some had nine children. Everybody knew everybody else. Like a little community.

44 The 'living streets' are playgrounds for children in the artisan's dwellings

45 Children in doorway of their home in artisan's dwellings

Children all mixed together and you'd be up at the corner there skipping rope. Everybody had open windows and your mother and father would be sitting there at the window looking out. People all had flower pots in the window and kept nice curtains. In the summer time everybody would be sitting out. They'd bring their chairs and there'd be another group on the other side. The men would sit and play cards and play handball at the top of the street. Women would chat, be sewing, knitting. We all left babies out in the prams at the window. If it was a warm night we'd be sitting out late at night talking, until 12:00 or 1:00.

'If someone was sick or died all they had to do was knock. My father was waked and everybody sat up day and night with my mother. We put the white card with black trimming on it on the door and pulled the blinds down to half mast. All the blinds along the street were pulled down to half mast out of respect. Then he was carried up the street to the church. At Christmas time you'd have a ding-dong-do at the neighbour's houses or at yours. And on New Year's Eve we'd all come out of our houses and make one big circle holding hands, maybe singing.

'Only about four years ago there was no mention of the street coming down. These houses are nearly a hundred years old. The Corporation didn't give us any clue that they were coming down. They kept saying it wasn't condemned, so we felt safe enough. Then they started to move people out. Once empty houses started to appear everything started to go down. When the tenants got out, squatters got in. We knew then the place was condemned. But when I came home from work one night a couple of weeks ago and saw the bulldozers, I was shocked. We should have been notified by letter that they were going to demolish the street. They came down like a ton of bricks at the last minute. You've no say in what they're doing because they own the buildings.

'They want us out. They want the street demolished. But we won't move till we get suitable accommodations. They think you'll take just anything that's around. They're just offering rubbish. Last year they built a new scheme at the top of Aughrim Street but they didn't give us one of those. Squatters got them! People only squatting twelve months, they got fixed up in new houses. And we're the longest tenants here on the street. You've lived all your life on this street. The anger is to see the way they've degraded the street, knocked it down and put out genuine tenants. Here we are living under this dirt. The rubble, that's the degrading part. It's just like Belfast, like a bombed-out place. It's depressing. It degrades you. It makes you want to scream.

'I don't want to leave the street but they're pressurising me. But I made up my mind that I'm not going. It's on principle. It makes you hardened to it. Now it's the winter I'm worried about. The rain. If you get a heavy rain the ceiling could fall. It's lonely now without neighbours and I'm scared at night. It'll be sad to leave the street, no doubt about it. There'll be tears. You know, all our family was reared in the one house and they all have great memories. My mother and father wouldn't believe it. I'll keep coming back.'

(*Postscript*: Four weeks after the taping of this oral narrative Bridget McDonagh and her sister were evicted and their houses demolished by Dublin Corporation bulldozers.)

MARY BOLTON – HOUSEWIFE, AGED 78

S he came to Stoneybatter when she was nine. Her father was a Sergeant in the Free State Army and the family lived in military housing. Today she resides in the artisan's dwellings. She loves the old neighbourhood and can't imagine living anywhere else.

'When we came here it was lovely and quiet. We went to school up at St. Gabriel's. Children all played in the streets, the best of games – skipping, marbles, tapping tin cans around with a stick, and ball against the wall. There was no vandalism and the respect we had for old people was unbelievable. You'd run a message for them or ask them what they wanted. Young boys, they'd curse if they got mad but they'd go "Shhh" if a woman came by. They'd have that much respect. But when I think now of the language they use in front of women!

'There was eight of us and me mother and father was ten. We were all one family and if something happened we were there to help the other. My father was a Sergeant in the army. Wages was small and it was a hard struggle. You just got by from week to week. But we never grumbled. Money was spent mostly on food and clothing. My mother was a cook in her day and could make a meal of anything. She'd make brown bread and home-made jam and your dinner might be a bit of stew. We passed clothes down on to another and you'd save for furniture. We had only the dressers and a kitchen table, nothing fancy. But we were happy.

'There was no doctors. You lived on old cures, home cures, like Castor oil, olive oil, a dose of Glauber's Salts ... a spoonful of that to clean out the whole system. People always suffered from the chest and a spoonful of Glauber's Salts would take it all out. We used to brush our teeth with (chimney) soot and salt and it would make them sparkling white. And me mother used to cure warts. She'd get a bit of mutton fat out of the butcher shop and bless them three times — "In the name of the Father, Son, and Holy Ghost" — and they'd go away.

'Another old cure at that time was with an ass and there were plenty of asses at that time around here. They always said that it was the ass that carried the Blessed Lady and St. Joseph into Egypt. Well, asses had a cross on their backside and they said if you put the child three times under the belly it would cure whooping cough. Actually, the first I ever heard of illness was when TB started. I always said that TB was the cancer of today. I don't care what anyone says because you go to skin and bone with cancer and you went to skin and bone with TB. And the loss of a child was very sad. It happened to us when we buried a little boy in 1918 when there was a heavy flu. He was only three and I can still see the hearse drawn by four horses coming to the door.

'When you were courting you'd stand for hours talking and chatting and there wasn't a bit of harm. Coming out of the Manor Picture House we'd walk home and stand at that wall talking. And we always went window shopping on O'Connell Street and Grafton Street. And you didn't hold hands then, you linked arms. Morals were very high. It wasn't acceptable at that time for a girl to invite the man into her home. When I think how harmless we were ... pure innocence at seventeen or eighteen. My father was very strict and if you weren't in by half ten me poor mother would have to leave the bedroom window open. This is no lie. Me poor mother would be hiding us and saying, "They're in bed." But now the young ones are going out all night to dances and not getting in until 3:00 and 4:00. I think it's terrible.

'Weddings were very quiet. You had weddings in your own house. The wife's family paid for it. You had to save up for it. You got the wedding cake and the beer, maybe a half dozen bottles of whiskey, maybe have a cooked ham and set up the table and have a dance that night. I remember when we got married we had a hundred and twenty-five pounds saved, which is nothing today. But we bought everything out of that — a honeymoon to London for a week, a bedroom suite, a dining-room suite, a kitchen dresser and two chairs. We covered everything.

'People got more out of life then. And I'll tell you, television was the *ruination* of the world. I used to have a crowd here and they all danced and that door was never closed. There was always, "knock, knock, knock, we're going to some ceili tonight or something on." But when television came in, the whole body seemed to go out of it, you know. It changed the whole atmosphere for me. And that old crowd are died away now and we're the last. Now about the next generation ... I couldn't tell you.'

KATHLEEN O'DONOGHUE – NEIGHBOURHOOD COQUETTE, AGED 70

She was, by popular consensus among male and female alike, the undisputed neighbourhood coquette – every young lad's imagined sweetheart. By age fourteen she possessed a striking face, statuesque figure, and appeared several years older. Flaunting her independent spirit and flair for stylish clothing, she attracted the roving eyes of all the young boys. By her own admission, she has broken more than a few hearts along life's road. But it was all innocent enough.

Today she lives along Oxmantown Road with her husband, Denis, a nice looking gentleman. Still vivacious and flirtatious, she plays out her girlish role with great elan. It's just her nature. Her winsome smile and beguiling manner still make a few old hearts flutter at Mulligan's and Kavanagh's pubs.

'I was born in this house. My father was in the British army for years and years. In fact, he was in the Boer War. He was sixteen or seventeen when he joined up. My mother was the eldest of thirty-three children. Now listen to that! Her father, John Murphy, his wife died on the twenty-first child. And she had one or two died in between. Four years after that, when he was forty-five, he married the sister of the wife and she had twelve more kids with him. And they were captains in the army and monks. There's more Murphy's ... I have about a hundred and twenty aunts and uncles. Anyway, my mother worked as a foreman down in the ammunition factory on Parkgate Street. And me father was in the war. She discovered some shells that were wrong and she was so good she was made a foreman there. My father, he come back from the war in 1918 and nine months later I was born. Then he worked in Guinness's and there were thirteen of us.

'There's not a neighbour on the road I don't know all me life. See, when we were teenagers there were lads up and down the road and always chasing me. I really had! See, when I was fourteen I was tall and thin and liked earrings and high-heeled shoes and I looked like I was nineteen. And I always liked a bit of glamour and clothes, little bits of style. I often made me own Tartan skirts and a lovely little scarf and coat and the devil knows what, and always with earrings on me and high-heeled shoes. And I went out like the Queen of Sheeba.

'Oh, I'm not denying I had a ball. I was tall and thin and full of beans. I was always very independent natured. I suppose I was a bit of an extrovert. Life is what you make of it. If I could count on me fingers all the fellas I met and went with. My fellas were very lovable. He'd put his arm around me, he'd squeeze me, the devil knows what, but he never wanted to be pulling me to bits. We were more pals and companions. I was going with a hundred fellas, going over the garden wall to meet a fella waiting for me at the corner. They were all good to me. Nowadays, if you go out with a young man he expects you to go home and go to bed with him. Years and years ago you didn't do that. The men around the Buildings weren't so hot-blooded. Now, I think it's all to do with them videos and reading books and imagination. We were better off because we knew nothing and imagined nothing. You didn't see all this on the telly. Now I'm not prudish but, Dear God, seeing how they jump into bed and the kids all looking on. And the kid's imagination.

'Then I met Denis and we'd hold hands and he'd put his arm around me waist. I was a friend, a mother, a sister to him, the whole lot. I just got started to like him. Denis was quieter and more reserved. We walked everywhere and went bicycling. We used to go to the Manor Cinema and see all those cowboys and indians and romantic pictures, "The Desert Song" and the sheik and all.

'It never changes here. No one changes. I knew lovely young men. Even now I can go up to the local pub and meet them, say hello, have a laugh and a chat with them ... cause they've all grown old like meself.'

SARAH HARTNEY – DOMESTIC MAID, AGED 67

At age sixteen, following the death of her mother, she was sent away to Dublin by her father to serve as house maid for a doctor. Long hours of daily drudgery, fear of the doctor's harsh wife, and loneliness, made for an unhappy life for the young girl. Three years later, when attending a movie matinee at the Manor Picture House, she met usher Bob Hartney (featured elsewhere in this book) and fell in love. His kind and gentle nature provided love and security she had never known. She was nineteen and he forty-one. Despite the generational gap, they married and have lived happily together for nearly half a century. As he nears age ninety, she affectionately calls him 'Dad' and attends lovingly to his every need. They are so close that it is difficult to visualise one without the other.

'I was born in the country in County Wexford. My mother died on the birth of her last baby at the age of forty-one in 1936. The doctor that attended my mother, he came to my father when she was a year dead and said that he was moving to Dublin and they were looking for a girl to do housework for them. I was up in bed and they called me down and asked would I like to go. In years gone by, you weren't allowed to say "yes" or "no". You were to do what your parents told you. So they took me. I was about sixteen and it was very hard work.

'You had to be up at six in the morning and have the veranda swept and washed and outside concrete steps scrubbed and brasses done and steps in the hall washed before the morning. We lit the fire at half-seven and had boiling water at eight for the doctor to wash himself. I was very young, had only just been in my own house doing housework. I never had the dealings of making big double beds, doing brass rods, and polishing the sides and wrungs. The doctor was nice but his wife got to dislike me. She was nice to the other girls who worked there. She was a red-headed person from Donegal. A beautiful head of red hair. I used to do whatever she would tell me. I'd never refuse because I'd get a box in the ear from her. She was that type. I was frightened by her.

'Now I was the poor unfortunate kitchen maid. Like a maid was terrible low. She wasn't equal to anybody. But I didn't dwell on it because you'd go crazy about it. It was cruel to have to wash and try to get dishes clean, greasy dishes, and the back of your hands would get chapped. I often cried from the pain from them. And I had to scrub a white and blue lino floor in the kitchen. It was black soap you had to scrub the floor with and the hands used to get chapped and the dirt would get into them and you couldn't get the dirt out. The doctor gave me a jar of vaseline for them but when that was gone I hadn't the money for anymore. Now they had a son and when I used to wash the floor he'd come in and do this (scuff it up with his shoes). He messed it up. One day she made me do it three times. But I never complained. I wanted to speak out but you weren't allowed to speak to your superiors in the way you'd like to do it. You wouldn't tell them to "Go to Hell", even though you'd like to do it.

'She used to have lovely rings. Gold and diamonds and little pearls. And a beautiful gold watch. One day I said to her, "Oh, I'd love to have a watch like that." She used to always send me up to get the watch for her. But after that she used to lock it away. "Why", I said, "are you locking it away?" "Because it'll be stolen on me", says she. "I wouldn't steal it", I said. It hurt my feelings. And on my day off when I wouldn't be there they'd come into my bedroom and search.

'Your wages were very poor and you have to have a uniform and keep your shoes heeled and soled. We weren't allowed to go in any rooms, only in the kitchen and your bedroom. My bedroom was a small little room ... but I hadn't much clothes. And you never asked anything about their private lives. It was lonely. The children used to say "Hello" but they never came out and stayed with you. Except on Christmas day when the Queen was speaking on the radio and they were sent out to stay with me in the kitchen until the speech was over. Christmas time used to be lonely. I used to have to help cook the dinner, the turkey, the roast, the ham, brussel sprouts, plum pudding. When they'd be finished with the turkey and the ham she'd cut a bit off and give it to you. I ate by myself in the kitchen. And they might give me five bob.

'I left the job when I was about eighteen and there was a person up here on Marlboro Road looking for a girl, someone reliable. And they said they'd take me. I had to do all the housework and washing and ironing. I had more freedom there because they hadn't got children to look after. She used to send me out now and again to a picture. Then on a Thursday I met Bob. And we'd meet and go out. He was so used to the cinema that we didn't always go to the pictures. We might go out to Dollymount for an evening in the summer. He was kind and gentle and you could go out with him and he wouldn't molest you or anything like the younger men used to do with girls. We got married on Aughrim Street and got a flat on the North Circular Road. I was nineteen and he was forty-one.

'When you got married you were innocent and you knew nothing. Marriage was very unknown. It was kind of a mystery to you. When I was growing up there was no one to tell you the facts of life. Girlfriends wouldn't talk. You had nobody to talk to. You had to figure it all out for yourself. You got married and you were really innocent. I was *so innocent* and it showed in my face. I was nineteen but I only looked sixteen. So you got married and you didn't know *anything*. You didn't know what was going to happen to you. An older woman I knew, she got married at eighteen and she said, "We went like lambs to the slaughter." When you got married – the intimate part – there was supposed to be a maiden head and if that wasn't burst and the blood wasn't on the sheet the next day, well, he'd always give you the life of a dog. That happened! And husbands would beat their wives. I don't think they ever retaliated. They just took it. They never let their husbands down to the neighbours. I never had any reason to say anything bad about Bob because he was always kind and gentle.

'In them days if you went to Confession and told the priest that you let the seed of life go to waste you weren't even given Absolution. Many a poor unfortunate woman had ten and eleven children and maybe died in the birth of another. That's the way it was with my mother, the Lord have mercy on her. There was nine of us alive and the little one died in 1936. And my mother died in November. When I look back, all I ever remember my mother in was a big kind of maternity thing on her with gathers ... something like Our Lady. Many a woman, she'd only be the six or seven weeks after having the baby and she'd be expecting again! With husbands it was like, "You were there and you were my satisfaction." You had to obey ... whether you liked it or not. That was the rule of the Catholic Church.

'I remember once a woman I knew, she had a baby and she didn't want it. He was drunk or something, but this priest was in to see her and he said, "You know it's God's will." Now she'd say the most outlandish sayings that you could ever hear. And, says she, "There's a hell of a lot of man behind it too!" The priest didn't know what to say. He just put on his hat and walked out.'

BEATRICE LUNNEY – PROTESTANT SUNDAY SCHOOL TEACHER, AGED 73

No, the church bells don't ring anymore at St. Paul's ... we've no one to ring them.' The local Protestant community was once thriving and the church over-spilling on Sundays – but those days are gone.

Always very well liked by Catholic neighbours, her roots in Stoney-batter are as deep as theirs. She always took great pride and satisfaction in the harmony between Protestants and Catholics in the neighbourhood. Now she is the last Protestant living along the street. Church membership has dwindled to a few dozen lingering families and a mere handful of children to teach on Sundays. She finds it a depressing situation but has no plans to abandon her family home on Oxmantown Road.

'I was born in this house and I've been associated with the parish for seventy-three years. My father and mother were very active in the Church. He was a church warden and I'm one now. There would have been 300 or 400 Protestant families in the church. Just in this little block here there were ten or eleven Protestant families. Now I'm the only one. In those days we had so many Protestants that we had a boy's school, a girl's school, and a kindergarten at St. Paul's. It wasn't a prosperous church, really, because they were only working people in it. It was prosperous with people but not with money.

'Morning service at 8:00 would be full and there was an after-noon children's service and a 7:00 night service. And we had a Boy's Brigade and Girl's Guide Rangers, a debating society, and a dramatic society. And we had very good concerts. My father had a black and white minstrel show. As a matter of fact, we had so many organisations in our church, dances and parties, that a lot of the Roman Catholics around here used to come to our parish and join in. Because there was nothing going for them in that nature in their own parish. But now for weddings and funerals they weren't allowed to come in. They would be excommunicated if they went into a Protestant church. They were brought up with that and it was a mortal sin. We were never told that, but they believed it. So they'd stand outside if there was a funeral or wedding till it was over. But now that's all changed.

'Catholics and Protestants did mix. But when it came to going out with a young man, that was the crunch. It was said that Roman Catholics shouldn't be allowed at our dances — therefore they wouldn't have got together. See, the trouble was that if you married a Roman Catholic you were always made to bring up the children Catholic. It was a *must* that they sign that paper. That was really the trouble. The crunch. I think people should be free to make up their own minds. Now there was a mixed marriage about three doors away and the rector of our parish was constantly paying them visits talking to them about it.

'Now my father was very broad-minded and we were quite friendly with the people. They all knew me. And I was manager at Bewley's for forty-eight years and the staff under me, they were nearly all Roman Catholics. But we'd go out carolling for the parish every Christmas around the neighbourhood and some people would ask you where you were from and you'd tell them St. Paul's Parish and they'd say, "Is that Catholic or Protestant?". I'd say, "Protestant" and they'd shut the door in your face. That's happened to me.

'Older members of the Church are dying off and there are no younger people coming up. Others went off to the suburbs. We're down to about fifty families now, if we have that. And we have only five children. We just have one service now on Sunday. It's really depressing now. Very depressing. Actually, we're very well off financially now, funny enough. See, we had a boy's school and we sold it and we had a Vicarage up on North Circular Road and we sold *it* ... and invested the money. That's how we got our money. So we've the money but no people!'

*46 Surviving two-storey Georgian brick houses along Manor Street enhance
the architectural character of Stoneybatter*

*47 The maze-like physical layout of the artisan's dwellings gives impression
of an enclosed community*

NELLIE KENT — RELIGIOUS DOWAGER, AGED 70

Born and reared on Oxmantown Road, she was within easy walking distance of Phoenix Park. Her happiest childhood memories revolve around park picnics, duck ponds, fields of flowers, and hiding places. Due to the death of her father, she had to go to work at age fourteen. Much of her life has been devoted to caring for her mother who suffered from an early heart condition.

Religion has always played a major role in her life and she is gratified to have lived long enough to witness profound changes within the Church, especially with regard to the place of women. She never married and today looks after an invalid sister in the home in which they were born.

'My father was a tradesman and died when I was only fourteen and there were four of us. My mother was left a widow and there was no pensions, no help given. She went to work as a waitress up in the Gard's Depot in Phoenix Park. She only lasted three years at the job because she had a heart attack. So I had to go to work at fourteen in a china and glass shop in Henry Street. Five shillings a week I got. You grew up fast and took responsibility. I worried about my mother ... thought she was going to die. That's very hard when you're a child. But the four of us and my mother, we were really united and had a terribly happy childhood. She lived to be eighty-five, even with the bad heart.

'We lived so near Phoenix Park. We were reared in the park from the time we were babies. Mothers would bring their children up and they'd knit and sew and crochet. They weren't idle up there. The park is huge and when you're kids it was great. We used to play hide and seek and all those games. You'd go to the People's Gardens and the Furry Glen and the nooks and crannies and steps. Down by the duck pond there were rockeries, huge big stones, and plants growing all around them and you could hide. Boys, they'd be climbing and the girls used to play with dolls. But you never put your hand on a flower. If your mother heard that you took a flower it would be murder. We were brought up like that.

'When we were twelvish a group of us would go on picnics ourselves. We'd get a bottle of milk — because minerals weren't things you got except on state occasions — and bread and jam and biscuits and we'd all walk to the park. We used to go to a place called the Private Woods. There was a lovely stream and woods but often you'd eat the stuff before you'd get there because we were starving. Then you could go wandering around but would be told not to go near the Hollow and the Furry Glen because they were sort of "known" places — secluded places — for courting couples.

'I have wonderful memories of the park. On a Thursday night the Garda band would play in the yard in front of the depot. And on Sundays the army band played in the Hollow on the bandstand there. Now at 11:00 Mass on Sunday the Garda band would parade down from the depot in uniform to Aughrim Street Church and the playing was beautiful. I suppose there'd be about sixty at a time. When they'd arrive they'd do a sort of drill and march into the church.

'The Church here played a very big part in people's lives. In this parish people went to daily Mass. It started their day. It's their life, really. I think all the changes in the Church are wonderful. Now I used to read my Missal in Mass when it was in Latin and you never really kept up with the priest. But with the Mass in English I think it's the *people's* Mass now. Now you can live the Mass because every word that's said you understand. And the ways women have been liberated in the Church I think are wonderful. I'm delighted that I've lived to see it. I really am. It used to worry me very much. It worried lots of women folk because they felt they were left out and now they're coming into their own. I think that's the way the Lord intended it to be. It was men who, I'm sorry to say, as priests and bishops, discriminated. I don't think they *meant* to, but it happened just the same and women felt that they were second all the time. They were never first. I never wanted to be first as a woman ... only have your right place. That's all you want.

'Like Nuns are being recognized more. Back when the Mass was in Latin there'd have to be a server, a lad. Well, weekdays the lads would be at school and a nun would answer, kneeling *outside* the altar railing. She'd leave the bread and wine in a convenient place for the priest. She was actually barred from going inside the altar. Like it reminds you of the "Holy of Holies" in the days of the Bible ... that only priests were allowed. People were unimportant because the priests were *everything*. They had no humility. It was wrong, I mean, Our Lord said that he came to serve the people and that's what the priests and clergy were to do as well. Now the nuns were women and dedicated their lives to God, really giving up everything, especially our Irish Sisters of Charity. But the priest is more with the people now and it's better for the priests too because I think their lives must have been very lonely.

'Old people, no matter what happens to them, they're always ready to say, "Well, God knows best and God is in his Heaven so all's right with the world." Even though things seem bad. They've got great hope. But I don't know about some of the young people. I think they're kind of living in fear with the threat of war. I don't think the youth of today are gay and carefree and happy. Not really. Their music, their songs... the words are about dying. I think they're searching, searching all the time for God.'

WINIFRED KEOGH – HOUSEWIFE, AGED 61

She came to Stoneybatter when she was one year old and considers it the only part of 'real Dublin' left. Her mother was a prominently known midwife in the neighbourhood and the 'Keogh' name is widely recognized and respected. Childhood was a happy and carefree period for her and she delights in recounting early Christmases and simple evenings at home with the family.

'I came to live here when I was one year old. Very good memories here, very good. My first memories was of Manor Place. There was all kind of cow sheds and I'd be brought there to have a look at all the cows going in there every evening. And I remember the horses coming up the road and there was a trough there and they'd be drinking water. And very good memories of Phoenix Park. We'd play Rounders, something like cricket, you'd throw the ball and run away and we'd watch polo matches. And have a picnic. Bring a few sandwiches and a bottle of milk. No worry whatsoever. You could play up there and nobody would ever harm you.

'My mother was a midwife in the area. There were about six midwives, all kept going because at that stage all children were born in the home. No such thing of people going into hospitals. She was paid by the people who paged her. I think it was about three pounds at that time. There was a brass plate on our door and it said "Midwife". So people would know where to come. They'd come at all hours of the night and she'd walk everywhere at night and nobody would ever touch her. She'd be out winter nights and always on foot to all those houses and some would be a mile and a half away.

'She'd go to their home and keep going for maybe six or eight days, twice a day after birth. She'd take a little bag with her, all lined and little divisions in it with all the different instruments. Now there'd be an inspector who'd come around about every six weeks to examine that bag. She used to inspect that bag and she'd also inspect your house and your room to see that it was clean. See, she'd know by your room if you were clean. My mother also had a big, big book and she'd have to mark in it all the births. Now if a baby was very small, premature, she'd have to go back maybe three or four times a day because the baby would have to be fed with a little tube like a fountain pen. But those babies survived. My mother always maintained that she never lost a patient or a baby and she was twenty-five years at midwifing. She boasted about that. And maybe in a year's time there'd be another baby and she'd be back to that family again because at that stage there were very big families.

'I can say that we had a very happy life. The weekend was kind of a family get-together and we always had cards. We were a terrible house for cards. We'd play "Whist" with six people and we might play for threepence. The most you would lose in a night may be ten pence and you'd have a good few hours enjoyment for that. And we had a Gramaphone and we'd play a lot of records ... John McCormick at that stage. And we had a piano and two of my sisters played on a Sunday. Ah, very happy times. And *conversation*, Oh, Lord, people *listened* to each other. The men would drink all right but not the women. Maybe at Christmas time at home the woman might take a drink or at a Christening or a death. Only on a very special occasion.

'Christmases were terrific. Really a family affair. The pudding would start to be made about October. It would be hung in a big white calico bag and it'd be like a football it was so hard. They maintained that the longer it was made, the better it was, that all the ingredients and spirits that went through it matured. And you'd make your own decorations like paper chains, coloured paper, crepe paper and that. But the main thing was the crib. And holly. Sometimes people would come around to the houses selling it. The wooden crib would have been made and then the figures bought. You'd go out and pick up a bit of straw and that would be the makings of the crib. And for presents you may get a doll. You'd really treasure that. You'd be making little clothes for it, looking for scraps of material in the local dressmaker's and they'd give it to you. Or threading beads to make necklaces out of them.

'Ah, I wouldn't want to leave this neighbourhood. An awful lot of memories here, childhood memories and that. This is *real* Dublin.'

KATHLEEN CANNON – WIDOW, AGED 68

Most mornings around ten she can be found outside her front door on Oxmantown Road in apron and house slippers chatting with neighbours. Born in the home, she knows everyone along the street. But so many old friends have died or gone away.

When nostalgically recalling her carefree childhood in the neighbourhood she muses, 'When I think of the days that are gone and how easily amused and happy we were it makes me feel lonely and feel like crying.'

'I was born in the front room upstairs. There were nine of us, six girls and three boys. My mother was very strict but my father was very soft. In our house my mother's word was law. She done the cooking, the ironing, the washing, the cleaning, and the spending of the money. My Dad would always mend the shoes and boots, do cobbling for us.

'Daddy would always explain everything to us. He wouldn't put you off. Like, "Where did I come from?" "From God's pocket", he'd say. "How did I not smother, Daddy?" And he said, "Now it was a big pocket, like a carpenter's pocket, and you didn't smother because there was plenty of room." He was great at explaining. Now I remember playing with my best friend and the thing came up about where babies come from. Well, I said that I was positive that I came from God's pocket. She had another story, but I stuck to my story because I believed what Daddy had said. It was the truth and it was the law.

'One day we looked in a window and discovered a lady breast feeding a baby. And we couldn't get over it. We kept looking. We had never even seen pups being fed, never mind babies. We were *fascinated* to see this baby being fed. Dumbfounded. Course we'd no authority to be looking in her window. And Eileen says to me, "How did that woman get that baby?" And I said, "I'll tell you. They just opened the woman's breast bones and lifted out the heart and they hold the heart while they lift out the baby. And then they put the heart back in." That was it!

'It was a lovely place to grow up. Lots of lovely music on the street. Long ago there was music in every house. Music seemed to be the life and soul of everywhere. We all learned music because my father played the flute. Over in the corner house there was a ceili band. They'd practice in the house and when we were school-girls we'd dance outside in the street. There was always music. And there was a family up the road and they had two sons and they had a bugle and on New Year's Eve they'd play music. We'd all be standing in the middle of the road holding hands — mothers and fathers and kids — and we'd all be singing "Auld Ange Syne" to let the New Year come in.

'But it was a hard life and there was a lot of TB. Now on number eighty-seven Oxmantown Road a girl lived there named Mary Corrigan, a delicate girl who intended to be a nun in Australia. But Mary got sick. She was dying of TB and was just waiting for God to call her. Now whether Mary was praying to St. Theresa or not I don't know but she must have been praying to St. Theresa because St. Theresa appeared on the wall in her brown habit, as she was a

Carmelite nun. That was the figure that came out. And she said, "Mary, you will get better and you will be a nun." And she disappeared. And Mary was able to get out of bed and was on the landing and her mother thought it was her ghost she saw on the landing. Mary recovered and the doctor attending her had her X-rayed and couldn't find anything wrong with her. Mary *must* have been praying to the Little Flower. She *really cured* Mary Corrigan, a neighbour of mine. To think that it was on Oxmantown Road! We all knew that house as the Little Flower's home. Anyway, she got stronger and she was a nun and did go to Australia. And she died in Australia of consumption. They erected a shrine to her (in Stoneybatter), "Mary Corrigan who was miraculously cured by the Little Flower."

'Now I had a sister, May, who died of TB. It was during a bad flu epidemic. She was beautiful and she was mad about Daddy. She had a bicycle and nothing would do her better than to go around the park with Daddy on her bike. She was beautiful. Black curly hair and big blue eyes. She loved Daddy. Daddy was her whole world. She trailed after Daddy like a little cub bear.

'It was a bad flu and May got it. They bled out of the nose and ears and all. And that developed into rapid TB. So they took May to the hospital and told her that her leg would have to come off. She said that she would rather go to Heaven with two legs than one leg. She didn't want to go to Heaven with one leg. After a week and a half in the hospital they knew May was going to die. Daddy would go over every morning at 6:00 on his bike to see her. And he went back again in the evening. It was very emotional. She kept saying, "It's not fair. It's not fair. I've seen so little of the world. Why should I have to die? It's not fair, Daddy." And Daddy says, "May, you'll go straight to Heaven and you'll have less to answer for." He kissed her and she still kept saying, "It's not fair, Daddy."

'He came back in the evening and he discovered that she was more reconciled to go. All she could say was, "I hope I die on Saturday." And this was Wednesday. And Daddy says, "Why Saturday, May?" "Because the nun said I'll go to purgatory but on Saturday Our Lady comes and takes you out of purgatory ... so I won't be so long in purgatory." "But", says Daddy, "May, you won't go to purgatory." "Oh, I will. The nun said I'll go to purgatory but I hope, Daddy, that it's Saturday."

'She fought death. You know, the young heart fighting death. When a young heart is dying it's a very hard death because you're going but your heart isn't letting you go. She was fighting, fighting death. Daddy saw the last of May and he had to go to work then.

He kissed her and said, "May, you're only a short time from Heaven."
He was broken-hearted. She was only sixteen and the most innocent
sixteen that the world ever knew. She died at 3:00 ... on Saturday.'

48 Typical family street socialisation scene in old Artisan's Dwellings

Chapter 10

Men Folk

He was born in the year of the Uprising, one of nine children, and since age fourteen worked hard at making a living. As a lad, he laboured long days delivering milk to hordes of tenement dwellers. Later, he went into his mother's fish shop on North King Street where she habitually dispensed food to the poor when they had no money. She was more saintly than business-wise, remembers Vincent.

Today he lives in retirement above his fish shop on Manor Street. A man of uncommonly strong convictions, he expresses his beliefs, opinions, and theories forcefully. When speaking, his steely blue eyes are so intense they seem penetrating. He likes to sit directly beside his guest so that he can tap on their knee with his finger to make powerful points. One is not apt to miss the thrust of his words at such close range.

He can be startlingly blunt, especially in criticism of his early Catholic training and the sexual morality taught back then. Yet he clearly retains respect for the Church believing simply that if it would modernise some of its archaic dogmas it would have more relevance in today's world.

'We were in the fish business since 1904. My mother ran the business. But we had a hundred milking cows as well and when I was a boy I went into the dairy business. I was a very good scholar but I left school at fourteen because my eldest brother, he was going away to be a priest and there was no one for to do the work. So I delivered the milk on a horse and cart, two pence a pint. I started at half four in the morning. There was no such thing as pasteurized milk in those years and in the summertime the milk wouldn't keep. The fish market opened at 5:00 and I had to be down there so they could get a cup of tea with milk in it. Then I'd make the rounds for the men who worked at Guinness's and the Post Office because they had to be in terribly early.

'I'd go around with horse and cart and twenty gallons in the churn. There'd be two churns and they were silver and you had to have them shined to look clean. And the horse had to be done perfectly with the harness polished. And you had to have a nice way with all the customers. You couldn't be abrupt. I could get to over 250 rooms in a day. I had to go up five flights of stairs with the loose milk in a can and a pint and a half pint measure. I was terribly active and never sick a day in me life and I flew up and down the stairs. And there'd be about ten cats smelling the milk and you'd nearly fall over them. And the poor unfortunate women, they'd be lucky to have an old can for to pour it in. Honest to God, you'd be glad to get down cause the rooms had no ventilation. As regards hygiene, there was only one tap down in the yard and maybe nine families living in that big house. If the children were going to make their Holy Communion or Confirmation that was one week you knew you were going to get no money because they'd be trying to get a suit. But you'd give them milk ... wouldn't cut them off. You forgot about it.

'Around the 1920's there was no work, only poverty. There was mass unemployment and mass hunger where we lived and all tenement houses, old Georgian houses, owned by Jews. Now don't misunderstand me, I'm not anti-Semitic or anything like that, but they were the landlords. Two shillings a week for a room this size. There was nine of us in my family. If you hadn't got eight or nine it would be a stigma. See, the Catholic Church at that time increased and multiplied. What they were concerned with was the penny on the plate every Sunday, and the more Catholics they had, the more pennies on the plate. It was a sin not to have large families.

'People were really hungry. Fish, shell coco, margarine, that was the staple diet. Fish was one of the cheapest foods. An awful lot of herrings sold at that time because it was the cheapest. There was no such thing as filleted fish. Women bought a cod from me mother with the head and all. She brought it home and put the whole lot in a pot. And when the children come in from school everything was et', the head and the whole thing. Not the bone, but there was a lot of flesh inside the head. And people would come down to me mother and get rabbits. We sold a thousand rabbits a week but we were only paid for about three hundred cause no one was working. They couldn't pay me mother ... maybe they could pay for a few. But me mother, she was a *Christian*, not a Catholic, if you know what I mean. She knew she wasn't being paid but she knew they were hungry and needed food. She was a saint, in other words. She never made any money in forty years there. She would have made a million if she was paid.

'So you'd have fish two or three times a week and stew that was called 'blind stew'. It was stew without meat and you'd have everything else in it — vegetables, onions, carrots and all that stuff that was cheap. On Sunday you'd often have pigs cheeks. Outside every grocer's shop was a big barrel of about forty pigs cheeks. It was full of brine and a poor old woman would come along and dip her hand in, cause she wanted the biggest pig's cheek. She'd go through them all and her hand would be black with coal and dirt. Talk about hygiene! And she'd pick it up, wrap it in a bit of newspaper, and throw it into her apron. If you were a young lad, the man who owned the shop would give you a shilling for the day to watch those six barrels. Watch the women if they took two and only paid for one. Ah, she'd take your life to feed her family. It was a necessity, this was the point!

'Before the 1916 Rising, the British were very liberal. British troops were decent people. They never stopped you from going to Mass. I'll tell you what changed it. When all the Republicans were captured and then James Connolly was shot on O'Connell Street and they executed him in Kilmainham Gaol, even though he was crippled in a wheelchair, that's what turned the people of Dublin against the British. You could shoot a British soldier when you were walking with your girlfriend and could slip the revolver into her handbag and the British soldiers could come up and search you but they dare not put their hand on a woman. They wouldn't touch her.

'But the British hated the Black and Tans. One Christmas morning my mother, she was stuffing the goose and two of these Black and Tans came in and they were half drunk. They were after breaking into a local public house down the street and they were full of whiskey and they had two big revolvers. They took these revolvers and pointed them at the goose. They were there for about five minutes and a British officer walked in and said to me mother, "Have they taken anything, Mrs. Muldoon? Have they molested you in any way? *Get out!*" he says. And he apologises to me mother. "We *hate* these people", he says, "They bring shame on us!"

'Family life was much closer forty, fifty years ago. Children respected parents. It was the law. Because the father, he used a belt on sons and daughters. Even though you could be sixteen or seventeen, your father could take out that belt and give it to you if you stepped out of line. You couldn't answer your father back. And Irish mothers were more possessive of their sons than daughters. Terribly possessive. Because the son was a more potential wage earner. The girls were brought up to learn how to sew, how to knit, how to bake, because that was the mother's role at that time. No doubt, a mother would favour a son over a daughter. When I was sixteen and nearly six feet I was still in short trousers and most young lads were the same. The mothers at that time, they didn't want to see the boys growing into manhood. They wanted to keep them children. That's why they were so terribly ignorant about sex.

'They knew nothing about intimacy ... just like animals in the field. Down around the fishmarket all the couples there used to do a bit of courting. Couples used to congregate in the archway near the vegetable market and no one saw you. Well, Father O'Farrell used to go down there at night time and have a black tarred stick and he beat the hell out of you. He'd strike her as well. Oh, it was considered sinful. Now if I went to confession in the 1930's and I said I was courting and took her out and put my hand on her leg, do you know what he'd want to know? How far up did I put me hand? He'd ask me that. How far did I put it? Well, what did he expect? You put it up as far as you possibly could! But, Jesus, no way you'd say that to him because he wouldn't give you absolution. He'd put you out of the confessional box. Now I'm not kidding you. I saw people being thrown out of the confessional box.

'We had a mission (retreat) given every year in the church by some different Order, the Passionists or Redemptionists. And the only sermons they ever gave was sins of the flesh. Once they would get on that theme they would give terrific sermons. But what *ignorant* sermons! Now, at seventy-three years of age, I can realise as a boy how stupid and thick the priests were at that time ... in terms of their attitude toward married life. Now if your wife went to the priests, the Passionists, and told him that she took pleasure, though she's married and has four or five children, if she went and told the priest that she enjoyed sex ... well, there was no way she could take pleasure out of it. She was just there for *your* pleasure.

'Can you imagine a husband and wife living together and she lying there and he coming home and falls into bed and having intercourse with his wife, but she was just like a statue? She wasn't even a *moving* statue! She just lay there rigid and her sexual desires were repressed. She was afraid for her life. And parents used to beat children and they didn't know the reasons why. Just the mere fact that they were suppressed, their sexual desires were repressed, and this was the only way she could vent her feelings. And he was the same. He had a big leather belt. This was very common in every family. And it came from pure ignorance. The Catholic Church has an awful lot to answer for.

'And, Oh, if a young woman became pregnant back then, it was England. England! And, naturally, you'd go to confession to tell the priest. Well, he'd get up the following Sunday and he'd say, "Mary Malloy, she's pregnant". He'd say that. He'd use the name and everyone in the parish knew that Mary Malloy was pregnant. The family would have to get rid of her, couldn't live it down. They'd get rid of her. Wouldn't have anything to do with her. She was an outcast. There was a double standard there. The man was all right. They blamed the girl. I knew a good few of them, girls, and they never came back.'

BILLY ENNIS – 'JACK OF ALL TRADES', AGED 76

He has always been, by his own definition, a 'Jack of all Trades'. He started out at age fourteen polishing and stacking apples and eventually worked as a messenger boy, bellboy, bootblack, waiter, barman, labourer, coal delivery man, and fisherman. But his favourite employment was at the City Arms Hotel on Prussia Street where he performed every imaginable task and relished the lively company of cattlemen. Those years hold his fondest memories.

'I was born on thirty-three Stoneybatter. It's real Dublin here, one of the oldest. This and the Liberties. Liberties is gone now ... they tried to hold on to it. But Stoneybatter has never changed. All them shops down there, they're all still the same, especially the pubs.

'It was all cobblestones and we'd go up to the cattle market in our bare feet chasing the sheep and cattle. We'd bring up an old sweet can and ramble up and one of the men would be milking cows and he'd give you a can of milk. They had to be milked after so many hours standing there overnight, so the men were glad to get rid of it. No hygiene there. Some cattle would get a bit ornery. Some of them often went into the shops. One cow went into a little vegetable shop and upset the applecart, nearly went down through the floor it was so heavy. And a bull got loose up there on Manor Street and they had to bring down an army man, a sharp-shooter, to shoot him there. Gone wild, he was.

'Me father was an ex-British soldier and there was an awful lot of IRA men around the neighbourhood and he used to knock around with them. Now the Black and Tans, they were bully boys. They were making their rounds in the tenement houses where we lived and they come in and saw his khaki uniform, and Parnell was hanging on the wall. They said a few languages and let it go at that. But I remember one of their lorries coming around and knocking down a gas lamp-post and an old man, Mr. Norton, he run out with a wet sack to stick it down into the gas main. And they wanted to shoot him just for wanting to stop that. That always sticks in me mind.

'I very seldom went to school. I took a chancer mitching. I was always by meself. The others wouldn't take the chance. Me parents didn't know. I'd go up to a little pond in Cabra to do a bit of fishing, catch little pinkeens. I'd been mitching for eighteen months before they summoned me. Brought up to court on Parliament Street for non-attendance at school. The court nearly sent me away for five years to Artane. Oh, thank Our Lord of Mercy that me mother was alive to plead for me. I got a few clappers, all right, from me mother. Me father'd just look at me. She was the boss. I went back to school and then me mother died before I was fourteen and that finished school altogether.

'I did everything in life. I started off polishing apples for six shillings a week and I'd build them up in pyramids in the window. Then I got a job in the City Arms Hotel. Very busy. All cattlemen. I done everything there. I was a bellboy, I was a barman, I was a boot polisher, I was a waiter, and I was a messenger boy. Did the whole lot. Now the Conroys owned the hotel and a very decent family they were. Oh my, they done great for the poor up around there. They'd send me around on me old messenger bike with little parcels of tea and sugar and bread for different families around the neighbourhood ... and fuel.

'It was really a cattleman's hotel. Then, you had the British and Dutchmen all coming over. They were very nice. Oh, they had money. They'd throw money around just the same as water. They'd make a sale, go into the bar and throw money over it. Live it up drinking and eating. Now on cattle market day, you wouldn't know whether you were out in the market or in the hotel. All you'd have to do was look at the floor. Everything was on their boots. It had to be cleaned out and it was done. And I used to clean their boots. They'd leave their boots here, good strong leather boots they were, and I'd have them ready for the following week. The British would tip you better. It was no bother handing you five shillings and that was a week's wages nearly at that time.

'Now there was one man, a jarvey, a *character*. He come from Queen Street and used to drive a horse and cart. He was a big man about six feet four. A big lump of a man he was. And he got religious mad, he did. One Sunday morning on Blackhall Street all the people were going to Mass. Well, he got the horse whip and the rosary beads and the people coming down to Mass, he made them all kneel down and say the rosary. Big whip and beads in his hands! Frightened the life out of them, he did.

'Cattlemen, they was heavy drinkers. They'd go to Hanlon's, Lenihan's, Cotter's. Some pubs, you wouldn't go into them because you didn't know when trouble was going to start. I seen dozens of rows in pubs. Fellas contradicting one another over sports or something. You'd be delighted when they come out. Just sit down there and watch two or three men boxing one another. I seen them in Stoneybatter, men from the pub, go at it. It was fair enough. Only with the hands, you know. Fists. No knives or sticks. They'd let them go at it. And when the fight was over you'd see them two men shaking hands and they'd probably go back into the pub and have a drink together.

'I seen a row one time between two gangs, one from the Liberties and one from Stoneybatter. It happened right in Chicken Lane there. It was a real street brawl. There was four fighting four and they all fought one another with their hands. They were boxing and boxing, beating one another up. Ah, if you seen these people fighting ... great fighters they were. A tough fight it was. Men were knocked out, they were. The south side gang happened to be beaten.'

DIXIE O'BRIEN – CABINET MAKER, AGED 75

Get old Dixie talking and he'll fill your book', promised publican Tom Ryan. He knew his man, all right. Dixie, a gifted conversationalist, is known by his mates as a man of strong feelings. He prefers to think of himself as a man of strong 'convictions'. Having been an All-Ireland hurler, he has a special status at Walsh's pub where he has been a regular for over forty years.

From childhood, his father instilled in him a strong sense of pride in his Celtic heritage. His flinty spirit and defiant character are most intensely exhibited when discussing two of his favourite topics – British domination and education under the Christian Brothers. Surrounding mates just smile and shake their heads.

'I was reared on Oxmantown Road. We had five boys and one little sister. My mother was a very gentle, lovely, saintly woman, a very religious woman. Went to Mass daily and said the rosary all her life. When I was seven she was taken away to die. My father was a powerful, strong man but a very gentle man at home. He was very staunch Irish, very fond of the Irish music and loved Irish dancing. He had that in him. We used to speak Irish at home. He'd pick us up and hug us and love us. He was a great man. He was the grandest man under the sun.

'The Black and Tans, you'd hear them shouting about the place,

49 Flinty and feisty Dixie O'Brien – a man of strong opinions and convictions

coming up the road, knocking at doors looking for Republicans. Me father would keep us in but he wasn't afraid of them. Course the trouble was that he had a few guns in the house and had to smuggle them away when they'd raid. He warned us, "Now you don't say a word about any guns". And we were very proud of that. It's in your blood, you know.

'I can remember when I was one. I fell down the stairs. Remember it clearly. See, with the Celtic temperament you don't forget. With the Celtic temperament it's intense feelings. Like what the British did in this country was horrifying. See, they call this the British Isles, which is wrong. Definitely wrong. This is the *Celtic* Isles. The Celtic people are fair and red and they're intense in their thoughts, in their feelings. I was real red-headed when I was young. Now when you consider the strangulation of 500 years of British in this country. ... They did more than the Nazis or even Stalin did on this country because they were so long at it. The country was put back at least three hundred years in progress.

'I went to school locally, the convent school first and then to North Brunswick Street. The nuns were kind. Lay teachers were nice enough, too. But the Christian Brothers were peculiar. They were ignorant. Once they had the black cloth, they thought they were somebody, something extra special ... God's gifts. Now the Christian Brothers, they might have been brothers, but they were never Christians. They didn't have a Christian attitude. They taught you to be afraid of them. See, they were too small for the guards and too lazy to work on a farm, so they were made Christian Brothers. Ah, it was no vocation. A vocation is a great thing to have from God but the Brothers, a lot of them were forced in by their mothers. There's an old Irish saying, "You can't make a silk purse out of a sow's ear". Which you cannot. The majority of them hadn't a vocation.

'They needed only the smallest excuse and they'd want to hit a kid. They were known for their illness. Very sadistic. They'd pick kids up by their ear and kick them or punch them. Now you never heard of Christ hurting a child, did you? I saw one kid, he was picked up six times by the ears, off the ground. That's the truth. I can swear before God to it. It could be only some small thing you'd do. The Brothers had leathers in their pocket and a stick. It was a specially made thing, a good quarter of an inch in thickness and sewed with a handle on it. About a foot long. They were suffering from sadism. They'd hit you on the hands and sometimes on the wrists and on the tops of your fingers. There's a man not too far from me on Oxmantown Road and he's completely deaf in one ear. That was from punching down here at school. But the Brothers never put the leather on me. My father put courage into us. I had a terribly independent spirit. They were wary of me.

'Near the school there was very poor people in tenement houses. And this kid came in and gave a note to the Brother to tell him that his little brother couldn't come to school, as his boots were being repaired. It was a cold, miserable, frosty morning and you'd want to be well muffled up. "Tell him to come!" Back came another note again that "He cannot come. He has no shoes". "*Send him in!*", says the Brother. He *had to come*. The kid walked in his bare feet and was put sitting at the stove for the rest of the day. That's how dictatorial they were. It was damned ignorance. It was "congenital bugmantitus", as I call it. I coined those words.

'But I'll tell you that they were very much afraid of anyone with authority. Now and again, parents would come in and complain. They'd straighten up, all right. They'd be afraid for their life. One of the fathers went down there and punched the head off this big Christian Brother because he had broke the kid's finger with the leg of a chair. The kid was only ten and he come home from school and couldn't hold a fork in his hand. The Brother was a coward. Only a coward will hit a child. Sure, Christ never did that to a child.

'What's happening now is priests and nuns are defecting from the Church. See, long ago they'd stick it out some way or another, but now they're defecting. Of course, it was prophesided. You've heard of the old Columcille's prophesies? The first thing was that cars would go without horses, and that meant, of course, motor cars. The ships would fly in the air. You have big airships flying now. And then the devil would walk the world. Well, he's walking the world now ... with the way children are being despoiled, corrupted, destroyed. And the number of murders. It was prophesided that the "elective" would have their doubts. Well, the priests now have their doubts. So you can see that these things are coming true.'

BILLY ARTHURS – NEWSPAPER VENDOR, AGED 68

No figure in Stoneybatter is more visible than Billy Arthurs who, for the past forty years, has been implanted on famous Hanlon's Corner at the top of Prussia Street and North Circular Road. In the newspaper vending trade it is one of the most coveted spots in all Dublin. Business is so hectic that Billy can't take time out to record this chat in some quiet setting. It will have to take place on the open street corner amid the clamour of traffic, customer interruptions, and intermittent angry spells of rain.

50 Billy Arthurs, local newspaper vendor and character who has been implanted on famous Hanlon's Corner for more than forty years

Until a few years ago, he shared the corner with his wife who, he
explains, was even more 'famous' than he. He idolised her and has saved
everything that belonged to her, even raggedy old coats. Since her passing, he has lived with a loneliness that won't go away.

'This corner was always a landmark. My wife's father had the corner
and his mother before him. In them days of the cattle market there
was more people around. There was about 400 or 500 people around
here in them days, all the drovers and English and German blokes.
Boarding houses were nearly always full along there. Pubs opened
at 6:00 and the men would come into Hanlon's here to have a few
whiskeys. There'd be 200 men in there. They'd even be drinking
out here on the corner. And there used to be more than a hundred
bikes along there and animals were all over the place. You might
get an odd one running a bit wild when he comes off the train.

'In the old days it was all a man's bar. No women allowed in
there. Men would do business in there. Have a bit of a deal, have a
drink and they'd come out and buy the paper off you. Cattle buyers
was good tippers in the olden days. Oh God, I used to make more
money on tips than I did selling papers. If a paper was three pence
they'd maybe give you six pence. In them days they'd say, "Keep
the change". I could get a pound tip! And at Christmas they might
say, "There's five bob, or there's ten cigarettes for you", or they
might give me a drink.

'They all know me as the paperman on Hanlon's Corner but my
wife, she was better known than I was. I was known as the paper-
lady's husband. She was the brains behind it all. Very brainy she
was and any money that was made, she made it. She had a great
personality for listening to people and she'd be down here sipping
tea and yapping and yapping. That was her life. You couldn't keep
her away from the corner because she loved to talk. People could
tell her their aches and pains and she'd be giving them advice. She
used to have about six coats on her and used to smoke sixty or
seventy cigarettes a day, even more. Ah, she was great.

'We had five sons, three daughters and two miscarriages. I used
to worry a lot when the kids were smaller, when we were poor. I
drew a horse in the Irish Sweeps in 1965 and wouldn't sell it to
the bookie up the road there for 3,000 pounds. I kept it. But when
the race was over I only got 300 pounds. If you've no money you're
not equal in this country. If you've no money nobody wants you.
It's what you call "dog eat dog". The real working people like meself, they're the best. I'm here in the morning at a quarter past
seven. People like to have a bit of a chat and I know nearly all that

goes on but there are people you can't talk to. Some people are story carriers looking to find out if you knew anything so they could talk about it. You keep your mouth shut, you know? Just play stupid. As me mother always said, "There's a time to be smart and a time to be stupid". You have to be a "yes" man and a "no" man. That's as far as you go.

"When my wife died people come to us. I got 174 Mass cards. She was well known. When she died we already had the grave bought because one of our sons died when he was only 100 days old. He was born with the caul on his face. So when the mother died we buried her with the caul. But I have everything that belonged to her, bar that. All her clothes and boots — everything. We were married forty years. It's never the same anymore. It's OK during the daytime but when I go home I still think she's alive ... but when I don't see her there it's very lonely.'

THOMAS MACKEY — BACHELOR, AGED 79

One is immediately struck by his Freudian visage — painfully thin, bald, short grey beard, eyes squinting with myopia and cataracts through thick glasses, and a large, toothy smile. 'I still have my own teeth', he boasts. Wearing high-waisted pants with suspenders, he takes his daily walk with cap and cane, chatting earnestly with young children along the way.

The early part of his adult life was spent working as a domestic servant in an 'upstairs, downstairs' sort of world. Latter decades were spent devotedly attending to his ageing mother for whom he had great reverence. Today he lives in St. Bricin's Old Folks Housing Estate. A lady friend, of whom he is very fond, visits each day, doting over him shamelessly. He relishes every morsel of attention. There is some speculation in the old folk's meal centre that they might marry. But having been a bachelor all his long life, he is happily mired in his little trench and gives no hint of matrimonial intent.

'It was just a small tenement house where I was born. I have four brothers and four sisters and I was the eldest. To tell you the truth, I went into domestic service because of overcrowding in me own home. Nine of us children growing up with mother and father in two tiny bedrooms. One bedroom was nine feet long and six feet wide and the other room was slightly larger. Me mother and the four girls all slept in one room and in the other room me father and me brothers. Mattresses had to be brought out and put on the floor at night. So I went into domestic service as a houseboy about 1930 for six shillings a week.

51 Thomas Mackey, the quintessential confirmed Irish bachelor

'My father was an ordinary boatman on the canal barges for the Grand Canal Company and they worked for Guinness's carrying the beer down in the country. I always remember seeing registered letters from my father. We'd look at the postmark to see. He might be in Portarlington or Arklow or Galway or Limerick. It took three weeks to go to Limerick in those days by canal barge. See, it was horse-drawn, only at a walking pace. A driver, he sat up on the horse's back and they used to travel night and day, weather permitting. The driver would fall asleep and still the horse was so surefooted along the little pathway at the edge of the canal. When they'd come to a bridge where there was no footpath going underneath, they'd unstrap the horse and bring him around. There was big poles to manoeuvre under the bridge.

'Our fathers, they were only labouring people. And in my day the men were hard drinkers. Now my father, he was away in the country but when he was in for a few days he'd go on the drink and just fall down. Me mother and I would have to bring him in and throw him into the bed. But he wasn't the only one ... that was the pattern. The men, they'd drink so much that there was very little for the wife and family. You'd depend on St. Vincent de Paul to come up and give you a loaf of bread or something. But the pattern, that was accepted ... that was the way it was.

'My first memories were happy memories. Now the children of the present day, they'll never know the happiness we had even though we lived in great poverty. On Sunday afternoons in the summertime the old women would sit on the steps by the hall door and the children would be playing ball in the streets. There'd be a football match going on and it would be a ragball. And we used to play "Relieve-ee-o" and there could be an unlimited number of boys. Little girls would amuse themselves playing shop. Pieces of little broken teapots was called chocolate and bits of glass supposed to be mixed sweets. For money they'd use the gold rim of an old broken saucer. It was all pretend ... their imagination, you know.

'Now for devilment I'll tell you what we did. In those days there were horse-drawn cabs and we'd get a piece of black thread and hitch it on to the landing windows and a boy would climb and attach a piece of it around a tree. And when the cabbie would be coming down we'd give it a chuck and it'd knock his hat off. His hat would fly off and it would be a bit of confusion. If the man was too tall you might get him here in the throat but the bit of twine would break, you see. It was only thread. No harm was done. He'd stop and lash his whip out at you.

'Another terrible thing we done in our block of flats, we often tied the opposite doors with a piece of rope and then knocked. And the unfortunate person on the other side of the door, they were pulling at it, couldn't open the door. Of course, we'd have to undo the rope and run. And another thing, in those days the old women always wore big white aprons and then they did their shopping in the local groceries they'd put all their groceries in the apron and fold it up. We'd often make up a parcel and tie it up and when we'd see her coming we'd throw it on the footpath and we'd have a string out on it. The poor creature would stoop down to pick it up and put it into her apron and then we'd give it a chuck and the unfortunate woman would probably spill everything out, even breakable eggs. But we'd no better sense. We'd be eight or nine, very young. It was just for fun.

'I went to the Christian Brothers' school around the corner from about age seven. And they beat the Irish into us. I used the word "beat" because that's the way they were. Very tough. Oh, the discipline was very strict. They were terrible on the Irish and I couldn't for the life of me learn it. Even to the present day I have a shocking bad memory. I'd get slaps with a strap on the wrists and your flesh would swell up. There was a lot of cruelty attached to it. You had absolute fear and there was no standing up to a Brother. They were lord and masters. I was born with myopia. I was always short-sighted and should have been wearing glasses. I couldn't see the blackboard and I'd have to be nudging the lad beside me to ask what was on the blackboard. And for talking I'd be hit with a duster, a wooden thing with a piece of cotton wool on it. You might get it in the face. Oh, it'd hurt you.

'In those days, if a child was naughty they'd threaten to "Bring Father-so-and-so" over to you. Mortal fear of the priest! Confession was a terrifying experience, no two ways about it, regarding going with a girl ... keeping company. I always remember at a retreat the Missioner's saying about keeping company, "A close embrace, that's a dreadful occasion of sin". Now I knew a girl, all right, and I remember going to confession and I asked the priest if there'd be any harm in putting me hand on a girl's knee. "Oh, no way", says he, "No way you should ever touch the girl at all. That would be an occasion for sin!" So when you met the girl you kept your hands in your pockets. Now in the cinemas, that was the only place you could steal an old kiss, in the back row. I think they were too strict.

'The first job I had as a domestic servant was out in Blackrock for the Callaghan family. They were in the saddlery business. I started serving the table as a parlour man and they had two sons and I had to look after the boys, like clean their shoes and serve a table. And do all the cleaning, brasses, and polishing. There was a cook and the maid was in the kitchen but mine was upstairs in the dining room. You may have heard of the show *Upstairs, Downstairs* on television. Well, it was something like that. I got six shillings a week and room and board.

'Now the reason why I'm a bachelor is that I was never in a position to financially get married, to afford a wife. I knew two girls who would have been willing to marry me because they said they loved me. Possibly I was in love with them as well. This one girl, she told me that she was madly in love with me. But this doubt was there in me ... is it right? So when I was in my thirties I went to me priest in Merchant's Quay and told him that I knew a girl and was very fond of her. He says, "You're only working in a house as a domestic servant and what can you offer? You're in no position to dictate terms to any girl." And I said, "All right, Father". I just conveyed that to my girlfriend and I never heard from her or seen her since. I've no regrets.

'I was the eldest of nine and all the others were married. In 1957 my sister, Lily, got married and she says to me, "Tom, will you be able to look after Mammy now?" "Certainly", says I, "Why not?" I stayed on with my mother for the last twenty-two years of her life. She died in 1979 at the age of ninety-four. They were the happiest years of my life. I looked after her like a baby and done all the cooking and cleaning and gave her breakfast in bed every morning. I had to think of what my mother had done for me. A mother brings you into the world and the least that a son or daughter can do is to look after them. That was the greatest blessing I ever had, being able to look after her. She died in me arms at 3:00 in the morning. I kept tapping on her face and she was completely lifeless.'

HARRY JOHNSON – LABOURER, AGED 83

He always had a very physically active life working as a van driver for Findlater's, at a flake oatmeal factory on the quays, at Guinness's cleaning barrels and sweeping, and assorted general labourer jobs. And he loved dancing. Therefore, it was a cruel blow when, at age seventy-nine, he lost both legs to amputation due to disease.

Others might be despondent and bitter, but not Harry. He exudes spirit and humour. A neighbour tells of his dry wit surfacing when her husband recently died. 'Did he leave any shoes behind?' queried Harry. Everyone enjoys his company and admires his courage. He is kind to a fault and neighbours reveal that he pays the electricity bills for those who can't manage it. His wife and son are very attentive but do not

coddle him. When they take him out in his wheelchair to catch the summer sun he seems at peace with the world.

'I was born in a place called Fountain Place at the back of Stoneybatter. They called it Fountain Place because there was a great big
iron pump, like a hydrant. You'd get your ordinary water out of
it, to boil. Fountain Place, they put a name on it — Virgin Alley —
because everybody up there used to be holy, very religious. They'd
go to church every morning and then to devotions every night. It
was moreless a mockery, a jeer, at the people going to church all
the time. Fountain Place was demolished when I was about thirteen
and we moved into number thirty-nine Stoneybatter.

'I had three brothers and one sister. My mother came from Dalkey
and my father was an Englishman. He fought in the 1914 War and
he came home then and lived with us for a while in Stoneybatter
and then he faded out. Went off with someone else. Me mother had
to go to court to get weekly support and at that time five shillings
was a lot of money. My sister was helping out doing a bit of factory
work and I was going to school. Our evening meal was mostly soup.
What me mother said was law. We abided by that. We had to.

'Stoneybatter was a great trading place with all the shops there.
And we'd go to the forge and the fire would be going all day and
we'd be delighted to see the sparks coming off the horses hoofs.
The blacksmiths were men with muscles of steel, always with the
hammer all day. On market day the cattle had to be herded through
the streets and if a shop sold fodder, bales of hay or anything like
that, the cattle would smell that and the shop would expand with
them going in. Then you'd have to back them out because they
couldn't turn. It was too little. Put them in reverse gear!

'I went to the National School on Queen Street. There was four
masters there. They were rough. Slapping. You might be reading
two or three lines from your lesson book and if you didn't know a
word, how to pronounce it, he'd say, "Now hand out!" He'd get
the cane and you'd get six slaps on the hand. It hurt. You'd see
them crying. You had fear. We got ideas then that if you'd wet
your hand, lick it, before he'd slap you, or get the hair of a horse
and put it across your hand, it wouldn't hurt. So if we were coming
home from school and saw a horse we'd get a hair off the horse
and put it in your pocket. Of course, there was no such thing.

'The Black and Tans were the worst curse on the earth. Oh, Jesus,
I ran into them. They were stationed down where Richmond Hospital is. At that time it was called the North Dublin Union. If you
were on the street after ten you'd see the point of a rifle. They

might say, "Bring him up!", and you'd get a boxing. We could do nothing because they had the guns. We had nothing. Couldn't even use our hands because they'd pull the trigger and you were gone. Some were brutal. They'd get into Mulligan's Pub down there, maybe twenty or thirty of them. They couldn't see your way at all. You were "Bloody Irish", that's all. "Bloody Irish pigs", they used to call us. The Black and Tans were scurrilous. Men my age now, we still have that little stigma against the British Crown. I still have it. It'll only leave you when you die. It'll die with you."

JOSEPH COX – TRUCK DRIVER, AGED 65

Born and reared on Oxmantown Road, he lost his mother in a tragic accident when he was a young lad. The seven children rallied around his father, a policeman, and pulled together to get the family through difficult times.

A large man of over six feet, powerfully built with barrel chest, thick hands, and a shock of white hair, he reminds one of some patriarchal Irish chieftan. For thirty-five years he was a truck driver for the Electricity Supply Board. After suffering a heart attack or, as he puts it, 'a little bang in my ticker', he was retired on medical grounds and draws a hefty pension of ninety-five pounds a week.

He and his wife live in Kirwan Cottages, a small enclave of multi-coloured dwellings. The country village flavour and community spirit is much to his liking. Possessing a jovial personality and wry sense of humour, he relishes socialisation. In fair weather he can always be found outside ambling about entertaining children, helping neighbours paint their cottage, or engaged in animated chat with fellow pensioners. He seems quite unfamiliar with boredom.

'I'm born up on Oxmantown Road at a place called Finn Street. My father was from Roscommon but me mother was Dublin – Lucy O'Neill. My mother died when I was eight. She was a cook for the Garda Depot there in the park (Phoenix) and her apron caught fire and she burned to death. So my father was rearing seven of us. Me young sister come out of school then and done the cooking and looked after all of us. Me father was a policeman and he was eighty-five when he died.

'You were living from day to day. Couldn't save money back then. Food was scarce but you'd always have something to eat. Bread and jam and your tea. I always remember that we had a big iron pot and everything went into that pot. Oh, I can see it now. A huge, big thing. We used to buy rabbits three for sixpence. They

52 Joseph Cox, proud resident of tiny Kirwan Cottages

used to hang in the butcher's shops with the skin and all on them. You'd walk down and say, "Give me that fella there." If you wanted, they'd skin the rabbit and cut its head off for you. You put them into a pot and put in potatoes and carrots, put thyme in it, the whole lot. Ah, a gorgeous smell.

'When I was a boy we had huxter shops. They'd sell anything. Very dull, drab and they had half doors. But you could get most anything you wanted at your door in those days. Mr. O'Toole had a horse and two-wheel cart with a big churn on the back and he used to sell the loose milk. He'd knock at your door and you went out with your milk jug. He had a measure, a tin can like, and he'd say, "Do you want a half pint or a pint?" And you always got a tiddler, that little bit extra. That was always the custom. And turf men came up from the bogs and then going home after a few jars the horse would take him home and he'd be asleep. And there was a man who would come around in a horse and cart selling mats made of straw. He'd be coming up the street and people would say, "Here's the mat man". Then there was a boot polish man used to carry a big wooden case. Knock at your door and sell you boot polish for your shoes. And the weight of that case ... any money he earned, he *earned it hard*.

'In those days we played Rounders with a hurling stick and a tennis ball. And we'd play soccer in the streets. It was against the law and a policeman would come around on a bike and summon all the kids, bring you up to court. It was a children's court. We'd be maybe only eight years old and they'd do it to frighten you. Oh, it was a mortal sin to play football in the street. The policeman would come around in uniform and hand your father the summons. Then you'd get a box across the ears for being caught ... not for playing football, but for being *caught*! And the minute he went around the corner, ah, sure, you'd be out in the street with the ball again.

'We used to play marbles. In my day they were like chalk marbles. If you'd throw them hard on the ground they'd break. It was only when I was coming into my teens that glass marbles were coming out. Kids loved the colours of the glass marbles. You'd be going to school and your school bag would be loaded down with marbles. See, we used to make three holes in the road just a little bit bigger than the marbles. We'd make the holes by just getting an old bit of iron. You had to get the marbles into the holes. If you didn't, the next fella coming up, he could knock you out of the way ... and the farther the better! Your own marble would stop dead but the other would go flying and you'd win the game. When you won, any marbles that were around, you took them up, they were yours.

Ah, there'd be a hole in your nail from the marbles.

'You'd be lucky to get toys ... no money. Now it sticks out in me mind that I got a little steam roller when I was about eight. It must have been for Christmas because you wouldn't get anything for your birthday. I don't remember getting anything for my birthday. They'd just say, "Oh, he's so old today" and "Happy Birthday." That's all. See, it's hard to understand. In those days nobody had nothing around here. Your neighbour had nothing. You had nothing. You were struggling. It was poverty. There was no money. Everybody was in the same boat. When I got that steamroller it was like the Bank of England. I can still see it going up and down there. Today you'd be ashamed to buy it, to give it to anyone.

'And characters. I remember "Bang-Bang". He used to go around with a big silver key, that was his gun, and run around going "bang-bang" shooting everybody. In them days you got on the platform on the back of the old buses and the conductors would shoot back at him. How he was never killed I don't know. He used to go up behind the busman and say, "Keep driving", with his key. He was harmless. There was another man around here called "Johnny Forty-Coats" because he wore all these coats. Ah, he was famous. And another man around Smithfield and Aran Quay, a tramp, with a huge big beard and his coat would be falling off of him. He used to carry old newspapers and that was his bed for the night. Wouldn't say anything to anyone. He used to get a penny dinner over on Meath Street. All the tramps of the city used to go in there.

'Big families were common back then. The clergy preached to have big families. The reason was because of the North — the Protestants — they were trying to outnumber the Protestants. They said that small families were wrong. In them days it was religion first and everything else second. People were more religious than today. You went to church and had retreats every year. You went to clean your soul. There were Missionaries, Jesuits and all, and these were hard men. They'd lay down the law. And if you broke them you burned in Hell. On the pulpit they were laying down the law and *no questions*. What they said was the Lord's word and that was it. They talked about the evils of drinking too much and long courtships. They said it was wrong, that it would lead to getting too familiar. It led to sin. And if a girl was expecting and she wasn't married she'd have to be married on the side altar. She wouldn't be married on the main altar. That was *wrong*. They'd say, "Oh, she had to get married." The women used to talk. Ah, the women would telegraph it. It was wrong.

'Life is better today ... financially. Today the State will look after you. You won't go hungry. And television, it's made life easier for pensioners. But TV has ruined conversation. Today it's "Come in, sit down, and shut up". Conversation is gone. And they shouldn't have it in the pub at all. I don't watch much TV but the "Misses" and my daughter does. Only when there's a soccer match on do I look at it, like the World Cup now. But my wife and daughter start cribbing because they couldn't see the programmes *Dallas* and *Dynasty*. "But", says I, "it only comes every four years!" Says she, "Too soon". They wanted me to switch over. Says I, "I will *not* … the men of 1916 died for me to have a look".'

53 Decorative iron railing along Prussia Street offers a fine example of surviving street furniture pleasing to the eye of pedestrians

54 Sarah Murray, gentle midwife and nurse to local residents for over sixty
years and the oldest resident in famous Chicken Lane

Chapter 11

Community Caretakers

SARAH MURRAY — MIDWIFE AND NURSE, AGED 87

She is the oldest resident in humble Chicken Lane and for nearly sixty years served unfailingly as neighbourhood nurse and midwife. Whenever necessary, it was Mrs. Murray who brought babies into the world, cajoled obstinate children into taking medicine, treated flu and Tuberculosis, cared for cancer patients, and waked the dead. She became Stoneybatter's 'Florence Nightingale'. Routinely called out of bed in black of night, she concocted home remedies with remarkable success and always refused payment for her services. It was, she felt, a 'gift from God' and regarded it as her natural duty to care for neighbours. Her sacrifice and selflessness are local legend.

Yet she has had her own crosses to bear. There would have been thirteen children but only eight survived. Her own infants died in her arms, she raised a retarded son, and lost her husband to cancer. But never was her great faith in God shaken. Today she lives alone in the same home that was once a stone cottage. The toilet is still outside in the rear yard. Racked by crippling arthritis, she moves about slowly with conspicuous pain. Most of the day is spent in a comfortable chair in the parlour.

'Stoneybatter was a pleasant place, like a little country district. It was like a little village in Galway, something like the Claddagh. There were little white-washed cottages on both sides of Chicken Lane. One cottage used to have flowers growing out the side. There were yards up there that had cows, sheep, goats and pigs and poultry running around. It used to be paved with stones and in the morning time about 4:00 you'd hear the milk carts. They made a horrible noise. They'd awaken the dead.

'This house is over one hundred years old. When I came here it was full of little brown bugs and when you'd kill them blood would come from them and you could smell a coffin. The place was alive with them. Very dirty people had lived here and they were evicted into the street. Had I known they were evicted, I wouldn't have come here because you're suppoed to have very bad luck if you moved into a house where there was an eviction. The kitchen was flagged and an old black stove in the middle of it. Anything I've done in this house to keep it standing, I've done myself. Not my husband, mind you, myself. I *had* to do it myself.

'I had eight children but if everything had went well I'd have thirteen. I'm sorry I hadn't the thirteen. Large families were very common and they were *happy* families. My babies were born here because it was convenient and I could be with the other children. Nurse O'Shea, a midwife, she lived up on Arbour Hill and attended me. My little boy, Michael, was born and he had fits, one after another. I'd say he had about fifty. She pulled her apron across so I couldn't see and I said, "Is he having fits, Nurse O'Shea?", and she said "Yes". She thought he would have died. He was just a fine baby, a handsome child, and looked normal and took his feeds. But the thought struck me that his heart wasn't quite right. That little boy died suddenly in my arms at seven months. I was making a dress for my sister and she had him in her arms and she was walking up and down the floor singing "There's a Long, Long Trail A-Winding", that old song. I folded up the dress and said, "Give me the baby" and I went to an old winged-back armchair in the kitchen and put him on my lap and he just stretched out and died. Seeing that he had fits at birth, I asked her to get me hot and cold water and put him into it immediately. But it was no use ... he was dead.

'The next birth was a little girl and she was a little premature. Very, very pretty little baby. But I knew something was wrong because I wasn't so very well myself during the time I was pregnant. The nurse didn't even know if the baby was alive. She says, "Can you feel life?", and I said, "Yes, very little". And the baby came into the world and it was a little girl and I was delighted because I'd only the one girl. She was delicate from birth. When she was into her fourth month she got bronchial pneumonia. Now this is a very, very damp house and it was winter time. I kept a big fire and had hot water in the kettle and put some Friar's Balsam into it and the steam of that come into the room and cleared her lungs. And I fed her on sherry whey, just milk and you put the half glass of sherry into it, heated and strained, and that's the whey. I fed her that and nursed her for three weeks out of bronchial pneumonia. I also made a jacket of cotton wool and soaked it with cod liver oil and put it on her so there wouldn't be a draft on her. I used every precaution.

'I remember the doctor came to me this day and says, "Mrs.

Murray, your little girl is all right". And I remember she put her little fist up in the air like that and smiled at me. And he whipped the cotton wool off her chest and threw it into the fire. Which was a very, very wrong thing to do. Naturally, after being on her for three weeks it was a bit soiled looking. But it was thrown into the fire. It was soaking into the little girl's body all the time and there's a cure in cod liver oil. That night I noticed her a little blue and the next morning she was bluer still. She had a relapse and died that evening. But had the cotton wool been left on it would still have gone on working.

'We had tough times rearing children ... clothing, feeding. It was hard to live. Not actual poverty, mind you, but hard to make ends meet. My husband, God rest him, was a bus driver and payday was an event each week. He'd hand his paycheque to me with the exception of ten shillings and he'd buy his own tobacco. But on Thursday he'd often say to me, "Sarah, could you spare me the price of a half ounce of tobacco?" I'd empty my purse on the table and give him the money for it. That's the way we lived. We never saved any money.

'I fed my family on stews. Used to get odds and ends of meat from the butcher. I'd get a pound and a half for maybe one and sixpence. And I'd put in all sorts of vegetables — carrots, leeks, celery, onions, barley. Now on Sundays we might have a chicken roasted. It all depended on how much money you had. There was always porridge in the morning and I made my own bread, so we never went hungry. I was very good with my hands and used to make the children's clothes out of old garments. I'd get them from my people in the country or from anyone who had something they didn't want. I'd cut it down and make little pants, all sorts. And we all knew how to knit socks. The only time they got anything new — and it was hard striving to get it — was for Confirmation or Holy Communion.

'I used to wash on the sink by hand. I still do my washing by hand. I have no washing machine. I don't want one because I've always maintained that mine are much whiter and cleaner than what comes out of the washing machine. Oh, I hated washing shirts. The collars used to be the worst. I used to get a little nail-brush and scrub them with Sunlight soap. I remember one day taking Jimmy out to the yard and I said, "Count the shirts on that line." And there was fifteen on it. And I'd iron everything. Now I never had the money to pay a sweep for sweeping my chimney. I used to set fire to it myself, put papers up it to burn the soot out. That's what we did around here, set fire to the chimney to burn the soot out. A policeman used to come and say, "Your chimney's on fire".

'I did all the nursing around this district. Nursed everyone around here when they were ill. I was a midwife and nursed cancer patients, did everything for them up till the time they died. Everything. There was only myself. I got my first-aid training during the War years and I learned practical nursing in different ways. It came natural to me because my father's mother was a nurse. God gave me the gift. I could always tell — more or less guess right — what was wrong with a patient. I never took money from anybody. I always felt it was my duty to do it. No way I'd accept money. I'm the only one to do it. Maybe at three o'clock in the morning there'd be a knock. And I've had stones thrown at my window in the middle of the night. I used to make up a bottle for chests that contained glycerine, orange juice, lemon, a jar of honey, and I'd put a drop of whiskey into it. That was very good for the chest. Now I'll tell you what was very good for consumption — garlic. To eat garlic would be good for you and you could have garlic in your shoes and through the soles you can absorb all sorts of things right up into your system. And we used to get dandelions and break the stems and the white substance would be put on warts. And if kids wouldn't take their medicine their parents would send down for me. I'd threaten to hold their noses if they didn't take it.

'And I used to prepare the person for waking. You washed them first, just to see if they were alive, you know what I mean? Then you'd tie up their chin and close their eyes and tie their ankles to keep their feet together. Then put on the habit and all the rest. I always insisted on putting a pajamas under a habit. And they always had beads or a crucifix in their hands. People coming in were given tea and cake and plenty of drink ... more sometimes than at a wedding.

'Now I was a midwife and long ago women had babies and that was just part of life when they were married. The babies came along and it didn't matter how many. Girls just got married and accepted it. Just went into marriage. But there was a very great lack of knowledge. A girl's mother wouldn't tell her anything in the majority of cases. Up to about twelve years old I was told that a baby was found under a head of cabbage. Or a gooseberry bush. I often remember going out and *looking under* the head of cabbage! Some girls, they'd be terrified if a boy kissed them. They got it into their heads that they could become pregnant. So much so, that there was a lot of young girls suffered phantom pregnancies. Absolutely. One mother, with her first baby, she became pregnant and didn't know where the baby was coming from. She was frightened. She didn't know how the baby would be born. She thought it was through her navel. That's true.

'A midwife, to the very last, would try natural means. For the woman, raspberry leaves boiled, made into tea and taken about a fortnight before birth, would help. Then you'd have to get a kettle of boiling water, towels, cotton wool and, in the case of a haemorrhage, burnt sugar was given to the mother to stop the haemorrhage. In the case of a haemorrhage it was important to call a doctor. And, Oh, you had to sterilize everything you used and scrub your hands up, rinse them in water, but not dry them. Because there's infection in towels, no matter how clean they are. Mothers just had to put up with the pain at that time, no injection or anything like that. A mother feels much better after a normal birth. In the case of a breach birth you'd have to go into a doctor, a hospital. You couldn't deliver the baby. But with bandaging, you can bring the baby's head into the right position. Then when the baby comes, you turn it on its side and put your finger into its mouth and clear the throat and clear the eyes because the baby is covered with mucus. If a baby showed any signed of death I'd baptize.

'Now some babies were born with a caul, a thick layer of skin over the face and head. It's taken off very gently, very carefully, and it's dried and preserved over the years. It goes down in the family from generation to generation. A baby who's born with a caul is supposed to be very lucky in life. Did you ever hear it said that sailors, when they go on board ship, going on a long journey, they'd have a caul? It was supposed to be very lucky on the ship.

'What worries me now is what's going to happen to my schizophrenic son when I'm gone. He's sixty now. He was always like a retarded boy. I always knew that something was wrong but I tried to ignore the fact. When I first took him to school the principal said to me, "That little boy shouldn't be here at all. He should be in a mental home", which I thought was very cruel. Well, he could never learn to read or write. He went into St. Brendan's when he was twenty-six and we were broken hearted. He's improved, all right. He's on five tablets. He comes down to me three times a week. But what worries me is what's going to happen to him when I'm gone.'

ROBERT HARTNEY – PICTURE HOUSE USHER, AGED 91

In this neighbourhood he was the boss. His word was law. If you'd get on the wrong side of him you were banished.' The parish priest? Local Garda? Neither. Pat Moylett, proprietor of the sweet shop directly adjacent to the old Manor Picture House, is speaking of 'Bob' Hartney, the usher he knew so well as a child. To small children he doubtless

*55 Ninety-year-old Robert Hartney, Stoneybatter's beloved neighbourhood
Picture House usher for nearly half a century*

seemed a tower of authority but, as everyone attests, Bob had a soft heart and gentle manner which endeared him to everyone.

Bob worked at the Manor (later known as the Broadway) from the day it opened in 1920 showing silent films to the final door closing in 1956 when the little neighbourhood picture house fell victim to the television age. He felt it was the end of the world. Says his wife, Sarah (whom he met in the cinema queue when she was seventeen and he forty-one), of that fateful day, 'He came home at 3:00 in the morning on his bike with the old cinema clock on the back and tears flowing out of his eyes.' The countless children he so lovingly cared for have all grown into adulthood and now and again one will stop him on the street, grasp his hand affectionately, and reminisce about the old Sunday afternoon matinees. It always makes Bob happy for the rest of the day.

'I had a liking for the cinema when I was a boy and I got me wish. An aunt of mine went to the people who were opening the show, the Fagan family of North Circular Road, and she recommended me to them. They opened the cinema in May of 1920 and I started the minute the doors opened. I was a junior usher, just a raw recruit, and there was a senior usher. We had four ushers and a couple of usherettes. I had a dark blue uniform and a cap. My duties were to seat people, look after them, and keep control. And I was in charge of the queues. I used to have to work in the mornings as well for two hours, sweeping in between the seats, cleaning brasses and all. And there used to be a red terrazzo, marble-like steps and we used to have to wash them down every morning.

'The theatre was very nice and would seat 630 people. We started off with the name of Manor Cinema. Then it was changed to the Palladium and then to the Broadway Manor Street Cinema. We had a big canopy of coloured glass over the front of the house. It was nicely lit up with lights and was quite a good shelter from the rain. But we started with no heating whatsoever. Eventually we got oil stoves, one heater upstairs and four downstairs. But they were no use. Sometimes the wick would burn up and they'd go smoking up the house. Eventually we got radiators but there was no heater out in the hall. I was standing out in the front and I often come home with no feet at all. I couldn't feel me feet it was so cold. I used to be petrified because the whole place was open. The Corporation inspector made us keep the doors open all the time during the show.

'The first film they showed was "He Comes Up Smiling" with Douglas Fairbanks. They were silent films at that time. And we had an orchestra comprised of the manageress, Miss Lily Fagan, and she was the pianist, and her sister was the cello player and there was a violinist. They played very high classics for the film on the screen. They were underneath the screen and they'd just look up and play the music to suit that particular part of the picture. Talkies didn't come in until about 1929, like "The Singing Fool" starring Al Jolson. We had what was known as "sound on disc". You had a projector and connected to it a turntable with a big disc about twice the size of a twelve-inch record. When they started the film they had to have the disc synchronized with it. Ah, the people would let you know if the sound wasn't synchronized. They'd say, "That fella's speaking out of his turn!" You'd have to stop and restart it. We were opened seven days a week. There'd be three shows and matinees on Sundays. Prices were nine pence and four pence for children. I always liked the cowboy pictures – William S. Hart, Gene Autry, Roy Rogers and Gary Cooper and John Wayne. And Nelson Eddie and Jeanette McDonald, the "Naughty Marietta" and quite a number of their films.

'I loved children. They were my favourites. On Sundays they used to come at half two and queue up on the path. They used to give me sweets out of their bags. Children's seats were in the front, long hard wooden seats. The manageress, she used to allow grownups in before the children and I used to give-out about that. I used to say, "What about the children?" It was because their money was nine pence and the children's was only four pence. The children's money was as good as the adults! If I found a child outside standing around with no money, and the other children gone in, I'd say, "Come here. What's wrong? Go on in". I used to let them in if they had no money. At Christmas the children used to bring me bars of chocolate and I often got cigarettes.

'Great excitement in the children. See, we had westerns and serial films called the "Purple Domino" and "Eddy Polo and the Broken Coin". They were chapter films that'd come every week. You'd be going around patrolling the cinema and you'd see the little faces looking up at the screen, all excited, and you could hear them all saying, "Look out there, he's behind you!" If they got too excited or scared you had to go around and tell them, "It's only a picture. It's not real." So as to comfort them.

'We had a platform, not actually a stage, in front of the screen. It was about six feet in length. We arranged children's competitions, singing and dancing, and gave prizes. We got quite a lot of little girls doing Irish dancing, fancy dancing, a variety. And they used to have a balloon competition. What you done was blew out the balloon. Whoever blew out the balloon first got the prize. Now some of the fellas, what they used to do, they'd have a pin stuck out in their shirt and they'd blow out the balloon and just tip it against the pin and it's burst. But we got wise to that.

'We had a few minstrel troupes. One was called the "Black Jesters". They weren't actually black, they were done with burned cork. They had a master, called him Master Johnson. They used to sing songs and tell jokes. And we had the "Carolina Minstrels", a white troupe, with a couple of comedians. And Jimmy O'Dea, the singer and comedian, was there for a week. He used to be in the Theatre Royal or the Gaiety. When he was a young man he came to us for a week. And we had Paddy Crosbie and the "School Around the Corner" for a week.

'We were told to make sure that everyone behaved themselves. A lot of the courting couples used to go upstairs to the balcony, the back seats, for privacy. Now embracing or kissing, that wasn't allowed. And misbehaving would be talking or disturbing others, like shouting. You'd have to go up and tell them to behave or else go out. We had to be diplomatic. Tell them in a nice way. You daren't start bullying them. Smart Alecs used to try and come in through the exits and sometimes we'd have rowdies. You know, cursing and swearing and that. We'd watch them and the next time they were barred. Now many a scrap we had at night time between crowds ... rows with each other. But we had a police barracks just opposite and we'd only have to call a guard.

'We always had to watch on Halloween. Fellas used to have stink bombs, little tubes, and the smell would go around the cinema. And sometimes they'd have little squibs (firecrackers) and they'd throw them down on the floor and they'd go off with a "bang" and people used to jump with fright. They were harmless squibs but they were a danger to anyone with a weak heart. You'd be sitting there watching the film and the next thing "bang" under their feet, an explosion. Now I remember one Sunday night – and this is a true story – a crowd of boys went upstairs. They had a dead cat wrapped up in a newspaper and they brought it up to the balcony and they dropped the dead cat into a woman's lap and she took a fright and ran off.

'Now there was a little fella used to come to us, Tommy Maher. He was nearly thirty years of age and he was very, very small. Tiny, with big hands and a lump on his back. He was deformed. He wasn't able to walk and he had a little pedal car. He'd come down to the cinema in the car and I used to lift him out and carry him into the cinema and put him sitting in a seat. We used to look after him. And some of the children used to push the car home for him.

'And we had this one man, a character. He was a bit mental,

you know. Not dangerous or anything. Used to take a drink. He had a horse that was blind in one eye. He used to come in occasionally, used to drive the horse down from the public house to the cinema. One time he went into the public house and called for two pints. And the barman says, "Where's the other man?" "Ah," he says, "he's outside." And do you know what he done? He went outside and put the pint glass down and the horse drank the pint. Drank the beer! Well, he come down to the cinema and, would you believe, he brought the horse up the steps and into the hall. And the manageress says, "Oh, don't attempt to go in there, you'll have the whole place upset". You know, the people would be running in panic. So he backed the horse down the steps and went off. Anyway, in the end, unfortunately, one day he made a bet with somebody that he could cross the bridge on the Liffey (walking on the railing). He went to cross the bridge and on this night the water was a bit on the rough side. He got half way across and he overbalanced, fell in and was drowned. That was the unfortunate end of him.

'One day in 1940 I saw this young lady coming along in the queue. I just looked at her and I knew that she was more respectable than most of the people. A little more superior. I didn't like the idea of her being in the four penny queue. Says I, "This is the four penny queue. There are dearer seats at the top." "I don't mind", says she. So after that we made a date. We were thirteen months engaged.

'When the television started, the cinema went down. Started to lose patronage then. Eventually they had to close down. I stuck me ground there the whole time. Thirty-six years. They were the happiest times I ever had. On the last day I felt terrible. Everyone said goodbye to me and I thought everything was finished. We had this old clock and I used to look after this clock. Always used to wind it. It was an eight day clock. It was there until we closed in 1956 and the manageress said to me, 'You've looked after that clock all those years. I think it's fitting that we should give you that clock for yourself. Take that clock home with you." And I was saying, "This must be the end of my life." I made hundreds of friends. Whenever I go by the old cinema today I nearly bless myself. It'll never live again.'

FATHER BRENDAN LAWLESS – PARISH PRIEST, AGED IN SIXTIES

A handsome, greying, strong looking man, he likes to term himself a 'traditional' priest. He has held his present position for the past twelve years and is obviously comfortable in the historic parish. Residing in a spacious and well-appointed red brick house directly adjacent to the church, he is looked after by a devoted housekeeper who at first seems wary of strangers seeking to take up some of his precious time. But with persistence and coaxing an appointment can be made. His busy schedule is alleviated by the four parish curates who assist him loyally and respect his wisdom and judgement.

In his comfortable drawing room he serves an excellent cup of coffee in elegant deep green and gold china cups brought from France years ago. A gracious host, he is witty, open-minded, and candid. He speaks warmly and caringly about his parishioners, almost as one would speak of their adopted children. In a paternal sense, they are his 'family'. He lauds the old-fashioned faith of the elderly yet understands the religious informality of today's youth. By all accounts, he is popular with every segment of the community. Settled securely in his Stoneybatter niche, it is his expectation and wish to finish out his years there. Unless, of course, he is made a Bishop.

'It's one of the oldest parishes in Dublin. Historically, the district is very ancient. Even the names of the streets, they're all going back to Danish times, like Sitric Street, Norseman Place, Ostman Place and Sigurd Road. You can sense that kind of antiquity in the Stoneybatter area. It's a lovely old parish, I must say. When I first came here I found it very traditional. We have a rather old type of Dublin person in the parish. We have a lot of old people. We're top heavy, in fact.

'I found that the people here have a great respect for the priest, a tremendous respect. It's still to be seen, especially among the older people. Now in the old days there was not just reverence for the priest, there was a certain *fear* of him. That has levelled out a little bit. But I still think the reverence is useful and necessary. You'd want to hear the older people talking to realise the *faith* they have, the love they have for the Church and the priest. And this is going fast in Ireland in cities. They have unquestioned faith. They were born with it. It's hard to define, but it's there. You can *sense* it but to put it into words and describe it is impossible. It's a faith with which they accepted everything they were told by the Church. If the Church says it's all right, if the priest says it, it must be all right. That type of faith will die out.

'You'll notice that there is a certain neighbourliness still in the parish. It's a village atmosphere. If you go down, say, Oxmantown Road there any afternoon you'll see people standing at their doors and talking in groups and it's nice to see this. Now I grew up in Clontarf and we lived on an ordinary Dublin road but you never associated that much with people on the road. You knew some of them but you never kind of stood together in groups having a chat. But down here on Oxmantown Road you will. You'll find the ladies out with their aprons on and the hall doors wide open and two or three from across the road would come over for a chat ... they'd be having a chat there on the footpath.

'We now have a certain amount of vandalism as you have in other inner-city parishes. A lot of the older people are living in fear now. Some perhaps had experiences of muggings themselves or their neighbour next door. They're afraid to go out of their houses, especially in the winter time when once it becomes dark. I know a number of people who tell me that they come out to Mass in the morning, on their way home they'll get a few messages, and then they go into their little house, close the door and lock it up and they're there until tomorrow morning. It's terribly sad. You know, at this hour of their life when they should be enjoying a certain amount of contentment.

'The Church is naturally falling off with the young. But I'd say that the majority of our young people are still coming to Mass. We're hoping that they'll stay with us. But nowadays the younger people coming up, they're so used to being brought into discussions on everything – on television and radio – whether it's the Church or anything else. They question everything. They won't take anything on faith anymore. They really won't. They have to get an explanation for it. And there's so many things in faith that you have to take because Christ said it and that's that! You can't explain it but it's there.

'I'm a traditionalist but I'm happy and I plan to remain that way. Some of the people in the parish might look upon me as being an "oldie" but it suits them. Ah, yes, I loved the old Mass. I still like the old things, the old devotions we used to have. And I love the old Latin. I very probably will be here in this parish till the end. Every parish priest here before me lived and died here, except for the one who was made a Bishop. I intend to go on in my own little furrow till the end.'

JOHN BYRNE – ENTERTAINER, AGED 79

Orphaned at a tender age, his childhood was an upward struggle all the way. He lived in the country, scrapped for food and was deprived of any normal, loving home environment. After knocking about in various Dublin jobs he was forced to emigrate to Britain during W.W. II in search of employment. Owing to his natural theatrical talents, he found a niche entertaining British factory workers. Upon returning to Dublin, he secured employment with the National Transport Company (CIE). His marriage, admittedly doomed from the outset and worsened by his long bout with alcoholism (which he eventually won), ended with his wife walking out on him. Unable to get a divorce under Irish law and marry a woman with whom he later fell in love, he is embittered toward the restrictive, moralistic system.

For the past forty-five years he has lived in the artisan's dwellings and is one of the most widely recognized figures in Stoneybatter. Nearing eighty, he is a small, handsome, blue-eyed man, spry in manner and appears a good ten years younger than his age. He is the inveterate entertainer with a dazzling repertoire of songs, jokes, poems and stories recited spontaneously and flawlessly from memory. He regularly entertains neighbourhood groups and when encountering friends along the street always has a cheery crack or whimsical comment.

'But when he enters the silence of his house a depressing transformation occurs. 'When I'm here alone I'm a different man', he confides. 'I'm schizophrenic.' The loneliess is often nearly insufferable. For company he has filled his home with music boxes and six simultaneously-ticking coo-coo clocks. They create a sense of sound, animation and life. Conscious of advancing age, he professes that he'll consider himself lucky if he has another four or five years left.

'I was born in the Liberties. There was eight of us but the big flu of 1919 took my mother and father and there was only three of us left. It wiped us out. I was an orphan. We were sent down to the country and we were kicked around. We were just like an animal at that time, an orphan was. You got two cuts of bread and your mug of tea. You were always hungry. We used to go out in the fields and get turnips. Pull one up and scoop it off on a stone and you'd eat it raw. Or get potatoes out of the field and light a fire and throw the potatoes in and when they'd be nice and black you'd take them out. You had to be tought to survive.

'When you were fifteen or sixteen you were sent out into the world. I was practically illiterate because I never got a chance to go to school. So I came back to Dublin and messed around the fruit market and got a bit of a job. A fella asked me one day to lift a barrel of apples onto a cart and I was fairly hefty despite what I'd gone through. And he asked if I'd like a job. I remember my first week's wages were eight bob. And every time I'd go up Bridgefoot Street I can see meself throwing that money up in the air and catching it. I was a millionaire, you know.

'The girl I married was also an orphan. I was twenty-five and she was nineteen when we started out in a tenement room. There was twelve and fourteen people reared in a room in these houses. We counted ninety people in one tenement house on Dominick Street. Hard to believe that. When I was married there was a half a barrel of beer on the table and a feed of bacon and cabbage and that was a wedding. That was it. And a melodion. I went to a wedding the other day and it cost 3,000 pounds!

'When we got married we were illiterate about married life. She didn't want to have children ... or like only one or two. But she was made to have six. Poverty was bad at that time and people had to buy shells of coco to get a drink, instead of tea. At that time pawnbrokers were the poor man's money lenders. People pawned their stuff on a Monday and on a Friday the wife takes the Sunday clothes out of the pawn. They even had a joke — "I have an indigo suit ... in-they-go on Monday and out-they-come on Friday". They actually ran a pawnbroker's express, the half-seven bus, from Cabra down to Gardiner's Street on a Monday morning. These were all people with parcels to be pawned. All the women queued up. And the Jewmen, they were a terrible curse around this area. They were money lenders, very bad. They were a necessary evil. The poverty was terrible and, oh, they got very involved. They'd knock at a door and say "There you are, there's a pair of blankets for you. Only two shillings a week." Some poor person would take them in and she'd pawn them and get fifty pence. And when she'd get the bill from your man it may be three pounds!

'People just existed. They helped each other. If you had something a little extra you'd give it to your neighbour next door. Drinking was terrible heavy. It was to forget their misery. Things were very bad and families broke up over it. Actually, my family broke up over it. Things weren't so good and then I started to take a few drinks and before I knew it everything was up in the air. So I went away to the War. Several hundred thousand of us had to leave this country to work in England. Despite all this talk about England and the hatred, we would have died of hunger only for England during the War because they kept supplying us with stuff and gave us work over there and we were able to send money home. Things were bad and you had to go away or starve. I got involved in what they called ENSA Shows, variety shows, working for the British Government. There were four variety shows and Gracie Fields would be in the top one and I was in the fourth. We went around to factories at night, like factories that made motors for aircraft, and there'd be an hour's break from 12:00 to 1:00 in the morning for the night workers and our job was to have a show for them. I sang a song and told a couple of stories. I met Gracie Fields and Tom Mix and saw Laurel and Hardy. Of course, the drink was flowing all the time and I became an alcoholic. When the War was over in 1945 we all got double week's pay and we had a great time in London.

'Then I came home here and the Transport Company was taking on people and I was given a job. But I had taken to drink and my wife, she just walked out. She'd had enough of married life. We'd no divorce. I feel terrible about that. I met a wonderful woman twelve years ago in England and we had an understanding of each other. We were on the same life line. We could have gotten married for the companionship ... somebody to talk to. Now that's the tragedy of no divorce. We're the greatest lot of hypocrites here. Why should anybody be forced to live with a person they don't want to? The terrible hypocrisy in this country, it's *unbelievable*. We're supposed to be so religious but it's all a sham. Now I'm not anti-religious. I believe in God ... at seventy-nine you should. But I saw so much hypocrisy over the years. If there was a little more Christianity and less religion. I hate saying this but the greatest hypocrites are religious. I'm not saying them all. We're all brainwashed in my time. Brainwashed into all this religion that you went to Hell if you looked the wrong way. It was religion based on bloody fear. There are supposed to be 90,000 bad marriages in this country but the people were told not to vote (for approval of divorce in the referendum election), that it would be a mortal sin. You see, it's the clergy. It's the *fear*.

'I work with old people now, bingo and all, to make their lives as comfortable as possible. And we do variety shows for the old people around here. We sing songs and give them tea and cakes. It's funny, you can bring them back to their childhood days. And we have this Neighbourhood Watch thing now and we look after each other. I found six people dead the last year. It's their own fault in a way. They have enough but they're still living in the poverty days. We find it where they haven't used it (pension money that they're hoarding). To be buried in a pauper's grave, that's the terrible fear of an old person. My mother was buried in a pauper's grave. People to this day still hold money for that although there's no danger today because the Government will come in. But they still have that fear of the pauper's grave and they'll hold that money, several thousand pounds. See, they grew up in a poverty age.

'An awful lot of them are very lonely around here. Loneliness is a sad thing, a terrible thing. And the callousness of relations, it's a thing I never could solve. A mother rears a family, she gives her whole life to her family, it's the instinct in the person. But when she gets incapable of looking after herself they put her into a home. I *never* could agree with that. What annoys me is you'll see a mother with a family around her ... "now, Mammy, we'll be up to see you every Sunday and don't you be worrying now." And they'd be around her for four or five Sundays and then down to one (a month) and then she'd be forgotten about.

'I often think of this old lady up the street there. I went in to check on her one day and I sat on this seat and I was thrown from here across the room! "How *dare* you sit on that seat." "Oh", says I, "I'm sorry." A neighbour said, "She's been waiting five years for him", but the son never came. However, I got through to her and we used to give her a few biscuits and sweets. But one days she says, "My son is coming next Thursday and he's bringing a melodion." Well, I forgot about it and I was calling on her the following week and she says, "Didn't I promise you something last week? I told you my son was going to call and he came last Thursday." "Oh", says I, "I'm delighted." "Now", says she, "I'm going to play you a tune." And she took up an imaginary melodion and I nearly broke down. There she was with her two hands pumping ... she had convinced herself that he had come.

'I understand what happens to a person living on their own. I know what it is because I'm nearly thirty years alone. When there's human beings together the house becomes alive. But when you go out, the place falls dead. As soon as you go out that door and I shut the door, it's like the iron curtain. As I say, I'm "Hail fellow, well met" outside. I talk to people, I tell stories, I sing songs. But the minute I come in here all I can hear is the bloody clocks ticking. It's a kind of company, all these things. Loneliness is a real hunger. It's worse than food hunger ... the hunger for company. You could *die* of loneliness. Loneliness is a killer. It is. It kills people. I know myself that I'm coming to the end of the road. You get that way. If I get another four or five years I reckon I'm lucky.'

WILLIAM HARMON – UNDERTAKER, AGED IN FIFTIES

Bourke's Undertaking establishment on Queen Street has been in his family since the days of the Great Famine. It occupies a two hundred year old brittle brick Georgian building. Dressed in a finely tailored dark suit with smart tie, he does not fit the stereotypical image of a sombre undertaker. He is friendly, humorous and a thoroughly modern businessman who has managed to successfully mix local tradition and personalised service with the economics of present-day funerals. His sense of local history and custom prompted him to retain horse-drawn hearses years after most other Dublin firms turned to motorisation.

Owing to the high population densities in Stoneybatter and the large elderly population, business is good. Custom holds strong in times of sorrow and local people have dealt faithfully with his family for generations. Even local folk who had been uprooted and transplanted in new vicinities customarily return to Bourke's to bury their dead. In a single year he can handle as many as five hundred funerals. The creeping trend toward cremation does not worry him, confident that it runs counter to the old-fashioned values of the local populace.

'Back in the 1840's the family business was established, but on a different site on Queen Street. It was established by Tom Bourke himself who was a granduncle of my father's. He moved down here to number seventy-one Queen Street in 1886. In the early days of undertaking here, before my father's time, an undertaker supplied carriages and coaches and hearses, all horse drawn. They also carried out a hackney service. We also had brakes ... they were an open wagon that would take maybe twelve people, six either side, with a driver up front. People might hire them to go to a race or that type of thing.

'Years ago a person died, was waked in the house, and went straight to the cemetery. Wakes got a lot of publicity here in Dublin from the likes of our writers like O'Casey and the boys, where they'd sit up all night and drink and then take yer' man off to the cemetery in the morning. The body was laid out on the bed and the fella that was dead was nearly part and parcel of the wake as well. Back then the families would just hire the horse hearse and carriages they wanted to do the funeral. People selected a coffin from the coffin shop and the undertaker just picked up the body at the home and coffined the deceased. No embalming or anything like that. See, at that time undertakers didn't make coffins on their premises. There were coffin shops over in a place called Cook Street. Around 1916 you could get a full funeral for about six pounds.

'With the Twenties and Thirties you had the advent of cars, motorised funerals. But they would have been few and far between because you must remember that at that time all your haulage was done by horse and cart. And undertakers saw it as more efficient to employ coffin makers on their own premises. That had the effect of closing the coffin making shops on Cook Street. Now at that time if somebody died one member of the family would go down to the church to see the priest, another to the cemetery to arrange for a grave, another to the undertakers to make arrangements, and a habit would be got from the local convent. Well, in the Thirties undertaking firms wanted to become more efficient, give a better type of service and bring all this together. So if a person died a member of the family could come to the undertaker and he would take over. He'd send his staff to dress the remains, supply the habit, contact the church, contact the cemetery, and make the grave arrangements.

'With the outbreak of War in 1939 motor cars were put off the road. You couldn't do motorised funerals. It was all horses at that time. Now say you were doing what we call a "country funeral", one outside Dublin. During the War if that town was served by a train you weren't allowed to go there by hearse. You see, petrol was so dear. You put the remains on the train and the undertaker there took over with his horses and continued the funeral. If it wasn't served by rail you could make your case to go by hearse. The Government supplied you with coupons for petrol. You supplied a log of the mileage that was put on the hearses and you got your coupons.

'After the War things started to change rapidly. Motor cars came up the road. Limousines started to come in but the undertakers like ouselves here in the older areas of the city still held onto horses ʻbecause the tradition had been horses. We had both horse hearses and motor hearses up until 1951. And we started to go into churches. We'd take the remains the night before into a church. Now that stopped the wakes because the body wasn't there. So we'd take them to the church that evening and bury them the following morning. And going to the cemetery there was still the tradition of passing by the house three times before going to the cemetery. That was an old tradition here in Dublin. Why I don't know but you just did it.

'At that time people started to put newspaper notices in the paper. That didn't happen in the Twenties and Thirties because in this area of the city all their relations lived around here and if a death occurred all you had to do was come out of your hall door and tell one person and everyone in the area knew. Now, families grow and get married and are all over the place. So in the 1950's and 1960's we started to delay funerals that extra day because we had a lot of emigration to England and you could hold up a funeral for a day to give them a chance to get over. To let the relatives get over. That's when embalming came in. We didn't have to, it wasn't the law, but we used it for obvious reasons.

'The coffins remained the same because the graves remained the same. See, unlike in the States where you bury side by side, we bury on top of each other. We go down to nine feet and might get five coffins in one grave over a period of time. It could be the same grave that you bought in 1870 that you're using in 1960. Three generations in three openings of that grave.

'In the Sixties any undertaker, if he wanted to stay in business, he did everything for everybody. He just took over. We had always been known as "Undertakers" but you began using "Funeral Directors". That's when we began to introduce funeral homes. If a death occurred in the house you took the body away to your funeral home. That took the pressure off the house straight away. Delays didn't mean anything if they wanted to wait until somebody came over.

'In this area generation is following generation. Families are so deep-rooted with ourselves right back through the years. They just call you and say, "Such a person has died. Go ahead, you make the arrangements." And the older people here stick to black at a funeral. The younger people will come out in colourful summer gear to attend a funeral. Just like they now accept cremation. The older people in this area don't accept cremation but for the younger people it's the only way to go. You wouldn't do many cremations in this type of area. Some would plead with you to make sure that they're not cremated.'

56 Walking along Sitric Road in the Artisan's Dwellings where high housing densities promote neighbourliness

Chapter 12

Pub and Betting People

THOMAS O'DOWD — PUBLICAN, AGED 63

O'Dowd's, on Grangegorman Street, is a classic old neighbourhood pub. For more than two centuries there has been a public house on the site. About eighty-five percent of the customers are hard-core regulars — it's as local as that. Patrons speak of Tom as a 'gifted' publican. He enjoys the reputation for running an unusually clean and orderly house. Egalitarian in philosophy, he abhors social snobbery and prides himself on serving labourer and doctor at the same counter without distinction. In short, he runs a 'people's pub' where customers are genuine friends.

After forty-seven years in the business he has learned much about human nature and it is evident in his handling of people. Constantly monitoring the socialisation around him, he has a knack for detecting early signs of discord. Knowing the men well, he immediately recognizes any irregularity in their speech or mannerisms that might signal a problem. If a man over-indulges it is best to simply prop him up comfortably in a corner and let him sleep it off. Or, if necessary, see that he is driven home safely and put to bed. To Tom, it is just a matter of psychology and common sense. One thing is certain — in this local pub his word is law and that's the way everyone wants it.

'My mother's people were publicans, over one hundred years in the business. So it's in the family. I've never worked at anything else in my life. I was sixteen when I started serving my time with my uncle in Christchurch Place. I served four years apprenticeship and then you did two year's juniorship after that before you became a qualified assistant.

'You started out doing normal, routine work. In those days they were much stricter on cleanliness in a place. In the mornings when we did the cleaning we used a black apron and that means that you weren't serving people. Our job was to keep ashtrays clean, keep tables clean, and keep the glasses washed. Publicans were fussier about cleanliness then and cleaning was a totally different type of

57 *Respected local publican, Thomas O'Dowd, at his establishment on Grangegorman Street*

58 *Tony Morris, flamboyant pub 'regular' and gifted conversationalist, at O'Dowd's Pub which is his local on Grangegorman Street*

job. You had plain hardwood which had to be scrubbed and all the shelves behind your counter where your glasses were had lead. No stainless steel in those days. You had to soak each glass back then individually in hot water, soap them with a brush. They were washed, dried, polished with a cloth and put away. That took a lot of time. And customers used to have their own pewter mugs identified by their names. People liked pewter mugs in those days. It was just traditional. But now they'd be too expensive. Then you had a tremendous amount of brasswork to clean. I was sick and tired of brass for years.

'Then you did the cellar work. In those days we did all our own bottling. We bottled our Guinness, we bottled our ale. The apprentice worked with the porter. You had to wash the bottles, fill all the bottles, put the corks in, and put them on trays. Filling was done by the Hog's Head (wooden cask) and there were seventy-two dozen bottles in a Hog's Head of stout. Then you had to put the labels on the bottles. You had an ordinary paste and you got the labels from Guinness's and dipped them in the paste and put them on the bottle. It was monotonous work, like an assembly line. Then in the evening you came back spotlessly clean, hands washed and nails cleaned, and wore a white apron and then you were ready to serve people. So you had to learn from the bottom up, from the cellar to serving people.

'Everybody back then drank porter. That was the working man's drink. Guinness had a plain porter which we called "single X" and "double X" which was a stout. The porter was eight pence a pint and the stout eleven pence. Porter was weaker and the ordinary working men drank porter all the time. We sold a lot of whiskey in those days and if men came in for gin you were very surprised because people didn't drink gin in those days — it was considered a woman's drink. There was no such thing then as vodka, and brandy was priced out of reach for the working man. So, seventy-five percent of the trade was porter or stout. And the stout was much better when it was in wooden barrels. There was much more grain used then. Today, with the metal containers, they use a lot more chemicals. The other was natural. It was yeast and barley and grain and it came up as God meant it to come up, not any pushing or shoving or putting gas into it.

'In the old days customers had their own seats. You just didn't sit on *that* seat. That was "Mr. X's" seat or "Mr. C's" seat. See, when I was serving my time you would *never, never* refer to a man by his name. If your name was Kelly, you'd be "Mr. K". In those days you had divisons all around the counter and you might get four people in one division and maybe four people in the next division and if I said "Hello, Mr. Brown" to the man in one section, the man in the next section might think that that was his boss. It might be somebody he didn't want to see. So, he was just "Mr. B" to me and that's all. That's the way I was told to do it. Confidence in a pub is a tremendous thing. You just didn't give people away. It was a very good idea, actually. It's not necessary today. But I still see some of those old people who I refer to as "Mr. C", "Mr. B", "Mr. K" — and I don't know what their names are!

'Conversation in a pub has never varied. It's simple — politics, religion, the price of drink, the cost of living, work, and football matches and hurling matches and such. We had no television in those days and the conversation was much better, much more interesting. Because you had people *discuss* things. They discussed their jobs. I learned a lot about different trades, like how they made biscuits at Jacob's Biscuit Company, just from listening to the men talking. You could learn an awful lot in a pub. Any person who doesn't go into a pub is missing an awful lot of life ... whether you drink or not. And there's nowhere else that I know where you'd meet the characters you meet in a pub. Every pub has its own characters.

'There's no subject that's not acceptable for conversation. But if it gets into a big argument and spreads around the pub, especially about religion, I try to hold it back. Because you can argue about religion for a million years and still not settle it. The political thing is a personal thing and religion, it's personal too, but it can get sticky with religion. Religion is one thing I'm nervous of because religion can be very hot-headed. It's something you can argue over for years and find no solution to. I mean, being a Catholic country we're based on *mysteries* and how can you *prove* anything if you believe in mysteries? In the last ten or twelve years priests come in and they can stand at the counter, have a pint and tell a joke and I like to see it. Now ten years ago that would have been unheard of.

'We get three generations of customers, probably four generations, in here. Regulars would be as high as eighty-five percent. It's as local as that. It's *tradition*. This is really an old Dublin neighbourhood pub. Eighty percent of the people have the same drink all the time, so when you're busy you don't have to ask him what he wants, you can just get it. Here you have to *care* for your local people. Anyone can serve a whiskey, serve a pint, but it's handling individuals that is the important thing. I wrote a poem one time about what makes a good publican ... "You're a doormat, a diplomat ...". Basically, you have to know about human nature. The important thing is *handling people*.

'You learn through experience. For instance, if we were just sitting here having a drink together and some fella comes in and he's
noisy, he's rowdy, or he's the type of character who wants to butt
in, it's my job to see that he doesn't butt into your company. Now
I can't tell him that he can't butt in, but I've got to be able to steer
him away from your company. There are people who just don't mix.
And you listen for any kind of row, whether it's political related
or football or whatever it may be. Your ear is trained to know when
the pitch goes a little bit high. Then you move in and say "Cool it
down, boys". You have to remember that people are good at heart
and you appeal to their good nature at first. If you don't get anywhere, then, well, then you just run up your sleeves and let fly at
them. I've never had a physical row in the place. We've had some
close ones. Funny thing about it is that when it comes to that, the
customer will say "Let's go outside" and once they go outside you
can sort them out very easily. They respect your house. If you're
strict, if you run a place properly, people will respect it. But there
are pubs around town that are very badly managed where there are
fights every night.

'Drink affects people differently. Get a few drinks in them and
people can change. You've got to watch those things. Some people
get boisterous, some people get funny, some people get very morose.
Drink changes people completely. You just couldn't believe it. You
have a responsibility to see that they don't get too drunk. It varies
how much a man can drink. An average man can drink six or seven
pints and no trouble. And our friend here (Tony Morris – to be
featured in following pages) can put down a bottle of whiskey and
still walk out. Women's personalities don't change nearly as much
as men's when they drink. They can hold a hell of a lot more.
Definitely! I don't know what their make-up is, but they can hold
a lot more.

'Now a wife will very rarely come to get her husband home. It's
a very awkward situation and it's very rarely done because it's just
one of these things that's been accepted over the generations, that
a wife doesn't call her husband out of a pub. She can do what she
likes with him when she gets him home. She can hammer hell out
of him, but she doesn't let him down in a pub. It's just one of those
taboos. Really, she can kill him when he goes home if she wants to,
she can beat him up on the road if she wants to, but she won't cross
that threshold and make a fool out of him in front of his mates.

'There have been some very prominent characters in here, either
going up to the hospital (St. Brendan's) to be "dried out" or coming back. Brendan Behan has been in here. Funny, but an alcoholic,

when he's going to the hospital, they have this thing that they just love that last drink before they go in. I've actually seen them come in that door on their hands and knees and we know that he's lookin for that last drink. And if he doesn't get that last drink he'll go beserk and give terrible trouble to the person that's taking him in — his brother, his father, his mother, his wife, the taximan. But if he just gets that one drink, nine times out of ten he'll walk back into that taxi and go up to the hospital with no trouble. It's psychological. He just *has* to get it. And if you don't give it to him it's wrong. I usually go to the person he's with and say, "Look, if I give him this he'll go easier" and they say "Whatever you say". And we give him the drink.

'For a while I had another pub, on the South side. People there weren't as friendly as people around here. They had more money than people around here and I didn't like their attitude of looking down on other people. I don't believe in class at all. I meet a man and make my own judgements. Over here no one gives a damn who you are. I've seen judges, labourers, doctors, every profession, mixing together at the counter and no one minds who everyone else is. But in the other pub if a doctor or a solicitor came in everyone looked up to them. I didn't like that. There are publicans who won't serve working class people if they're in working clothes. I don't go for that myself at all. I don't know if they're trying to lift themselves or their pub to a higher standard. People are people as far as I'm concerned. I don't give a damn as long as they behave themselves and have a few jars and enjoy themselves. That's all I'm interested in. Who they are, what they are, makes no difference to me. There is no class distinction whatsoever here.

'To the local people the pub is the centre of the whole neighbourhood. If you did away with the neighbourhood pubs in Dublin where the man comes in after a day's work for a few drinks, where he can relax and chat with his old pals ... if you closed down these pubs you'd just have to build mental asylums all over the place.'

TONY MORRIS — PUB REGULAR, AGED 42

S aid by publican Thomas O'Dowd to be the 'greatest talker in the place', he unfailingly lives up to his reputation. It comes naturally. Tony was born and reared in 'the buildings', works just up the street at St. Brendan's Hospital as a psychiatric nurse, and O'Dowd's has always been his local pub. He ritualistically visits the pub twice a day — every day. His capacity for putting away a bottle of hard whiskey yet walking gingerly out the door quite lucid is part of the pub's lore.

Everyone in the place likes Tony, drawn by his charm and wit. Gregarious and mildly philosophical, he tells a good story, delivers a quick crack, and embellishes a news item or local event in some colourful or amusing manner. But he is also a good listener. Seated on the stool at the bar, which is indisputably his 'throne', he can listen compassionately to a troubled friend, offer consoling advice, and then issue a wry crack to cheer him up. That's what makes him a good pub mate.

'I was born up in "the buildings" just above Arbour Hill on Malachi Road. It was a good area to grow up in. There were forty-one houses on Malachi Road and everybody knew everyone else. If the door wasn't open by half-nine in the morning somebody would go over to find out what was wrong. They averaged about five children along our street and there was thirteen children in the family two doors down from us. There were seven of us reared in two bedrooms. Four of us slept in one bed. It was rough in terms of physical comfort but you had great camaraderie.

'Everybody knew what everybody else had. And everybody shared. Like, we were the house with the pram. See, with seven children me mother got a pram. So no one else had to go down and buy one, they'd just borrow from us. Two doors down from us was a man with a hair cutting machine. The machine was used by the whole street. But my favourite story is the Christmas pudding cloth. There was only one in the street, that's all. It was only a square of calico and it was a Mrs. Murphy had that. And she had a little notebook to go with it, you see. Everybody had to decide when they were going to make their Christmas pudding. And it would go around. My mother might have to make it in early September and she had to have it made by a certain date because somebody else was waiting for it. I'd often ask my mother about that and the reason was that a new one was no good ... had to be seasoned.

'My mother was born in our home. She carried guns for the IRA. It was always a woman carried the guns under their dresses. The soldiers were comparative gentlemen at that time and wouldn't search women. So, if a man wanted to use a gun she'd just hand it to him. Pre-1916, nobody liked the IRA but after 1916 everybody was sympathetic. And once the Black and Tans came in, everybody hated them. When word would spread that there was a raid going on everybody would open their doors, front and back. You know the way the buildings go, back on back, and the walls about six feet high between the houses. Well, the dust bin brigade would get the lids, metal lids, and bang them on the footpaths and that would tell everybody that the lads (IRA members) were coming up. All the doors would open, you see, and they could run into any house, out the back, over the wall, into the next house and they were lost.

'It would be very fair to say that I spend a good portion of my life here in this pub. I usually come in twice a day, seven days a week. We normally drink with the same fellas. About six of us join together but some days there could be fifteen of us. It's a nice feeling to know that you're wanted. The customers, this is *our* pub ... where we come to drink, where we come for our social life. I mean, the publican only *thinks* he owns the pub, but it's *our* pub. Actually, it isn't really a pub as such, it's more of a club. Some of us even have our own stool or chair. That's my spot there on the corner.

'It's very relaxing to come in and have a couple of Paddies. We talk about all sorts of things. Could be something from the news or something that happened at work. An awful lot of bull is spoken. You can hear the same thing over and over but with a different slant on it. I don't know how many times we've fought World War II down here. You know, "If Churchill had done this, and such and such had done that." It's all bull but it gets rid of all your tensions. You just get rid of pent-up energy. And you can tell the biggest lies under the sun and you know everybody doesn't believe you but you still keep telling them. We actually start arguments here just to get an argument going, just for fun, because when you drink you just don't care. But you won't have much bull if you have no drink because you'll think of what you say first.

'Now language in a pub depends on the company. If there's females in the company there has to be a limit on language. There *must* be. Now when I started drinking, women wouldn't be allowed into the bar. But I remember once a man came in the bar with two women and I was arguing with a fella down at the far end of the counter and I didn't see the women coming in. Of course, I let a bit of bad language fly the length of the counter, which was accepted in a man's bar. That's why it was all male, so you could use invective. And the whole pub went quiet. Because, you see, at that time you didn't swear in front of women. That was an awful sin. I apologised, but the man complained to the barman. But he said, "There's a lounge upstairs if you want to bring the women up, but this is the *men's* bar here and if they want to use bad language, they can use bad language." And it was grand because you didn't have to be on your best behaviour all the time. Nowadays, the women swear as well as the men, so it doesn't make any difference.

'Those of us that regularly drink together, we discuss our problems. I find that if you have a problem it's very easy to talk about it over a beer ... some fella has a problem with the wife or one of the kids is sick. The last problem was when one of our lad's kids was making their First Holy Communion and he hadn't enough money to buy the dress. We just said, "That's no problem" and we just dressed out the kid. Just dipped into our pockets and threw a few quid on the counter and said, "If that's not enough, come back to us." And I remember when my youngster was christened and I was on strike, out of work, and God knows when I would get paid again. Well, the normal thing when a child is born — at least that's the custom in this neighbourhood — is you throw a pound into the pram. But it was ten pound notes that went into the crib that night. It wasn't really for the kid ... it was for me. Ten pounds at that time was an awful lot of money. You remember it for the rest of your life if somebody does a good turn for you.

'It used to be that we'd buy rounds for the whole company. But we stopped. Now, we just buy our own drink ... unless somebody is broke and you'd drop him a few quid. It comes back to you. Everybody can be down on their luck now and again. Normally I'd have about four or five — about a half bottle of whiskey — twice a day. Most of us know our limit but now and again a few go over their limit, which is acceptable. I never drink during Lent. Just an old quirk I have. But I still come in. I'll drink a pint of lemonade. At the beginning it was difficult. I tried staying away from the pub one year and it was very, very difficult. I found that it's easier to come down, drink a lemonade, and chat away with the lads. And one day I was standing there at the bar listening to the fellas talking away and I remember saying to myself, "That's the greatest load of bull I've ever heard spoken in my life." Cause I was *sober*, you see. And I said to myself, "If I was drinking I'd be in the middle of it and I'd be worse than any of them.'

'A publican and the barman make a pub. You can have the nicest decor and everything else, but it mightn't be a good pub as far as customers are concerned. It depends on the publican and the barman because they know everybody's business who comes in. Some publicans are the cream of the country. Tom (O'Dowd) is actually a brilliant publican. He's a fella who can mind his own business when it has to be minded and mind your business when it should be minded. I remember one night I was sitting there, about broke, nursing two drinks, and Tom knew that I was broke. And a couple of pals come in I haven't seen for years. And without even batting an eyelid, he come over and put down three drinks and gave me the change for a twenty pound note. Never said, "You owe me that". He knew that I owed it to him.

'He also knows if I don't want my wife to know that I'm here and if she rings on the phone he'll say I'm not here. And there was never a row in this pub because he's quick enough to notice that there was the makings of a row starting. I never heard him giving-out to anyone. He'd just say, "Now you've had enough, go home and get something to eat and come back." And at Christmas he gives you what's called the "Christmas drink". What he gives you depends on how much you drink. If you normally drink a pint, he'll give you two pints and say "Happy Christmas". But now he gives me a bottle of whiskey here every Christmas. I often play the accordion here on Christmas Eve night and we have a sing-song. It's the only night you're allowed to sing in this pub.

'The way I feel, if alcohol wasn't discovered — there was no such thing as drink — and it was discovered tomorrow, it would be the wonder drug of the century. Because it keeps more people out of mental hospitals. It really does. OK, it puts a few in, you have a few alcoholics, but if you compare the number of alcoholics to the fellas it keeps out.... A fella comes home and the wife starts giving-out to him. He'll go down to the pub, have a few drinks, get a bit jarred, then if she starts giving-out to him he's half jarred, so he doesn't mind. So you go up to your bed, get up the next morning feeling sick, but you feel good because the row is over.'

JIM HIGGINS — PUB REGULAR, AGED 65

He was born and reared in Stoneybatter and for the past thirty years O'Dowd's has been his local pub. A dapper dresser in tweed coat and tie, he prefers 'Jim' to the formality of 'James'. He is well liked for his congenial nature. A week ago his mother passed away but being surrounded by caring pub mates is therapeutic and comforting. That's what his local pub is all about.

'I was born on Manor Street and now I live in Kirwan Street cottages. This is a very working-class area. We were working-class people and growing up we hadn't got a great deal of money but we had something special. In the artisan's dwellings area it's a small community of people. If someone became unemployed people would help out with simple things, maybe a pound of sugar. When a woman had a baby when she come out of the hospital in those days she couldn't do anything until she was Churched. A neighbour would come in and do all the washing, scrub the floors, cook the meals. And if the mother wasn't too well she'd come in and nurse her and look after the children. There was never a big thing made of it. It was done as a neighbour. That's the type of people you have around here. Very closely-knit people.

'Now we had a great character, a Granny Dolan. She'd look after the dead. Dress them up, wash them, shave them if necessary. She was renowned. A wonderful old lady and she never wanted money. It was a matter of helping each other. Granny would have a few baby Power's whiskeys and she'd get to work, no bother. And when she was finished she'd get another baby Power's to compensate her for her time.

'I've been coming to this pub now for thirty years. This is my local. There's always an invitation here. Go in and have a drink, meet somebody, exchange pleasantries. You can talk, have a game of cards. It's a social thing, an experience that adds to life. You develop friends and share the trials and tribulations of life and the joys as well. A local pub like here, it's like a pulse of the neighbourhood. You can guage how the area is going. My mother died only last week and my friends here got a Mass said and sent a wreath and a card that read, "From the staff and customers of O'Dowd's Public House". They sympathised and that's how they showed it. So we share the good times and the bad.

'In my book a good publican makes the place itself. The personality of the man behind the counter. A man who will listen, not pry, sympathise, not pity. A good man, a decent man and he's (Tom O'Dowd) one of them. He keeps a very good pub. Now you can measure a pub by its toilet. Now that's a very odd thing to say. It's spotless how he cleans that toilet. Now if you got one or two unruly animals come into the pub they'd immediately sense that there was a local crowd of fellas here and if they were haggling for a row this is the last place they'd pick. They'd be out the door. For instance, this pub was raided some time ago by two young hoodlums and the customers beat the hell out of them. They had come in to rob it. They had a bar and a stick. And a number of men here physically hammered them. Ah, you have to stand up and be counted. Ah, those two hoodlums who came in here that night, they won't come back here anymore. No way.

'There's a few characters in the place. We have a man called "The Dead Man". He's a patient up in the Gorman (St. Brendan's Hospital) and he says he's dead and he just comes up now and again to have a drink. And he *looks* dead! His face is a dreadful colour and he has a mouth full of bad teeth. He's dreadful looking. But he's convinced he's dead. He's a character. He'll come in and look for a drink off anybody. Then we have "Paddy Carwash" who washes cars for want of something better to do. Again, he's a patient, a day patient, in and out, you know. No bother, the lads will get him a pint for washing their car. Paddy, on a good day, he'll drink twenty pints. But he's harmless ... and "The Dead Man" is harmless.

'I think that a pub is a man's domain. A pub is a man's refuge, if you like. It used to be almost unknown for a woman to go into a pub. It was *verboten*. Wouldn't be done. It's awkward. See, the atmosphere would be more guarded because sometimes men express themselves rather vulgarly and very outspoken. They'd never do that if their wives or girlfriends were here. Basically, the man is working all day, he comes home, has a meal, talks to his wife. But then he wants relaxation and he comes up here and has a drink. It's just a safety valve. Now I've seen where a woman comes into the pub and said, "You come home. Your dinner is ready on the table and that's it." And he was shamed. He wasn't seen in that pub for two or three weeks. But I don't think it would happen now. There isn't a dominant male as perhaps there was in my day. There's a different style attached to marriage. The woman is equal to the man now ... almost.'

MICHAEL McDERMOTT – BOOKIE, AGED 43

His sign reads 'M & M Racing Services – All Sporting Events'. It's a prime location for a betting shop, smack in the centre of Stoney-batter Street and directly across from the Post Office where pensions are collected. Dressed in a dark suit and tie, looking very much the business-man, Michael arrives about an hour before opening time each morning and intently pores over the racing forms he has posted on the walls. In this trade one had better do his homework. Taking risks and coping with pressure is part of the game. He has developed a high blood pres-sure condition from the unrelenting tension. But he wouldn't want to be doing anything else.

Michael has all the right attributes for his role. He has a gregarious personality, glib tongue, knack for deciphering human nature, and a fair bit of sheer luck. Able to get along easily with every type of customer, he has been remarkably well accepted by the locals and business is good. In his shop patrons know that they will get a fair deal and be treated respectfully. He has a special affinity for old pensioners who are not always welcome in other shops because of their modest betting habits. He gladly accepts their twenty-pence wagers and makes them feel at home beside the big bettors. In short, locals consider him a 'bookie with a heart'.

'I've been in the business for twenty years. My family were all horsey people. I sold my house to start. And I lost the whole lot. Every penny of it. Lost it all in a year and a half. See, when I started I thought I knew it all. But I didn't. Thought I knew it all and you knew *nothing*. I was going to give it up, pack it in, but I had relatives that kind of stumped up a few quid and kept me going. After I lost everything I saw myself going into my betting office on a Saturday morning with twenty-four pounds. I said to the board marker, "You won't guess what I'm starting with today". "Well", says he, "I hope it's not two hundred quid". And I says, "No, it's less. I'm down to twenty-four quid". And he says to me, "Oh, I'm getting out of here". But it was a Saturday and I won seven hundred pounds! And I haven't looked back since.

'When I came here they didn't want another bookie in the place. I was just living up the road and my kids were going to school here. And my wife was from the area. Lived all her life here. See, once my wife was from the area I was accepted. I was one of their own, so to say. I never saw an area attract back folk as much as here. Fellas born and reared in the area can live outside in Finglas, Blanchardstown, everywhere, but they'll come back here to Stoneybatter to their friends and their pubs. I find that they all come back. This shop is packed every Saturday and on Derby Day I had fifty-two people in here.

'There's always something new in this game. You never get two days the same. Different types of bets that you have to sweat out. There's pressure. Fierce amount of pressure in the game. Because you're taking on *everybody*. If there's a race going you're taking on the whole shop but every individual is only taking on you personally. So all the bets are running and there can be big money involved. You can win big or lose big here. I'd say it's ninety percent skill and ten percent luck. But you must have luck. I have a certain amount of luck, I know it. But I lost 2,000 quid on one horse last Saturday. The biggest bet I ever had to pay out was 4,600 quid. There's a lot of pressure in that. There's an old saying about bookmakers – "You have to have nerves of steel".

'There's a lot of what you call "mug money" around now, just the ordinary punters. The fella with ten 'P's" and twenty "P's". The ordinary small punter, you can fall asleep with him. You don't have to worry because you'll get your percentage at the end of the day. But the "strokers", the fellas that get information from the stables and that, they're intelligent. They get first-hand, first-class information. I have regular strokers who come in daily. There's certain fellas I run out ... the real professionals. If they walk in the door I *know* them, by their looks and all. I just say "Goodbye". They'll just hit you once and be gone. But I'll entertain fellas that'll back with me every time there's something on. What I do now, I cater for them and maybe back-bet the horse that they bet. If they bet a hundred quid here I'll have two hundred backing it. See, I'll phone another bookie and say, "Two hundred pounds to win." So I back a hundred pounds for myself. That's how I survive.

'Then you've got "hookey" races where you've got ten horses in a race and nine aren't trying. I was at the races in Leopardstown three weeks ago and the jockey on the second favourite horse had backed the favourite! I knew that because he had given five hundred pounds to a friend of mine to put on the favourite. So, what chance have you? Oh, it's illegal but they do it. Ah, we get that inside information. In the terms they use, the second favourite is a "dead one". That's the word. Just like the dogs. I go to the dogs nearly every night. Last Saturday night there was a dog race with six dogs ... five duds and one live one. Five of them just stopped dead. The live one had to win. So a stranger coming in has no chance. No chance whatsoever. You've got to be in the circle of bookmaking, the "clique" they call it. That's the way bookmaking at the moment has gone.

'With bookmaking you have to be fair. If you're fair with them the customers will be fair with you. First thing I tried here was to build a bit of atmosphere in the place. I'd come out from behind the counter and talk to the lads, socialise around the shop, and it means an awful lot to them. Other bookies would look down on them like "I'm only here to grab your money." And I treat the man who puts on ten "P" the same as the man who puts on a hundred pounds. Like I cater for the pensioners who have their ten "P" bets and that. I give them little perks, like I'd pay the tax myself for them. Now the bookie next door, he didn't want old age pensioners in his shop. Said they were no good to him, just taking up room. He's gone out of business now. It caught up with him.

'I have no pensioners here betting heavy and I wouldn't encourage it anyway. I'd tell them to go easy. Even fellas that do in their wages, I don't go in for that. See, I can tell. I can read into their minds if they're betting their wages. Or a fella after collecting the scratcher, as we call it, the dole. I'll say to them, "I suppose you've the best part of it done in. Won't you go home now with the rest of it?" I don't like that kind of money at all. Some bookies don't care where their money comes from. They'll grab pensions from old ladies or anything. I try to avoid fellas on the dole. I find that sometimes a fella might lose his dole here and I'd know by him standing around like he's edgy at going home. Often I took twenty quid out of the till and threw it at him and told him to take that home. But some never learn their lesson.

'Everybody thinks turf accountants are loaded with money. If I was paid what I was owed I'd be a lot wealthier. There's no protection. Credit customers and phone customers, you're at their mercy to pay it. You have so many good clients but you'll always get a bad apple in the box. You'll find the "dodge-pots" as we call them. I have to deal in cheques and I have a cheque there now for six hundred quid that's come back twice. Now a lot of bookies would send a "heavy" to their door but that's not my scene. I just try and get the money over a period of time and then once it's in I just say, "OK, I don't want your business anymore".'

JOHN McCARTHY – BETTOR, AGED 50

Most mornings around 11:00 he can be found in Mulligan's Pub sipping his pint and poring intently over his fresh copy of *Sporting Life* – the 'bible' as he calls it. Fingering his beard contemplatively, he calculates the odds for the day.

His father was a jockey and he has been around the tracks all his life. Around Stoneybatter he is regarded as a very knowledgeable man about the betting game. To him it is a serious and methodological business. "I don't enjoy it', he claims, 'I do it for the money.' But one can't miss the spirit of challenge tinged in his tone. He has seen betting become far more sophisticated over the years and knows that today he is competing with computers which set odds. Matching his mind with a computer only seems to heighten the sport of it. His mates know not to begin the morning chat until he has plotted the day's strategy.

'My father, God rest him, was an ex-jockey. He was bringing me to the races since I was about seven. He had a great eye for a horse. He was never able to pass it on to me. I'm not brilliant but I know when a horse is fit, all right. Now I don't just bet on horses. I bet on football, cricket, hurling, boxing, Wimbleton. But betting on politics now is too cut and dried. Since opinion polls became more exact, seldom the favourite gets beaten. It's removed the gambling.

'Betting is a sport. It's a game played slow. And it's therapeutic, especially for pensioners. People like old Jocko spend the day in the betting shop. They've got papers there to read. The local betting shop is a fairly social occasion so I think it's a social good. In all these shops around here everybody knows everybody else. With the price of drink now you can't afford to spend your whole day in a pub anyway.

'A betting shop is very much like a pub. You like good service behind the counter and you like people to be pleasant to you. The reputation of betting shops is even more important than the reputation of pubs because you're dealing with money to money. As far as integrity is concerned you have to be whiter than white. Bookies have to give the benefit to the punter every time. And they should be good losers. Even if it hurts. A punter can afford not to be a good loser but the bookmaker *has* to be a good loser. You have to smile even when you're losing, otherwise you get a bad reputation. A bookmaker friend of mine, whenever a fella won a few hundred pounds, he always had a bottle of whiskey for him as well and he'd say, "There, now that's to celebrate with." He had style.

'The only way you'll make money out of this is hard work and study and I can assure you it's harder than going out and digging roads. I treat it seriously. To a lot of people it can be a really enjoyable thing but I don't really enjoy it myself. I do it for the money. Now I get this *Sporting Life* first thing every morning. I'd spend a couple of hours with it. Some races would need an hour's study before you'd be entitled to have an opinion on them. And a lot of people follow jockeys blindly or a stable blindly but I believe in horses first because I don't believe that there are many bad jockeys. There are some brilliant ones but there aren't may bad ones. Usually, if a competent jockey has the gear under him he'll get the horse home. So the horse is far more important. You have to know your horses. Ah, and the weather has a big effect. Soft going is not as reliable as firm going.

'You get so many tips, bad tips, but you can sift them. But if you get a source of good information it can be a pure goldmine. You can become a rich man by it. Come in here on a Saturday morning and I'll guarantee there'll be a half dozen tips running about. I'll take it with a grain of salt. I won't back a tip unless I have good assurance where it's coming from. The biggest bet I ever had was two hundred pounds and I was getting information. The horse won. Now that's not a big bet today. And I don't believe that luck plays too big a part in it. The luck factor is like spinning the wheel or a toss of a coin. You'll have a run of good luck and a run of bad luck. It'll balance out. You'll break even.

'Now we'll bet on anything here (Mulligan's Pub). Usually, what happens if a bet is made in a pub it's money across the counter and it's put in a glass. That's the normal routine here. Memory is an awful lot of it, like who won an All-Ireland in such a year. Now one year I bet on the Miss World finals. This friend of mine is betting too and we're studying all the pictures of the Miss World's. But we had a tip that it was *bent*, that Miss South Africa would win it. It's bent practically every year. Ah, yes. We don't suspect it, we *know* it. We know this through a casino (British). The information was that of the nine judges, three of them were committed beforehand to vote for Miss South Africa. So three should be enough to swing it and she was a fine looking girl anyway. But what we didn't know was that it was *double bent* for Miss Great Britain!

'I think gambling can be a worse addiction than drink. You can only drink so much but you can gamble your house and everything away. My father had a great saying about gambling and he never really encouraged us to gamble. He always said that you can have success all your life in gambling, you can win every day of your life, and you can lose it all in one day. Like poor Mick who always sits in this corner here. He's managed to knock out twelve grand in the past couple of years. With him it's just compulsive and when he has a drink he gambles too much. I view betting same as drinking. As long as nobody's suffering, it's OK. I've got no children and me dogs never go hungry. I've got only meself to answer to.

'Now the one-armed bandits, Ah, they're completely anti-social. They're very popular with younger people and, funny enough, with married women. It's boredom. They'll go to these arcades, spend an afternoon and maybe the housekeeping money on them. They're a social evil because there's no socialising. You're only feeding a machine. And now I don't like women in betting shops to be honest with you. The reason is a little bit the same as a pub. A punter who has had a bad time, he's entitled to use bad language and it doesn't go down well. The two don't mix. A punter is waiting on a result and a photo finish goes against him and the language can be choice. Some people are performers. They'll roar, they'll scream and their language will be beautiful. They'll curse the jockey, curse the trainer, kick the counter.

'It's not an exact science. Anything but an exact science. I've tried to compute the odds and all. Nowadays handicapping is all done by computers. But it still needs a man to actually see the horse before he can pass the information into the computer. They press buttons and it's all computerised for setting bets. But I still do it quicker in me head than they can press the button.'

59 Scrubbing the front pavement in the tradition of tidiness among artisan's dwellers

60 The house-proud tradition along Aughrim Street

Chapter 13

Public Servants

DAVY SHERIDAN – POSTMAN, AGED 77

I know everyone by name', he boasts. Certainly everyone knows him. For fifty-two years he daily trekked the streets of Stoney-batter dutifully delivering the post. He was always proud of the dark blue uniform. The brass buttons bearing the Irish harp, always polished, gleamed in the sunlight as he trod up to the houses. He was always a welcome sight in the neighbourhood, especially to the elderly and shut-ins for whom a letter was a small treasure.

Walking the countless thousands of miles on hard pavement has resulted in serious knee problems. Today, in retirement, he still takes daily strolls around the familiar terrain, but at a decidedly slower gait. Along the way are many old friends with whom to chat.

'Oh, I'm real Dublin, born on Oxmantown Road. It was always known as "Cowtown" and we called ourselves "Cowtowners". Nothing derogatory about it. My father was a postman like myself. I followed suit, of course, because in those days you had to do what your father told you and there was no work anywhere and you were very lucky to get a Government job.

'You had to sit for an examination when you were about fourteen years of age and if you passed it you were called as a boy messenger. A messenger delivered telegrams around the city on a bicycle. You'd start off at 6:00 in the morning till 2:00. Oh, you could do fifteen miles in a day. You enjoyed it because when you're young nothing is hard. Up here in the cattle market I delivered telegrams to English buyers from big stock owners in England. "Buy more at such a price!" That was urgent. They might give me threepence or six-pence tip.

'At eighteen, a boy messenger went to a postman. You were trained by another postman. You'd go around with him. Now in the morning you'd have to do the sorting, get your stuff ready in little stacks and boxes in numerical order along the streets. I'd start at 6:00 and you got one hour for sorting. You had to be fast. I'd go through about 600 pieces of mail in an hour. I was a bit smart and had me own system. Then I'd start out at 7:00 to do the first delivery and it was very heavy because everyone posted at night time for the morning post. I'd come back and do a second delivery at half past ten. That would be the English mail that came in by boat and at that time it wouldn't be so bad. Then at a quarter to three you done a mid-day delivery. From 6:00 in the morning till 5:00 in the evening. And Saturdays the very same. I'd do 500 or 600 houses in a day. It was tiresome.

'You had a canvas bag, a beige one, and you had to carry forty-five pounds. Now that's very heavy. But I loved the job in the summer time. You wore a light uniform, navy blue, and you had to wear a tie and you couldn't take off your coat walking around. It wasn't allowed. The rules were very severe. And you had to wear a hat. Now I took pride in me uniform. I used to burnish the brass buttons ... and then they changed to silver ones. I was very particular about that. And I'd get an artificial crease put in my pants, sewn in. So my pants were always creasy. The winter uniform was a heavier material and if the weather was bad you had a big heavy overcoat, pull-ups, and a rain cape. It was rubberized. And black laced boots, pure leather they were. We weren't supplied with gloves. You couldn't deliver letters with gloves. Too awkward. Your hands wouldn't freeze because you had so much motion all the time. The only thing that'd happen in the winter time was the frost would slit your fingers. Ah, the tips of your fingers would be sore, terrible sore.

'I loved being a postman. I knew *everyone* around here and everyone knew me as "Davy". I knew what they had for their breakfast. See, I'm a bit of a chatterbox and I like people and I speak to everyone. It was a pleasure delivering the mail, especially to elderly people who'd be waiting at the door. Mail is especially important to elderly people, very much so. Very often they'd be waiting at the door. And the next day they'd say, "Mr. Sheridan, I had happy news. The son is doing very well and he wants me to come over for the holidays." It made me happy too. But, God, you'd get some sad mail too. You'd know from the envelope if it was bills or an official thing, like from the local sheriff, or a death notice letter with a black braid around it. It was very sad, very difficult.

'People would invite me in very often for chat and tea. Now the rules said "No". But sometimes you'd even go in for breakfast. A batch of eggs and black and white pudding. Then you'd have to make up your time. And at Christmas people would give me little gifts like a half crown or two shillings. And if I got tea they might put a little something in it. Payne's, the pork butchers, and a printing firm there on North Circular Road would give me a pound every year in an envelope. Now do you know that I delivered letters on Christmas day for years and years and years? It was terrible. Christmas Eve at maybe 10:00 we finished up, getting ready for the next morning, and we'd have to be in at 6:00 on Christmas day. And what a delivery it was on Christmas morning because everyone had the idea to post on Christmas Eve so that they'd get the letters on Christmas morning. Which was very nice ... but not for the postman! We were flooded out. It'd be 5:00 in the evening before we'd be finished. Oh, I'd come home beaten. God, Christmas Eve and Christmas day, imagine that. It was really awful.

'Now why dogs went for postmen I don't know. I think it's the bag. You'd have to take the bag and swing it at them. This man up on Prussia Street had two Alsatian dogs and this one grabbed me bag and I got afraid for me life. I couldn't go up to the house with the letters so I brought them back and endorsed them "Unable to effect delivery – mad dogs at large". Now I had quite an experience one time. I came to this house and put the letter in and the box was very tight. So I shoved it like that. And the next thing, I got a dart. There was a dog behind the door and me whole hand was tore off, skin and all was off. The woman came up and said, "I'm very, very sorry." I went down to the hospital to get an injection and get it dressed and I was out for a week.

'I was fifty-two years in the Post Office. I'm on pension now for a retired post office official. But I don't get anything else. I got a gratuity of 3,000 pounds and we bought a few things for the house and went on a holiday, but it didn't last very long. The amazing thing about it is there's an old age pensioner that has stamps, that's getting social welfare, and he has more money than I have after fifty-two years. It doesn't seem fair.'

JOHN BARRY – GARDA, AGED 52

His dark, rugged, balding handsomeness and large, solid frame bear a strong resemblance to Victor McLaughlin in *The Quiet Man*. Even his massive knobby hands are those of a prize-fighter. In Stoneybatter, his old beat, he is remembered as a 'good cop' – and a tough one.

After nearly thirty years of front-line duty at the Bridewell station in Dublin's inner-city he is seasoned and savvy. Now graduated to plain clothes detective, he is noted for his thief-catching abilities. Tough on criminals, he has a soft spot in his heart for Dublin city people, especially those in Stoneybatter, his favourite neighbourhood.

'I'm a Cork man. My father was a farmer and I'm kind of a runaway really. My brothers are professional people and my father kept me home to be the farmer of the family. I was up at four and five in the morning milking cows. I gave it a try for about a year but I kept saying to my father, "I can't live this life." So he saw an ad in the paper and said, "Why don't you join the Garda?" In the Fifties life was very tough in Ireland and he said I should join until something better comes along. And I said, "OK".

'When I joined the force I was sent to Bridewell on the beat. I was twenty-one then and a country boy thrown into the deep end of Dublin. Into all kinds of things I never dreamed would happen. In my part of the world everybody was in bed at 11:00 at night and you got up and milked the cows in the morning. I wasn't brought up to believe that this existed in Ireland, not these places along the quays. You'd see the dregs of society travelling along the quays at night. All this was something alien. To be honest with you, I felt very disoriented. Such a contrast, and I began to wonder, "Was my upbringing all wrong? Is this really what life is all about?" Not the way I knew it down on the farm.

'I hated it when I was starting. Hated the life of it. I said, "I'm leaving this job." My first Christmas here walking the beat I was very lonely, feeling very far from home. I was lost and lonely walking along the quays during the Christmas period. Anyway, I was told about the artisan's buildings up around there and I met a fella up there on the beat. We got to be really good friends and I went to his house and had my first dinner in Dublin and they were the *loveliest* people and couldn't have done more for me if they had been my own people. And I got to know all the neighbours through them, got to know everybody up there. They were the loveliest people I could ever wish to meet.

'Stoneybatter is the best part of Dublin to me. Those people up around Oxmantown Road and Ivar Street were a special people, the salt of the earth as far as I was concerned. I felt very much a part of them. It's a real little close-knit community up there. This was my neighbourhood. I got to know everybody. People knew me as a fair cop and I always treated them as humans and they respected me for that. If it were raining the shopowners would say to come in and have a cup of tea. Having a little chat was part of getting a good look at the locality. Today the police shoot past in squad cars and they're not on the beat and they don't get to know the people.

'When I was walking the beat my word was law. They'd say, "OK, Sir". I used to be up at the cattle market there at 6:00 in the morning. You'd hear them shouting at the cattle driving them. My responsibility was just to ensure that traffic was moving reasonably free around the market. Pubs would be open early in the morning and everybody would be up early and there'd be roaring and shaking at very early hours. It broke up the old monotony. It brought me back to my roots, really ... you know, the old country way of life with poop on your boots and all.

'Now when you'd be on duty at night from 10:00 until 6:00 a.m. you'd be watching on the beat for rows in pubs and people stealing. I got a great kick out of catching thieves. I love catching thieves. Still do. Back then it was just one officer walking the beat and no radios in those days. I never raided a pub unless there was a fight. And if there was a fight you would never go into it unless you were in control of the situation. Wait for help or ring up a squad car because when people are loaded up with beer you're the common enemy. If they're fighting each other and they see the blue uniform coming, you become the enemy.

'If there was a family dispute between husband and wife I went in and sat down in the most comfortable chair and I'd call the two of them around me and try to talk a bit of sense into them. I'd say, "What advantage is there for me to charge either of you, because it will just drive you farther apart?" Because I've seen family rows and women, the first morning after a black eye they want vengeance on the man. But after a week passes, they say, "We've made it up. We're back again." I saw many of them with black eyes and their men had been out drinking her housekeeping allowance and yet she'd forgive him a week later. The women in Dublin are the most decent people you'll meet in all your life.'

EAMONN O'BRIEN – COMMUNITY WORKER, AGED 45

In his rumpled tweed coat and skewed tie, he is one of the most familiar figures along neighbourhood streets, daily shuffling back and forth between meetings with various groups and chatting away with virtually everyone he passes. His stocky frame, dark features, and full beard make him an imposing sight. He could well be mistaken for one of the original Viking settlers of Old Stoneybatter – an identity he would doubtless relish.

Eamonn is the leading community worker and activist in the area. He does everything from arranging youth projects to working with organisations for the elderly. Perhaps most important, he is an indis-

61 Ambling down Stoneybatter Street to shopping area

pensable liaison between the local community and city planning officials. Intelligent, well-informed, and articulate, he is most effective in this role. That he is also jolly, optimistic and fair-minded is an additional asset. He is openly affectionate toward his neighbourhood and determined that it not be corrupted or destroyed by outsiders.

'I was very young when I came to live in the area, about fifteen months old. My father and his father was born and reared around here. So the O'Brien family would be well known. There's a unique character about the Stoneybatter area and the people born and reared here. There's still very much a rural, country atmosphere about the place and neighbouring is still a part of life here. They've always been great neighbours. People who cared about others. I can remember up around Findlater Street when I was growing up there. Nobody had very much. Everybody was working-class people and there was a lot of poverty but everybody shared.

'I can remember the night my father died and I was only five years of age. Too young to really appreciate what was happening but I remember neighbours coming in with two or three eggs for my mother and a half a loaf of bread and a bottle of milk from somebody else. That's the kind of people that tended to live around the artisan's area because it was a very close-knit community. After my father died my mother had to go to work for economic reasons and I was reared by neighbours. They made sure that nothing happened to us, that we were never without a meal.

'When I was growing up grandparents and parents and children all tended to live in the one area. We were very close. On a Sunday afternoon they all used to congregate. If the parents were dead it would be the elder brother or sister that they would congregate with. Now a lot of the lads I grew up with tend to be scattered out to Tallaght or Blanchardstown or Swords. But they'll come back to visit and you might find them in a pub or around Stoneybatter. And special occasions bring them back, a wedding or funeral or christening. Anybody that has been reared in the area has got certain feelings for it and will always speak affectionately about the place.

'People always tended to be very house proud. That was a tradition. There might have been an odd one in the neighbourhood that wasn't and it certainly would have been frowned upon. There's always been a high degree of upkeep and maintenance. People have always been very conscious of the appearance of houses. Not just their own house but the whole row of houses. I can remember as a boy that Tuesday was always the day that women came out and scrubbed their paths and window sills. And all the houses had their front doors painted green ... with one or two exceptions with people that would be a little more adventurous. That's changed. People now paint their own doors their own colours.

'In the early history of the artisan's dwellings, to qualify for a house you had to be born and reared in them. Outsiders couldn't come in and get an accommodation. It went from children to children. Then, in the 1960's, the Artisan's Company started to sell the houses to tenants. And when an old tenant died they became vacant and they'd be put up for sale on the market. People worried that if it became an area of just old people that when they died off speculators would take over the property and it might become a very unsettled area. So the elderly people today are pleased to see young couples moving in because that's how the area is going to keep its character, how it's going to survive. It's great to see young children out in the street playing again. It's more natural.

'But people feel less secure than they did years ago. People never locked their houses. They would go out and leave the key in the door and go down the road shopping. But now it's not so. People now have guards on their back windows and double locks on their doors. Robbery is now a daily occurrence. That's certainly not my memory of growing up in the area. As a child that just *didn't* happen. I can remember the first robbery in my neighbourhood when I was about seventeen years of age. It happened on a Saturday afternoon when somebody went to the shop to buy a paper and came back and their gas meter had been robbed. I can remember the reaction of the neighbours. The whole neighbourhood was absolutely numbed.

'I was talking to Chris Carr (featured elsewhere in this book) the other day and she reckons that Stoneybatter is the same today as it was seventy-five years ago when she was a girl. None of the shops have changed. Only the names over the doors may have changed on a few of them. That is unique for this area. Now the Dublin Corporation wanted to demolish the street of Stoneybatter, to widen the road. It would have destroyed the whole area. Now they've said that they recognize that Stoneybatter is an old inner-city neighbourhood with a unique character of its own that's well worth preserving.'

THOMAS BARRY – SOLDIER, AGED 81

In 1922, concealing his age of only fifteen, he joined the raw recruits in the new Irish Army. 'Proud as a peacock' of the green uniform,

he spent forty-three years in the service. Toughness and loyalty were his
proudest traits.

Today he resides in St. Bricin's Old Folks Housing Estate just across
the road from Arbour Hill Barracks where he was stationed throughout
his long career. On the wall is a photograph of his brigade being inspected
by DeValera. Though he moves about more slowly these days, there is
still the strong, erect military bearing and prideful recounting of the old
army days in the struggling Republic.

'I was born in County Cork and came to Dublin in 1922 when we
started a new army. Of course, it was the "in thing", the first time
Ireland had its own army. We were *proud* of our green uniforms.
We were known as the "Green Linnets" at that time. Oh, you'd be
proud as a peacock to wear the new uniform on the street. I was a
Corporal at sixteen years of age, the youngest Corporal, but I was
supposed to be eighteen. I became a Quartermaster Sergeant. Once
you got into the army life you didn't like to leave it. Like in the
Hungry Thirties there was very little work unless you emigrated.
So there was security and everything was very cheap.

'It was a young army and we were only after getting over the
Civil War end of it and life in the army was tough at that time. Ah,
it was tough going. I can compare it to the Foreign Legion because
we had a lot of ex-British army men at the top, from the First World
War. They were all eliminated shortly afterwards, a clean sweep of
all ex-British army officers. Now the *Irish* officers in the early days
were all out in the hills during the British army years. All men that
made their way with Connelly's Flying Column. They were men
who had been fighting the British in 1919, 1920, and 1921. Some
had been shot. They had to be courageous. When Michael Collins
formed the army in 1922 he brought in all those fellas and gave
them the rank because they were under him during the Troubled
Times. He knew his men. They were all good men, tough men, after
doing some damage to the British. Oh, God, we had great respect
for those men. But some weren't able to write their name.

'Discipline was very hard. We come under the hammer all the
time but nevertheless it was very exciting. All types of drills. We used
the Enfield rifle with a big long bayonet and the Webley revolver.
We were young and tough and got up at 6:00. You had to do an
hour's drill and physical training before your breakfast and then
you'd eat the leg off the table. The food was, what would you say,
rough and ready. But good food and plenty of it. When I joined,
the pay was one pound, four and sixpence a week. Of course, you
could go into the Sergeants' Mess and get big pints of the black

62 Examining racing forms posted in window of local turf accountant

stout for sixpence and a packet of twenty cigarettes were ten pence.

'Back in 1927 and 1928 the army was very low on men and the duties were very heavy. You'd be twenty-four hours on and twenty-four hours off. See, when DeValera took over he started rounding up all the blue shirts, that crowd, and the army had to guard all those people at the prison on Arbour Hill. And the prisoners at Mountjoy Prison. And soldiers had to guard the Bank of Ireland and Dublin Castle and Crown Alley which was the centre of the telephone system. See, there was still opposition and all those establishments were guarded because of the troubles still going on underneath. It was difficult duty. You got very little sleep. Oh, God, after you'd done twenty-four hours you'd know it!

'Now the best part of our time at night was cleaning all the different brass and equipment. Brass buttons and buckles and little buttons on the cap and the pouches and belts and straps. If there was a speck found on them in the morning you were sure to be charged a couple days "CB" — confined to barracks. And fellas would spend hours and hours at the boots, getting a sheen. The boots were a reddish colour, a real good leather. You'd rub away with Kiwi polish and a toothbrush, wetting it and rubbing it. After weeks and weeks there'd be a skin on that boot and all you'd have to do is rub it with a cloth and you could shave in it. Every morning they'd check for everything, buttons and all. Real regimental. And you had to be clean shaven. If you had a little speck there you'd be charged. Oh, my God, you had to be glittering!

'If a man didn't pass inspection he'd get seven days confined, maybe in the kitchen peeling potatoes. And if a man would be drinking on duty he'd be brought out into the square and there'd be a realy jildy — that's strict — sergeant and he'd have him there loaded down with his pack and rifle, the old British army accoutrements which would weigh about fifty pounds, and he'd be marching for an hour in a space of a few feet. And at that time there was a way of cooling bad boys, those fellas who'd start a row at night and upset the lives of others. There'd be a fella tougher than him and in the morning he'd take him over to the gym and that's where they'd settle it. There were some naughty little boys but they were quieted very fast.

'In 1940 we were expecting an invasion of the Germans. The whole place was mapped out and we had our defences. We were getting ready for this invasion, getting toughened up. We had to march from Dublin to Cork and back. It was for the training. One night we were taking up defences where the Germans were to be invading and I remember well the priest giving us his blessing. We were worried, all right.

'Now the army is three times stronger and you have a better life and men have privileges that we never had. Conditions and pay are far advanced. The top brass now would be the fellas that were in cadetship. They brought in intelligent people, more educated fellas, put them through the college and they finished up as Colonels and Generals.'

THOMAS LINEHAN – GARDA & COMMUNITY LEADER, AGED 34

Apart from discharging his duties as a Dublin Garda, Tom is committed to the preservation of Stoneybatter, his native neighbourhood. He exudes pride in being able to trace his family back to the creation of the artisan's dwellings. Wary of external forces which might threaten the historical environment, he emerged as one of the principal forgers of the Stoneybatter Development Plan which alerts local residents to the need to protect their home community.

   Too often, Tom has witnessed the demolition of historic inner-city architecture which led to the desecration of entire streetscapes. This, he believes, would be the death blow to Stoneybatter's distinctive character. He regularly champions the cause of neighbourhood preservation before the Dublin Corporation and other private and Government bodies.

'I was born on Murtagh Road and I have a deep sense of roots in the area. I know exactly how far back I go, how far my family goes back. They've been in the area since the Buildings went up. I have an inclination toward local history. There's quite a lot of oral history left. It goes back to the oldest residents that's articulate enough to tell you about it. You'd really want to pry it out of some of the old lads in the pub over several drinks. Now "Stoneybatter" was long synonymous with the area. But another name for the area, known throughout the city, was "Cow Town". I remember all my relations calling it Cow Town. It might sound a bit derogatory but the old people would know what you meant. There was nothing here but cattle and horses and dairies and piggeries. It was all cobbled and great piles of cow dung in the middle of the street. Now Chicken Lane, known as that from time *adinfinitum*, that's a place that still has piggeries. They're dreadful. You'd want to smell that!

   'This is a very old, staid, conservative parish. Families perpetuated themselves. A lot of elderly people today, their people came from the same street. A tradition that people *born* in the Buildings *stayed* in the Buildings. Genuine, honest Dublin working-class people. The salt of the earth. You have this trait in people that they believe in an honest day's work for an honest day's pay.

'There's nothing very glamorous about the Buildings. They are what they are – artisan's dwellings. And they're stereotyped. People on Murtagh Road, their homes were only two up and two down. Two bedrooms upstairs and two rooms downstairs. A small scullery where you cooked and the parlour. You had a small back yard that you washed and dried clothes in. And families were so much bigger then. You could get up to fifteen people in a house. I can remember family rows and it must have been the fact that people didn't have enough room to breathe. A very small house and an element of unemployment and a lot of the time it was drink related. Sometimes you'd even have the eldest son and the father coming to blows.

'You'd see house-proud touches. Old ladies polishing the door knockers and numbers on the door and polishing the windows. And I remember seeing women, they'd sweep a whole area of the street and then light a little fire of all the rubbish. And on a Friday night women would scrub the footpath, the pavement, outside their house with a deck scrubber and water and vin (vinegar). Some kind of whitener, I suppose it was just vin. Housewives would go out as far as their hand could go with a scrubbing brush and you'd get this semi or half-moon shape outside every door.

'I don't know what's going to happen to the Buildings when all these elderly people die off. Are new people going to move in? As long as the houses don't become dilapidated. Areas like St. Paul's Street (just off Stoneybatter) where similar houses have become dilapidated, it's now completely de-tenanted and it's going to be flattened. It could happen here. Once the artisan's dwellings start to go Stoneybatter as such will have vanished. The whole nature of Stoneybatter will change completely and utterly.

'What grieves me is to see good old buildings being torn down. Buildings that of themselves are not much to look at but as a *pattern* are intrinsic to the shape of an area. They have a certain *style*. There's a sense about this area that it is worth preserving. There's an *aura*, a feeling, about it that it is worthy of preservation. But it can be chipped away little by little and buildings disappear. There's no tradition here of a community group going in and speaking to the Dublin Corporation but we went down and spoke to them about the buildings in the area that were being torn down. But it's very difficult. You're writing letters and meeting officials and after two or three years people in a community association say, "Ah, I'm wasting my time." They become cynical and leave it. You just become discouraged.'

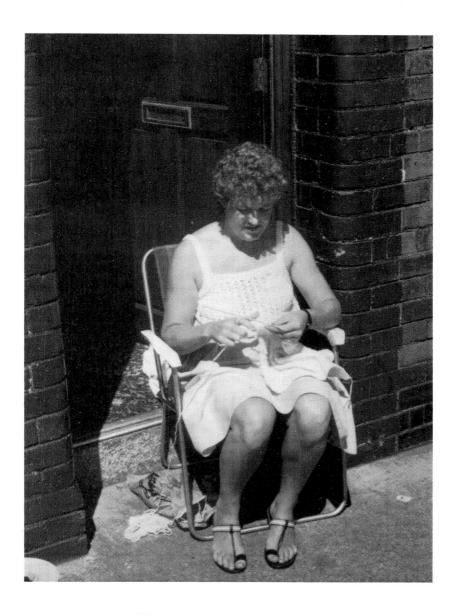

63 Catching a bit of precious sun

Chapter 14

The Need for Preservation

'Dublin's city communities are disappearing, producing a soulless environment. Without an inner-city population the urban life blood is drained, resulting in a place without identity or meaning.'

(Gerry Cahill, *Back to the Street*, 1980)

'Stoneybatter should be protected and preserved.'

(*Stoneybatter Development Plan*, 1985)

THE CULTURAL APARTHEID PROBLEM

The personal oral histories in this book are powerful testimony to the life and spirit of Stoneybatter. Regrettably, 'planners never take into consideration the spirit of the community', theirs is strictly a 'bricks and mortar mentality'.[1] This attitude has allowed greedy developers to perpetrate what many have called the 'rape' of Dublin's environment. Violation of the capital city has been exposed and documented in Frank McDonald's *The Destruction of Dublin*, my own *Georgian Dublin: Ireland's Imperilled Architectural Heritage* and several other revealing works.[2] All recognize that no single group of villains can be held solely responsible for the ruination of the cityscape. Blame filters through many levels of Irish society. Even the ordinary 'good citizens' must accept a significant share of culpability for their passivity.

Much of the problem is due to a cultural abyss between native inner-city dwellers and outsiders. Suburbanites, as well as Dublin city planners and decision-makers who hail from other parts of the country, often have appallingly little genuine understanding of, and feeling for, central city communities. A type of cultural apartheid exists, based on misconception and bias. To many outsiders, the term 'inner-city' is a pejorative one, associated with decay, dereliction, economic depression, social deprivation and crime. In short, a grimly dilapidated, dangerous wasteland or 'no man's land' populated by social rejects or poor unfortunate souls 'stuck' in the 'pit' and unable to escape to the leafy, 'civilised' suburbs. Such negatively

250

stereotyped images and attitudes have *devalued* the inner-city to the point where its destruction is considered no real loss to those living outside the area.

Dublin's heartland people are a different breed within a separate culture. They possess their own distinctive history, values and social views. Their whole life experience has been profoundly different to that of others born and reared elsewhere. Outsiders couldn't begin to comprehend their attachment to home, street, neighbourhood. It is emotionally and psychologically part of their very being. This is their ancestral ground — their roots and identity rest here. Being a *city person* is a source of great pride, like being of pioneer stock. 'My grandparents were from this street' is a mighty boast in these parts. For many, it would be unthinkable — almost a betrayal — to willingly leave the area of their forebears.

Outside Dubliners who may disparage or pity their inner-city brethren might find it unfathomable that, given the choice, they would have no desire to resettle in the posh, upwardly mobile suburbs. As Leslie Foy so simply vouched, 'I was born in this house. I know who my people were. It's something that's part of you. I *belong* here.' Ironically, city people often feel that it is the suburbanites who are actually the deprived ones, living in a new, rootless, socially sterile environment devoid of history or meaningful human investment. As Foy's daughter, Grainne, bluntly declares, 'I could not live in a nothing, in a satellite that has no centre, no heart, no tradition and no life.'

PERILS AND PROTECTIONISM

Stoneybatterites have witnessed with alarm the destruction around them. They are especially sensitive to the lessons to be learned from the lost Liberties because, as their own Paddy Crosbie so aptly put it, Stoneybatter is the 'other side of the Dublin coin'. Since they see themselves as the Liberties counterpart across the Liffey, they understandably fear a fate similar to that described by Mairin Johnston:[3]

> With the passage of time the tenements were depleted and demolished, the families banished to the outskirts of the city to housing estates ... but their relations, friends, and neighbours weren't there, the shops, schools, churches, dealers, pawnshops, hustle, bustle, atmosphere, bumping into people they knew all their lives. The security of the community was gone.

Though not tenement dwellers, they are keenly aware that they reside in century-old artisan's structures which are doubtless viewed by developers as outmoded and expendable. They also know the premium value placed on their central city property. Hence, many are wary and fearful. These fears are not unwarranted. An article in *City Views* warned of threats to the historic area:[4]

> (It) will suffer heavily under the Dublin Corporation's ill-planned road proposals. It would mean the demolition of most of Prussia Street and part of Stoneybatter and will affect everybody living there ... through the destruction of shops, pubs, businesses, and houses – all things that make up a successful community.

Similar clarion alarms have been sounded in the *Stoneybatter Community News*, telling of the 'constant threat to the area if the Corporation's bulldozers and wreckers are not stopped finally in their tracks'.[5] In response to these perils, people have become more protection-minded and some defensive actions taken. The community newsletter now regularly disseminates information alerting people to threatening developments and calling for strategy meetings to counteract the dangers. Also, in 1985 the *Stoneybatter Development Plan* was published, documenting housing stock, citing buildings of architectural merit and arguing persuasively for preservation. Despite these protectionist efforts, Stoneybatter suffered a brutal blow in the summer of 1987 which exposed its vulnerability. St. Paul Street, part of the artisan's dwellings, was de-tenanted and hurriedly demolished before local action groups could muster forces to prevent it – an all too familiar story. Over seventy structurally-sound historic houses were destroyed in a matter of days. That this occurred in the heart of the community was especially ominous. Feeling shock and anger, people heeded Thomas Linehan's prophesy that 'once the artisan's dwellings start to go, Stoneybatter, as such, will have vanished'.

Stoneybatter is manifestly the grand 'last stand' on the Dublin preservation scene. Here is an opportunity to finally learn from past painful lessons and exhibit the wisdom and vision to act honourably to preserve this surviving inner-urban village for future generations. There is no more staunch defender of old Dublin than Larry Dillon whose anguished lament and plea, prompted by sorrow over the loss of his beloved Liberties, now holds profound meaning for Stoneybatter:[6]

> Our ancient Dublin is dying before our eyes and the Dubliner, like his ancient city, is vanishing, all in the name of bureaucratic planning – and we are told it is progress. For God's sake, you people, speak up, this is a tragedy that need not happen.

Notes

INTRODUCTION

1 Cathal O'Byrne, 'Stoneybatter', *The Irish Bookman*, October, 1946, p. 22.
2 Paddy Crosbie, *Your Dinner's Poured Out!*, (Dublin: The O'Brien Press, 1981).
3 Gerry Cahill, *Back to the Street*, (Dublin: Housing Research Unit, University College, Dublin, 1980), p. 36.
4 For examples, refer to the following: John Healy, *The Death of an Irish Town*, (Cork: The Mercier Press, 1968); Hugh Brody, *Inishkillane: Change and Decline in the West of Ireland*, (London: Allen Lane, The Penguin Press, 1973); and F.H.A. Aalen and Hugh Brody, *Gola: The Life and Last Days of an Island Community*, (Cork: The Mercier Press, 1969).

HISTORY AND HERITAGE

1 *Record of the Parish of the Holy Family, Aughrim Street, Dublin*, (Dublin: The Irish Annals Press, 1940), p. 3.
2 Rev. M. Donnelly, *Short Histories of Dublin Parishes, Part X, Parishes of St. Paul, Arran Quay, and Holy Family, Aughrim Street*, (Blackrock, County Dublin: Carraig Books — reprint of original circa 1912 publication), p. 4.
3 John T. Gilbert, *A History of the City of Dublin*, (Dublin: Gill and Macmillan, 1978), p. 322. This is a reprint of the original three-volume work from 1854-59.
4 Frederick Falkiner, *Foundations of the Hospital and Free School of King Charles II, Oxmantown, Dublin*, (Dublin: Sealy, Bryers, and Walkers, 1906), p. 23.
5. *Ibid.*, p. 22.
6 *Record of the Parish of the Holy Family*, *op. cit.*, p. 7.
7 Donnelly, *op. cit.*, p. 8, footnote 2.
8 *Ibid.*, p. 9.
9 James Collins, *Life in Old Dublin*, (Cork: Tower Books, 1978), p. 71. This is a reprint of original 1913 work.
10 Rev. Nathaniel Burton, *Oxmantown and Its Environs*, (Dublin: T. O'Gorman, 1845), p. 3.
11 Thomas King Moylan, 'The District of Grangegorman', *Dublin Historical Record*, Vol. VII, No. 1, 1945, p. 65.
12 Collins, *op. cit.*, p. 77, footnote 9.
13 Leo Bowes, 'The Case of the Stoneybatter Strangler', *The Irish Digest*, July, 1964, p. 70.
14 Patrick F. Byrne, 'Ghosts of Old Dublin', *Dublin Historical Record*, Vol. XXX, No. 1, 1976, p. 30.
15 'The Artisan's Dwellings Act', *The Irish Builder*, Vol. XXIII, June 15, 1880, p. 171.
16 *The Irish Builder*, September 15, 1880, p. 225.
17 'Dublin's Artisan's Dwellings Company', *The Irish Builder*, Vol. XXXVI, August 15, 1895, p. 189.
18 Donnelly, *op. cit.*, p. 5, footnote 2.

19 *Stoneybatter Development Plan*, (Dublin: Dublin Inner City Group, 1985), p. 9.
20 Moira Lysaght, 'A North City Childhood in the Early Century', *Dublin Historical Record*, Vol. XXXVIII, No. 2, 1985, p. 76.
21 Robert Gahan, 'Some Old Street Characters of Dublin', *Dublin Historical Record*, Vol. II, 1939, p. 98.
22 *Stoneybatter Development Plan, op. cit.*, 9. 9, footnote 19.
23 Moylan, *op. cit.*, p. 67, footnote 11.

SURVIVAL AS AN URBAN VILLAGE COMMUNITY

1 Herbert Gans, *The Urban Villagers*, (New York: The Free Press, 1962), pp. 14-15.
2 For clarification of the differences between neighbourhoods, communities, and villages, refer to: Paul Knox, *Urban Social Geography*, (London: Longman's Ltd., 1982); and R.D. McKenzie, 'The Neighbourhood: A Study of Local Life in the City of Columbus, Ohio', *American Journal of Sociology*, Vol. 27, 1921, pp. 344-346.
3 Adrian McLoughlin, *Guide to Historic Dublin*, (Dublin: Gill and Macmillan, 1979), p. 124.
4 Deirdre Kelly, *Hands Off Dublin*, (Dublin: The O'Brien Press, 1976), p. 21.
5 J. Douglas Porteous, *Environment and Behavior*, (Reading, Massachusetts: Addison-Wesley Publishing Co., 1977), p. 69.
6 *Stoneybatter Community News*, January, 1987, p. 1.
7 *Stoneybatter Community News*, October, 1986, p. 2.
8 Alexander J. Humphreys, *New Dubliners*, (London: Routledge and Kegan Paul, 1966), p. 224.
9 John Jackle, Stanley Brunn, and Curtis C. Roseman, *Human Spatial Behavior*, (North Scituate, Massachusetts: Duxbury Press, 1976), p. 224.
10 Gerry Cahill, *Back to the Street*, (Dublin: Housing Research Unit, University College, Dublin, 1980), p. 21.
11 Jackle, Brunn and Roseman, *op. cit.*, p. 54, footnote 9.
12 Porteous, *op. cit.*, p. 72, footnote 5.

ORAL HISTORY AND THE SEARCH FOR SOURCES

1 Alice Hoffman, 'Reliability and Validity in Oral History', in Willa K. Baum and David K. Dunaway (Eds.) *Oral History: An Interdisciplinary Anthology*, (Nashville, Tennessee: American Association for State and Local History, 1984), p. 68.
2 Trevor Lummis, 'Structure and Validity in Oral Evidence', *International Journal of Oral History*, No. 2, 1984, p. 111.
3 Hoffman, *op. cit.*, p. 72, footnote 1.
4 *Ibid.*, p. 72.
5 Desmond McCourt, 'The Use of Oral Tradition in Irish Historical Geography', *Irish Geography*, Vol. VI, No. 4, 1972, p. 394.
6 Mary Maloney, 'Dublin – Before All is Lost', *Evening Press*, 17 May, 1980, p. 9.
7 Sherna Gluck, 'What's So Special About Women? Women's Oral History', in Willa K. Baum and David K. Dunaway (Eds.) *Oral History: An Interdisciplinary Anthology*, (Nashville, Tennessee: American Association for State and Local History, 1984), p. 227.
8 Hoffman, *op. cit.*, p. 68, footnote 1.

THE NEED FOR PRESERVATION

1 Bairbre Power, 'Farewell to the "Diamond" – With Songs and Sorrow', *Sunday Independent*, 6 September, 1981, p. 20.
2 For detailed coverage of this subject, refer to: Frank McDonald, *The Destruction of Dublin*, (Dublin: Gill and Macmillan, 1985); Kevin C. Kearns, *Georgian Dublin: Ireland's Imperilled Architectural Heritage*, (London: David & Charles, Ltd., 1983); Ronan Sheehan and Brendan Walsh, *The Heart of the City*, (Dingle: Brandon Books, 1988); and *The Urban Plunge*, (Dublin: Veritas Publications, 1988).
3 Mairin Johnston, *Around the Banks of Pimlico*, (Dublin: Attic Press, 1985), p. 94.
4 'North City – Now What?', *City News*, No. 18, December, 1980, p. 7.
5 *Stoneybatter Community News*, February, 1987, p. 4.
6 Larry P. Dillon, 'The Liberties of Tomorrow', in Elgy Gillespie (Ed.) *The Liberties of Dublin*, (Dublin: The O'Brien Press, 1973), p. 106.

Bibliography

Aalen, F.H.A. 'The Working-Class Housing Movement in Dublin, 1850-1920', in M.J. Bannon (Editor), *The Emergence of Irish Planning, 1880-1920*, (Dublin: Turoe Press, 1985), pp. 131-153.

An Taisce. *Amenity Study of Dublin and Dun Laoghaire*, (Dublin: An Taisce, 1967).

'The Artisan's Dwelling Act', *The Irish Builder*, Vol. XXII, 15 June, 1880, p. 171.

Bowes, Leo. 'The Case of the Stoneybatter Strangler', *The Irish Digest*, July, 1964, pp. 70-72.

Boydell, Barra. 'Impressions of Dublin – 1934', *Dublin Historical Record*, Vol. XXXVIII, No. 3, 1984, pp. 88-103.

Burton, Rev. Nathaniel. *Oxmantown and Its Environs*, (Dublin: T. O'Gorman, 1845).

Byrne, Patrick F. 'Ghosts of Old Dublin', *Dublin Historical Record*, Vol. XXX, No. 1, 1976, pp. 26-36.

Cahill, Gerry. *Back to the Streets*, (Dublin: Housing Research Unit, University College, Dublin, 1980).

Clarke, Desmond. *Dublin*, (London: B.T. Batsford, 1977).

Collins, James. *Life in Old Dublin*, (Cork: Tower Books, 1978). Reprint of original 1913 edition.

'The Corporation New Cattle Market', *The Dublin Builder*, 15 February, 1861.

Cosgrave, Augustine D. 'North Dublin City', *Dublin Historical Record*, Vol. XXIII, 1969, pp. 3-22.

Cosgrave, Dillon. *North Dublin: City and Environs*, (Dublin: M.H. Gill & Sons, Ltd., 1909).

Craig, Maurice. *Dublin: 1660-1860*, (Dublin: Allen Figgis, Ltd., 1980).

Crosbie, Paddy. *Your Dinner's Poured Out!*, (Dublin, The O'Brien Press, 1981).

Curtis, Edmund. 'Norse Dublin', *Dublin Historical Record*, Vol. IV, 1941-42, pp. 96-107.

Daly, M.H. 'A Ramble from St. Mary's Abbey to Oxmantown', *Dublin Historical Record*, Vol. XXI, No. 3, 1967, pp. 99-108.

D'Arcy, Fergus. *Dublin Artisan Activity, Opinion and Organization, 1820-1850*, (Dublin: M.A. Thesis, University College, Dublin, 1968).

De Burca, Seamus. 'Growing Up in Dublin', *Dublin Historical Record*, Vol. XXIX, No. 3, 1976, pp. 82-97.

De Burca, Mairin. 'Stoneybatter Gets Its Own DIY Plan', *Sunday Tribune*, 3 March, 1985.

Dillon, Larry P. 'The Liberties of Tomorrow', in Elgy Gillespie (Editor), *The Liberties of Dublin*, (Dublin: The O'Brien Press, 1973), pp. 106-108.

Donnelly, Reverend M. *Short Histories of Dublin Parishes, Part X. Parishes of St. Paul, Arran Quay, and Holy Family, Aughrim Street*, (Blackrock, County Dublin: Carraig Books, no date).

Dublin: A City in Crisis, (Dublin: Royal Institute of the Architects of Ireland, no date).

'Dublin Artisan's Dwellings', *The Irish Builder*, Vol. XL, 1 February, 1898, p. 18.

'Dublin Artisan's Dwellings Company', *The Irish Builder*, Vol. XXXVI, 15 August, 1894, p. 189.

The Dublin Civic Survey Report, Published by the Civic Institute of Ireland, (London: Hodder & Stoughton, 1925).

Dublin's Future, (Dublin: An Taisce, 1980).

Dunne, John J. *Streets Broad and Narrow*, (Dublin: Helicon, Ltd., 1982).

'A Fair Day in Smithfield', *Stoneybatter Community News*, April, 1987, p. 2.

Flood, Donal T. 'Eighteenth Century Dublin', *Dublin Historical Record*, XXXIII, No. 3, 1980, pp. 109-111.

Gahan, Robert. 'Some Old Street Characters of Dublin', *Dublin Historical Record*, Vol. II, 1939, pp. 98-105.

Gans, Herbert. *The Urban Villagers*, (New York: The Free Press, 1962).

Gilbert, John T. *A History of the City of Dublin*, (Dublin: Gill & Macmillan, 1978). A reprint of the original three volumes, 1854-59.

Gillespie, Elgy. 'Dublin Town is Falling Down', *Irish Times*, 6 December, 1978, p. 12.

Gillespie, Elgy. *The Liberties of Dublin*, (Dublin: The O'Brien Press, 1973).

Gillespie, Elgy. 'The Sick Heart of Dublin', *Irish Times*, 9 December, 1982, p. 10.

Gillespie, Elgy. 'Trying to Hold Together the Body and Soul of the City', *Irish Times*, 7 December, 1982, p. 10.

Glassie, Henry. *Irish Folk History*, (Philadelphia: University of Pennsylvania Press, 1982).

Glassie, Henry. *Passing the Time in Ballymenone*, (Philadelphia: University of Pennsylvania Press, 1982).

Gluck, Sherna. 'What's So Special About Women? Women's Oral History' in Willa K. Baum and David K. Dunaway (Editors), *Oral History: An Inter-*

disciplinary Anthology, (Nashville, Tennessee: American Association for State and Local History, 1984), pp. 221-237.

Henchy, Deirdre. 'Dublin 80 Years Ago', *Dublin Historical Record*, Vol. XXVI, No. 1, 1972, pp. 18-34.

Hoffman, Alice. 'Reliability and Validity in Oral History', in Willa K. Baum and David K. Dunaway (Editors), *Oral History: An Interdisciplinary Anthology*, (Nashville, Tennessee: Association for State and Local History, 1984), pp. 67-73.

Humphreys, Alexander J. *New Dubliners*, (London: Routledge & Kegan Paul, 1966).

Jackle, John, Brunn, Stanley and Roseman, Curtis. *Human Spatial Behavior*, (North Scituate, Massachusetts: The Duxbury Press, 1976).

Johnston, Mairin. *Around the Banks of Pimlico*, (Dublin: The Attic Press, 1985).

Joyce, Weston St. John. *The Neighbourhood of Dublin*, (Dublin: M.H. Gill & Son, 1939).

Kearns, Kevin C. *Dublin's Vanishing Craftsmen*, (Belfast: Appletree Press, 1986).

Kearns, Kevin C. *Georgian Dublin: Ireland's Imperilled Architectural Heritage*, (Newton Abbot: David & Charles Publishers, 1983).

Keatinge, Edgar F. 'Colourful, Tuneful Dublin', *Dublin Historical Record*, Vol. IX, No. 3, 1947, pp. 73-83.

Kelly, Deirdre. *Hands Off Dublin*, (Dublin: The O'Brien Press, 1976).

Kennedy, Tom. 'Dublin's Ironwork', *Ireland of the Welcomes*, Vol. 18, No. 5, 1970, pp. 8-12.

Kennedy, Tom. (Editor). *Victorian Dublin*, (Dublin: Albertine Kennedy Publishers, 1980).

Keogh, Dermot. *The Rise of the Irish Working Class*, (Belfast: Appletree Press, 1982).

Know, Paul. *Urban Social Geography*, (London: Longman Press, Ltd., 1982).

LeHane, Brendan. *Dublin*, (Amsterdam: Time-Life International, 1978).

Longford, Christine. *A Biography of Dublin*, (London: Methuen & Co., 1936).

Lummis, Tevor. 'Structure and Validity in Oral Evidence', *International Journal of Oral History*, No. 2, June, 1984, pp. 109-120.

Lysaght, Moira. 'My Dublin', *Dublin Historical Record*, Vol. XXX, No. 4, 1977, pp. 122-135.

Lysaght, Moira. 'A North City Childhood in the Early Century', *Dublin Historical Record*, Vol. XXXVIII, No. 2, 1985, pp. 74-87.

MacThomais, Eamonn. *Gur Cake and Coal Blocks*, (Dublin: The O'Brien Press, 1976).

MacThomais, Eamonn. *Me Jewel and Darlin' Dublin*, (Dublin: The O'Brien Press, 1974).

MacThomais, Eamonn. 'Seven Hills of Dublin', *Dublin Historical Record*, Vol. XXIII, No. 2, 1969, pp. 86-94.

Maloney, Mary. 'Dublin Before All is Lost', *Evening Press*, 17 May, 1980, p. 91.

McCourt, Desmond. 'The Use of Oral Tradition in Irish Historical Geography', *Irish Geography*, Vol. VI, No. 4, 1972, pp. 394-410.

McDonald, Frank. *The Destruction of Dublin*, (Dublin: Gill & Macmillan, 1985).

McGrath, Raymond. 'Dublin Panorama', *The Bell*, Vol. 2, No. 5, 1941, pp. 35-48.

McGregor, John James. *New Picture of Dublin*, (Dublin: Sealy, Bryers and Walker, 1907).

McKenzie, R.D. 'The Neighborhood: A Study of Local Life in the City of Columbus, Ohio', *American Journal of Sociology*, Vol. 27, 1921, pp. 344-364.

McLoughlin, Adrian. *Guide to Historic Dublin*, (Dublin: Gill & Macmillan, 1979).

Millman, Laurence. *Our Like Will Not Be There Again*, (Boston: Little Brown and Company, 1977).

Moylan, Thomas. 'The District of Grangegorman', *Dublin Historical Record*, Vol. VII, No. 2, 1945, pp. 66-70.

Moylan, Thomas. 'Dubliners — 1200-1500', *Dublin Historical Record*, Vol. XIII, 1953, pp. 79-93.

'The Mysteries of Smithfield', *The Dublin Builder*, 15 February, 1861.

'North City History', *City Views*, December, 1980, pp. 4-5.

'North City — What Now?', *City Views*, December, 1980, pp. 6-7.

O'Brien, Joseph V. *Dear, Dirty Dublin*, (California: University of California Press, 1982).

O'Byrne, Cathal. 'Stoneybatter', *The Irish Bookman*, October, 1946, pp. 22-24.

O'Connor, Deirdre. *Housing in Dublin's Inner City*, (Dublin: Housing Research Unit, University College, Dublin, 1979).

Peter, A. *Sketches of Old Dublin*, (Dublin: Sealy, Bryers and Walker, 1907).

Phadraig, Brian M. 'Dublin One Hundred Years Ago', *Dublin Historical Record*, Vol. XXIII, 1969, pp. 56-71.

'Plan Launched for Stoneybatter', *Irish Times*, 26 February, 1985.

Porteous, J. Douglas. *Environment and Behavior*, (Reading: Massachusetts: Addison-Wesley Publishing Co., 1977).

Power, Bairbre. 'Farewell to the "Diamond" — With Songs and Sorrow', *Sunday Independent*, 6 September, 1981, p. 20.

'Proposed New Street to Blackhall Place', *The Irish Builder*, 15 August, 1881.

Record of the Parish of the Holy Family, Aughrim Street, Dublin, (Dublin: The Irish Annuals Press, 1940).

Shaffrey, Patrick. *The Irish Town: An Approach to Survival*, (Dublin: The O'Brien Press, 1975).

Sheehan, Ronan and Walsh, Brendan. *The Heart of the City*, (Dingle: Brandon Book Publishers, 1988).

Somerville-Large, Peter. *Dublin*, (London: Hamish Hamilton, 1979).

'Stoneybatter: An Unfinished Prologue', *The Irish Builder*, 15 December, 1871.

Stoneybatter Community News, December, 1986.

Stoneybatter Community News, January, 1987.

Stoneybatter Community News, February, 1987.

Stoneybatter Development Plan, (Dublin: Stoneybatter and District Youth and Community Council, 1985).

'The Street Life of Old Dublin', *The Lady of the House*, Vol. XXIII, No. 248, 1909.
Urbana: Study of Dublin, (Dublin: An Taisce, 1982).
Urbanization: Problems of Growth and Decay in Dublin, (Dublin: National Economic and Social Council, 1982).
The Urban Plunge, (Dublin: Veritas Publications, 1988).
Wren, Jimmy. *The Villages of Dublin*, (Dublin: Tomar Publishers, 1982).

Index